A HISTORY OF
AMERICAN IMMIGRATION

1820–1924

A HISTORY OF
AMERICAN IMMIGRATION

1820–1924

BY

GEORGE M. STEPHENSON, Ph.D.

NEW YORK
RUSSELL & RUSSELL · INC
1964

FIRST PUBLISHED IN 1926
REISSUED, 1964, BY RUSSELL & RUSSELL, INC.
BY ARRANGEMENT WITH GINN & CO.
L. C. CATALOG CARD NO: 64—15022

PRINTED IN THE UNITED STATES OF AMERICA

PREFACE

The present volume attempts to deal with immigration as a factor in American political development. The author has sought to set forth the part that immigration and the immigrants have played in the political history of the United States, an aspect of the subject that has been much neglected. It is hoped that without unduly stressing the subject the student will gain from the volume a better historical perspective. The ever-present temptation to elaborate and to enter into details has been constantly repressed.

The chapters on the European background have been prepared with the purpose of introducing the reader to some of the conditions and events which have set in motion, accelerated, or retarded the great migration and of supplying the link between conditions in Europe and those in America.

The limits of the volume have prevented the discussion of many important subjects, and chapters on the cultural contributions of the immigrant stocks have been entirely omitted —certainly not through the failure to appreciate their importance, but in the expectation of incorporating them into another volume.

In dealing with such a highly controversial subject the author lays himself open to criticism on almost every page. Conscious of the vast amount of unexplored material and of the difficulty of compressing the material at hand into a single volume, he can only plead that he has made a reverent search for truth and hope that his effort will stimulate others to carry the search further.

GEORGE M. STEPHENSON

THE UNIVERSITY OF MINNESOTA

iii

CONTENTS

PART IV. SELECT BIBLIOGRAPHY

A HISTORY OF AMERICAN IMMIGRATION
1820–1924

PART I. THE EUROPEAN BACKGROUND

CHAPTER I

INTRODUCTION

When the Congress of the United States enacted the immigration law of 1924, it closed a momentous chapter in American and European history, and indeed in world history. The operation of forces which brought to the great western republic within the span of a century some thirty million people of various languages and of diverse customs, traditions, and ideals, the great bulk of whom remained to share the opportunities of the adopted country, is in itself worthy of study by those who seek to understand the events which shape the destiny of nations and determine the fortunes of individuals. How shall we understand the jostling of races, the clash of cultures and creeds, the political activity of the foreign-born, and in general the problems of our composite population without a knowledge of the Old World environment?

Volumes have been written on the European background of American history. One of the first lessons in American history portrays the conditions in the Old World which set men to thinking about possible routes of travel and intercourse. The rivalry of the newborn states of Europe for trade, precious metals, and colonies prompted men to brave the hazards of uncharted seas and to explore regions where Europeans had never set foot. The motives which determined the Pilgrim Fathers to establish a settlement beyond the sea are analyzed, and their reactions to the new environment are studied. A study of nineteenth-century Europe is as important for the student of American immigration as is a knowledge of seventeenth-century Europe for the study of American colonial history. Immigration legislation, political-party platforms, the policy of labor organizations, naturalization laws, the relations between immigrant stocks, the process of assimilation, the efforts to foster loyalty, the propaganda of states, organizations, and individuals to stimulate immigration, foreign policy,—all these and many more are directly and indirectly related to the background of immigration.

During the nineteenth century students were conscious of the far-reaching results of the great migration of population across the Atlantic, but no very serious efforts were made to sound the depths of the movement. Perhaps the phenomenon was too obvious and prosaic: it was heralded by no catastrophe and it produced no leaders of heroic stature. In the beginning the newspapers in the countries of departure commented on the spectacle of whole trains of wagons closely packed with household gear and children moving through the streets, followed by men and women on foot, en route from the interior to the ports of embarkation, and American papers chronicled the arrival of these hosts. But soon these events became too common to record.

The emigrant himself at the time of his departure, as well as in later years, was incapable of analyzing the complex forces operating over a long period of time which created his environment and brought him to the decision to cast loose from the old moorings. Whether or not he was conscious of it, the emigrant was essentially a nonconformist—in economic, social, political, or religious matters. He was the creature of his environment, but he chafed under it; and when he arrived in the country of his choice, he found himself a nonconformist. He usually learned to understand and speak the language of the new country, he adopted American ways and customs, but he could never entirely shake off the influences of his early life. America, however, did work a marvelous transformation. The emigrant who returned to his native land was the most conspicuous individual in his community. He wore American clothes, shoes, and cap; he had new ideas; and above all he had money. He was a living advertisement of American prosperity. The returned emigrant was often an unbearable person, but he preached the gospel of America in a language that could not be misunderstood. Perhaps he was illiterate, but he usually returned with a broader vision and knowledge and the ability to answer with some intelligence questions about the far-away land.

The immigrant came to America with an imperfect understanding of its history, government, and institutions. He knew America was rich and great; he had heard of its great factories and large farms; he knew something of the spirit of America, for he had heard of or read about Washington, Jefferson, Jackson, and Lincoln. But a perspective of three thousand miles was distorting. The letters written by prosperous and enthusiastic emigrants to friends and relatives at home were often exaggerated. In his own country the upper classes and those who opposed emigration, by seizing upon every opportunity to belittle the opportunities America offered and to paint America in the blackest colors, augmented his perplexity. Emigration agents, employed by industrial organizations, states, and railway, steamship, and land companies, in their eagerness to swell their commissions, made promises that could only be realized in a Utopia. On the journey to the port of embarkation the emigrant was frequently preyed upon by unscrupulous persons; on the ship which transported him across the ocean he was exploited and packed into the ill-smelling steerage; on his arrival at the American port sharks and runners lay in wait to cheat him at exchange, to steal his baggage and money, to direct him to disreputable lodging-houses, and to send him to false destinations.

Immigration is distinctly a nineteenth-century and twentieth-century phenomenon. Although the migration of groups and of individuals from one country to another is as old as history, nothing comparable to the movement of population from Europe to America in the last hundred years is recorded in the annals of the past. Even to the superficial student of history it is obvious that no such movement could have taken place without the discoveries and inventions of modern times. With the passing of each year the earth grows smaller; the steamship, railway, telegraph, cable, telephone, wireless, radio, automobile, and aëroplane have annihilated distance. The printing press has aroused man's curiosity and stimulated his ambition; the railway and steamship have made it possible to satisfy his curiosity and realize his ambition. The observant and studious resident of Naples in this century is better informed about the United States than his grandfather was about Italy. Samuel Topliff, a Bostonian traveling in France in 1828 and 1829, was astonished to find how ignorant the people in general were of America:

Many did not know of such a country, but as I spoke English, thought it somehow or other connected with England. Some appeared to stare and look as if they never before heard the name.

Some inquired if Genl. Washington was still President. The enlightened and educated, however, know full well the history of our country, and entertain for it the most exalted opinion.[1]

Lord Macaulay in a brilliant chapter describing the state of England in 1685 wrote as follows:

The chief cause which made the fusion of the different elements of society so imperfect was the extreme difficulty which our ancestors found in passing from place to place. Of all inventions, the alphabet and the printing press alone excepted, those inventions which abridge distance have done most for the civilization of our species. Every improvement of the means of locomotion benefits mankind morally and intellectually as well as materially, and not only facilitates the interchange of the various productions of nature and art, but tends to remove national and provincial antipathies, and to bind together all the branches of the great human family.

He confidently affirms that of the squires whose names were in the king's commissions of peace and lieutenancy not one in twenty went to town once in five years, or had ever wandered so far as Paris.

The student who aspires to understand the causes and motives which underlie the exodus from Europe to America will not steep himself in the documents and literature which relate the exploits of the battlefield or describe the pleasures of kings and nobles; on the contrary, his researches will lead him to the cottages of the peasants and to the humble dwellings of the laborers in the factory and on the farm. The task of writing the history of the commoner is immeasurably more difficult than that of portraying the lot of those upon whom fortune has smiled more graciously. The material is scattered and scanty, colored by prejudice, and difficult for later generations to interpret and animate. Nations have always

[1] Samuel Topliff, *Letters from Abroad in the Years 1828-1829*, p. 198.

had difficulty in understanding each other, and with the universal unrest and feverish activity of the present century, augmented by racial animosities let loose by the World War, the historian is never sure of his ground.

Nationality is elusive of definition. A nation with all its common attributes embraces numerous contradictions. A state may incase many nationalities, and a nation may include a variety of characteristics. The subjects of the king of Great Britain call themselves Englishmen, Scotchmen, and Welshmen. Ireland is a part of the British Empire, but the Irishman is most eloquent in denouncing in almost perfect English the iniquity of English rule. The French provinces of Canada accept the fact of British sovereignty, but language and religion set them apart from their sister provinces in the Dominion. The people of the United States are united by a common language, by history, traditions, and theory of government; yet a plethora of religions, diverse economic and geographical conditions, and a mixture of races have raised doubts about their constituting a nation.

Says an English writer:

In the new folk-wanderings of all peoples, nations and languages, which in North America to-day are preparing the future of the world, English speech and in some sort English ideas and customs have become the mould into which the outpourings of all Europe are cast year by year to dissolve, mingle and be transformed. . . .[1]

The people of European countries are sprung from stocks which for generations and even centuries have contributed to their development. The peasant tills the soil which gave sustenance to his grandfather, and the artisan walks the village streets which were familiar to his forbears. He is born

[1] G. M. Trevelyan, *England under the Stuarts*, p. 174. London, 1910.

into a society hoary with age, and with customs and traditions dating centuries back. Millions of Americans now living, on the other hand, have been uprooted from an older environment and transplanted into a country where traditions are in the making, where society is fluid, where races and ideas are fused, where distances are vast, where the language is strange, —everything different beyond imagination.

The great bulk of immigrants have come within the last hundred years. Within the span of that time wave after wave has reached our shores—English, Irish, Germans, French, Dutch, Scandinavians, Slavs, Jews, Italians, Magyars, Greeks, peoples from the Balkan Peninsula, Asia Minor, China, and Japan.[1]

It has become the custom to distinguish between the old immigration and the new. Bearing in mind the limitations of this classification, we may accept it for convenience. Prior to 1883 about 95 per cent of the immigrants came from England, Ireland, Scotland, Wales, Belgium, France, Denmark, the Netherlands, Norway, and Sweden—the so-called "old immigration"; in 1907 fully 81 per cent embarked from Austria-Hungary, Bulgaria, Greece, Italy, Montenegro, Poland, Rumania, Russia, Serbia, Spain, Syria, and Turkey —usually designated as the "new immigration."

American immigration in a sense may be said to constitute a chapter in the expansion of Europe, a movement which has been in process for over four centuries, beginning with the discovery of America by Columbus. In the large, the factors underlying the European colonization of America, using that term in the narrower sense, have operated to stimulate immigration.

[1] See valuable chart accompanying Jenks and Lauck's *Immigration Problem*, and also pages 25, 26. New York, 1917.

The impulses for colonization may be summarized as follows: (1) pressure of population; (2) religious zeal and persecution; (3) economic motives; (4) love of adventure; (5) political ambition.

The pressure of population has driven many people to wars of conquest, especially in primitive times. Primitive people require a great deal of room. The pressure of population brought the Germanic tribes into the Roman Empire. Modern Germany and Japan furnish examples of people seeking additional territory to furnish outlets for their rapidly increasing numbers.

The religious impulse is often closely allied with political considerations. The Spanish explorers were largely impelled by religious zeal, and Mohammedanism has spread over vast areas by force of arms. In general, religion has figured prominently in political expansion, but it has played a relatively small part in swelling the tide of immigration.

The history of the colonial expansion of Europe embraces several centuries, but it has remained for the nineteenth and twentieth centuries to furnish the historian with material which reveals colonial rivalry in the highest degree, with economic motives dominating. In previous centuries there was the desire to find and control certain commodities; for example, gold, silver, furs, and spices. In more recent times nations have desired colonies to furnish markets for manufactured articles; hence the mad scramble for territory.

American immigration, therefore, is contemporaneous with fundamental changes in the lives of peoples in every part of the world. It is the product of forces a long time in the making, and the change of residence of millions from Europe to America not only reshaped the career of individuals but wrought great changes in Europe as well as in America.

CHAPTER II

THE UNITED KINGDOM

The causes underlying great historical movements and changes admit of classification, but for every generalization there are usually a multitude of exceptions. The historian who seeks the causes for nineteenth-century and twentieth-century immigration faces a most complicated problem, for in most instances the major cause is supplemented by more or less minor contributory factors. Dissatisfaction springing from a most serious grievance may be intensified by a complicated environment. The immigrants have left comparatively few records of themselves; and the statistics, data, and observations which have come down to us are at best only approximations.

Students of immigration are in agreement that the great bulk of immigrants to America were impelled by the desire to get a better living: that economic causes overshadowed all others. While this is true of the whole immigration movement, religious and political causes play a relatively greater part in the case of the "old" immigrants than of the "new." Economic discontent in England, Ireland, Germany, Scandinavia, and the Netherlands was fanned at times by religious and political dissatisfaction. This may possibly be explained by the temperament of the peoples of those countries, or by the relatively more advanced state of education, or by the political and religious changes peculiar to the first half of the nineteenth century.

The industrial revolution, with the accompanying and re-
sultant readjustments which affected the life of every individual who came within its domain, is certainly one of the
greatest phenomena of modern times. Speaking broadly, the
transition from domestic manufacture to factory manufacture was most marked in the years from 1750 to 1850; and
in England, the cradle of the industrial revolution, the period
of greatest readjustment falls in the years between 1800 and
1840. The inventions and discoveries of the previous century had laid the foundations of a new industrial society, but
the new social relationships which followed appeared most
conspicuously in the generation after the close of the Napoleonic wars. Then England became the scene of those trans-
formations which every civilized country has experienced
since then, although in less aggravated form.

The beginning of emigration from England on a large scale
coincides with the changes wrought by the establishment of
the modern factory city. With the rise of the corporation
the relations between employer and employee tend to become
less intimate, resulting frequently in open hostility. Fluctua-
tions in trade resulted in business depressions and widespread
unemployment. Incredibly low wages prevented the laborers
from accumulating a reserve to fall back upon in days of
adversity. In the time of transition from hand manufacture
to machine manufacture the workmen skilled in the older
methods found it difficult and even impossible to adapt themselves to the new conditions. In the House of Commons, in
December, 1826, Sir James Graham declared it necessary to
do something to relieve the distress under which many arti-
sans were sinking. He was sorry to inform the House that
he had received information that the distress was increasing.
Hand weavers received no more than five shillings per week

for a fourteen-hour day. Most of them, he declared, were a year's rent in arrears; their diet consisted of oatmeal and potatoes; and their appearance showed that they were reduced to an extremity of want. One of the principal reasons for their unfortunate condition was assigned to the improvements in power looms: hand-loom weavers could not be converted into power-loom weavers.[1] In the same month a petition from the weavers of Glasgow represented their extreme distress—they were destitute of clothing—and asked from the government the means of emigrating.[2]

Macaulay, writing at the time when these conditions existed in the main, minimizes the suffering of his countrymen. "It is, in some sense," he writes, "unreasonable and ungrateful in us to be constantly discontented with a condition which is constantly improving." The very fact that Macaulay sees fit to make this comparison testifies to the numerous expressions of discontent which reached his ears.[3] Of great significance to us, however, is the fact that writers and speakers were fond of making contrasts between conditions in America and England, to the detriment of the latter.[4] That the misery of the people was somewhat exaggerated is probable; that discontent was rife is certain; and that many immigrated to America, Canada, and Australia to gain relief from poverty is equally certain. Indeed, the large number of paupers stimulated emigration directly and indirectly.

From the days of Queen Elizabeth every parish had to provide for the maintenance of its infirm poor and to provide

---

[1] *Hansard's Parliamentary Debates*, Vol. XVI, pp. 298, 299.

[2] Ibid. pp. 227–232.

[3] *History of England*, Vol. I, pp. 333–335. Boston, 1849.

[4] See William Cobbett's "Letter to the Journeymen and Labourers of England, Wales, Scotland, and Ireland," in *Political Pamphlets*, edited by George Saintsbury, pp. 182–224. New York, 1892.

work for those who were able to work but who for one reason
or another could not or would not secure employment. By
the poor-law amendment of 1796 the system of outdoor relief
was inaugurated, resulting in a large increase in the sums
levied for the poor rates. These lavish grants of outdoor
relief are explained partly by the circumstance that the poor-
law administration was in the hands of large employers of
labor, whose interest it was to keep wages down and to compel the parish to provide for those whose wages were insufficient to support themselves and their families. The law,
therefore, proved an incentive to improvidence. The number
of persons in receipt of relief increased from 1,040,000 in
1801 to 1,850,000 in 1827. It can be readily understood that
the burden of the taxpayer grew constantly heavier. In order to make the burden lighter, parishes tried to shift a portion of it to other parishes by deporting recent arrivals who
applied for charity. Under the law of apprentices the parish
could apprentice children of poor parents to any trade, and
the master was compelled to receive them. Children were
separated from parents, transported to distant parts of the
realm,—from London to the cotton mills in Lancashire and
Yorkshire, a distance of two hundred miles,—where living
conditions were unsanitary and moral safeguards unknown.
There were no laws regulating hours of labor, providing
education, or insuring humane treatment.

After much agitation outdoor relief was superseded by the
poor-law amendment of 1834, which provided for a union of
several parishes under an elective board of guardians as the
local administrative unit, and a Parliamentary commission of
three members as the central administrative board. Thereafter poor relief was not to be offered to able-bodied persons other than in workhouses. This change of system was

vehemently opposed by the working people because in their economic state at that time it presented to them the probability of ending their days in the workhouse.

To augment these unhappy conditions the generation following the battle of Waterloo developed an increasing criminal tendency. The penal code was antiquated, including no less than two hundred felonies punishable by death. Conscious of the unreasonable severity of punishments, juries often declined to convict. Deportation to the convict colony in Australia was in some cases worse than death.[1]

Having in mind a vivid picture of conditions in the manufacturing districts in England and Scotland, William Thomson, a Scotch weaver who traveled for his health in the Southern states of the American Union in 1841–1842, made the following statement:

After witnessing negro slavery in mostly all the slave-holding states,—having lived for weeks in cotton plantations, observing closely the actual condition of the negroes,—I can assert, without fear of contradiction from any man who has any knowledge of the subject, that I have never witnessed one-fifth of the real suffering that I have seen in the manufacturing establishments in Great Britain. . . . The members of the same family of negroes are not so much scattered as are those of working men in Scotland, whose necessities compel them to separate at an age when the American slave is running about gathering health and strength.[2]

In part the history of England is the story of attempts to alleviate the distress caused by unemployment, low wages, overpopulated districts, conditions which the ambitious man

[1] For a graphic account of conditions related in this paragraph, see Spencer Walpole's *A History of England from the Conclusion of the Great War in 1815*, Vol. I, pp. 167 ff. New York, 1902.

[2] Sir Charles Lyell, *A Second Visit to the United States of North America*, Vol. II, pp. 93, 94. London, 1849.

sought to escape,—if not for himself, then for the sake of his children whom the tide of misfortune might engulf in the years to come.[1]

The farmer in the British Isles, no less than the factory hand, felt the pinch of readjustments and changes in agriculture.[2] Overcrowded numbers explain in part the exodus from certain rural districts. Until 1834 the practice of supplementing wages from the poor rates impelled overlords to eject from their estates tenants who might apply for poor relief, in order to escape the taxes which would fall upon their property to provide funds for that purpose. In the communities to which the ejected tenants drifted the lands and residences of the small farmers were assessed lavishly to support these unfortunate people. Thus the poor laws were directly responsible for the emigration of two types of farmers. In addition to these factors the process of converting arable land into pasture and the consolidation of several small farms into one lessened the demand for labor.

Petitions to Parliament, speeches in Parliament, discussions at public meetings, innumerable pamphlets, newspapers, and political magazines, all bear witness to the misery and degradation of the people. Vice, misery, wretchedness, ignorance, degradation, depravity, drunkenness, crime, and discontent were rampant. The mere fact of discontent, however, explains very little, except as it affected, consciously or un-

---

[1] Edward Bottomley, in his letters, *An English Settler in Pioneer Wisconsin* (Wisconsin Historical Society, Collections, Vol. XXV), states that his emigration from England was prompted by the desire to assure his children escape from the unfortunate conditions which surrounded them. Milo M. Quaife, in his introduction to the letters, says that Bottomley is representative of the sober, hard-working, middle-class population.

[2] S. C. Johnson, *A History of Emigration from the United Kingdom to North America, 1763–1912*, chap. iii. London, 1913.

the existing industrial system. The emigrant from England, as well as from Scandinavia, Holland, and Germany, soon became aware of the fact that America was a land not only of economic opportunity but also of religious freedom. This circumstance was frequently mentioned in letters written by immigrants, and it contributed in no small degree to the optimistic tone of these letters. In America the ministers followed the example of the Wesleys and Whitefield, who brought the gospel to the toilers in the factories, mines, and fields.

In the established church a few favored ones enjoyed the lion's share of privileges and prizes, although the mass of the clergy lived in poverty. By various methods, including marriage alliances, prelates reached their high stations and often controlled numerous offices. Frequently the clergymen were sportsmen, and enjoyed the pleasures of the huntsman and angler without giving much thought to the duties of their offices. Their sermons, often second-hand opinions of dogmaticians, lacked fire and were read listlessly from manuscript.[1]

The dominant social and political classes belonged to the Anglican church; the dissenters were of the lower classes, and for that reason it was unfashionable to be a dissenter. Dissenters had to pay rates for the repair of the parish church and had to register their place of worship with the archbishop or bishop of the diocese. Roman Catholics were under even greater disabilities. Even after the laws were modified or repealed, dissenters felt the sting of social discrimination.

The condition of the people of Ireland in the nineteenth and twentieth centuries may be summed up in the one word

[1] Reverend George Crabbe's "The Village" presents an interesting picture of the country parson at the close of the eighteenth century. The author presents village life as one of severe labor and toil, in which the rustics are dissatisfied and overburdened with work. Oliver Goldsmith, on the other hand, in "The Deserted Village" brings out the cheerful side.

"unhappy." In proportion to the population no other country has experienced such a large emigration, the population of the island having been materially reduced, partly, though not entirely, as a result of the exodus. The chronic state of discontent has its roots deep in political, religious, and economic conditions. Dissatisfaction with the policy of the British king and Parliament has brought rebellion after rebellion, followed by repressive measures and confiscation of lands. Restraints on trade and commerce and the system of absentee landlords had reduced the Irish people to such a state of poverty at the beginning of the nineteenth century as to make one wonder that the people were able to exist at all. The small holdings of the tenants had made Ireland a one-crop country; potatoes constituted almost the entire crop. When that crop failed, the people were reduced to an extremity of want.

Ireland's scanty resources and system of agriculture brought a series of famines. The most serious famine occurred in 1846 and 1847 and was "probably the most potent factor which has ever influenced the flow of emigration." Stanley C. Johnson writes:

To appreciate the extent of this disaster, we must remember that the population of the country had reached a point of unusual density, being just over eight millions, and also that the peasants depended on the potato as their staple article of food. The state of the country, even prior to the failure of the crop, was none too satisfactory, for poverty had risen to such a degree that all attempts to cope with it had seemed to be of no avail. The famine, however, solved the problem, sweeping away thousands by starvation and death, and causing a still greater number to leave their country owing to the fear of sharing in a like fate.[1]

[1] *A History of Emigration from the United Kingdom*, p. 50.

Within a period of seven years 1,656,044 people emigrated; and in the decade from 1841 to 1851 the population was reduced by over two million. The exact number of deaths will never be known. Years after, in bogs and out-of-the-way places, were found the remains of people who had perished. Many succumbed in after years to diseases left in the wake of the terrible calamity. The rush for ships was so great that emigrants were crowded almost to suffocation in miserable quarters, without privacy and sufficient provisions, many of them dying at sea or shortly after their arrival from the long and trying voyage.[1]

The emigrant left Ireland with bitter memories of his life in his native land, and he has bequeathed his hatred for England to his children and children's children. The violation of the treaty of Limerick (1691), which followed the struggle between the army of the Protestant king, William, and the Catholics who favored the deposed James II, made an intolerable situation in Ireland. Roman Catholics in a land where the vast majority of the inhabitants were of that faith were excluded from the Parliament and were not allowed to hold office. Catholics were compelled to transmit their lands to all their sons; but if a single son renounced Catholicism, he received the entire inheritance. Catholics were forbidden to serve as guardians of children. Prelates were banished, and priests were compelled to take oaths entirely incompatible with their conscientious scruples. An English author writes:

In addition to these and similar enactments, the Irishman who was true to his religion had to bear the daily scorn and contumely

[1] Thomas Aldis Emmet, in *Ireland under English Rule, or a Plea for the Plaintiff* (New York, 1913), Vol. I, pp. 301 ff., presents a graphic picture of the miserable emigrants.

of men of English or Scottish descent and religion, who looked upon him as a being of an inferior race, and scarcely deigned to admit him even to their presence.

One immediate result of these conditions was a great emigration from Ireland in the eighteenth century. It remained for the great famine in the following century to fill Ireland's cup of woe and to swell the tide of emigration. A rapid succession of coercive acts and frequent suspensions of the writ of habeas corpus are evidence that the Irish immigrant was a refugee from political oppression as well as from extreme poverty. At the earliest possible moment his letters from America were accompanied by remittances, made possible by saving from his earnings, to enable a father, mother, brother, or sister to share with him the opportunities and freedom which the republic had bestowed upon him.

Statistics show that the number of immigrants to America from Scotland was much smaller than the number from England and Ireland; but in proportion to the population unfavorable economic conditions produced similar results. Overpopulation in certain districts, the conversion of large districts into sheepwalks, agricultural depression, the collapse of certain industries, and the changes in society are among the most important causes.

Prior to the year 1840 more than one half the emigrants of British nationality went to British North America; but since that date, with the exception of a very few years, the United States has attracted the greater number. The amazing prosperity of the United States, the existence of millions of acres of public lands which could be acquired on very liberal terms, the activity of certain states,[1] and the disinclination of the

[1] See Theodore C. Blegen, "The Competition of the Northwestern States for Immigrants," in *Wisconsin Magazine of History*, Vol. III, pp. 1-29.

Irish to settle anywhere under the British flag are the out-standing reasons for this development.

In the famous report of Lord Durham, submitted to the British government in 1839, after a careful study of conditions in Canada, a most striking contrast between the state of affairs in the United States and that in Canada is presented.[1] He attributes the progress south of the boundary to the excellence and uniformity of the public-land system, and the backward state of Canada to the lack of such a system. In Canada, he writes:

Large tracts become the property of individuals, who leave their lands unsettled and untouched. Deserts are thus interposed between the industrious settlers; the natural difficulties of communication are greatly enhanced; the inhabitants are not merely scattered over a wide space of country, but are separated from each other by impassable wastes; the cultivator is cut off or far removed from a market in which to dispose of his surplus produce, and procure other commodities; and the greatest obstacles exist to co-operation in labour, to exchange, to the division of employments, to combination for municipal or other public purposes, to the growth of towns, to public worship, to regular education, to the spread of news, to the acquisition of common knowledge, and even to the civilizing influences of mere intercourse for amusement.

On the other hand,

The system of the United States appears to combine all the chief requisites of the greatest efficiency. It is uniform throughout the vast federation; it is unchangeable save by Congress, and has never been materially altered; it renders the acquisition of new land easy, and yet, by means of a price, restricts appropriation to the actual wants of the settler; it is so simple as to be readily understood; it provides for accurate surveys and against needless delays; it

[1] *The Report of the Earl of Durham, Her Majesty's High Commissioner and Governor General of British North America*, pp. 144 ff. New York, 1902.

gives an instant and secure title; and it admits of no favouritism, but distributes the public property amongst all classes and persons upon precisely equal terms. That system has promoted an amount of immigration and settlement, of which the history of the world affords no other example.

The British government, unlike the governments of nearly every other country of Europe,[1] has looked with favor upon the emigration of its subjects and has even appropriated money to encourage it. This is explained in part by the problems created by the industrial revolution and in part by the possession of colonies in which emigrants might be converted into prosperous and loyal subjects, which would redound to the advantage of the whole empire.

In March, 1826, Mr. Wilmot Horton brought before the House of Commons a motion to appoint a select committee "to inquire into the expediency of encouraging emigration from the United Kingdom." Mr. Horton informed the House that in 1823 the sum of £50,000 had been voted for the purpose of enabling a certain number of men, women, and children to emigrate to the North American colonies. The expense incurred to assist the 268 persons who availed themselves of the assistance of the government amounted to £22 for each individual. They were now placed in upper Canada, he said, and from a state of wretchedness and misery were now comfortably and prosperously situated. Two years later (1825) 2024 were sent out, when the expense per person was £20. He read letters from immigrants who expressed satisfaction with their situation. The government did not propose to defray all the expenses for carrying the experiment further, continued the speaker, but the object was to show, by a few trials, the ease with which it might be carried

[1] Italy is the most conspicuous exception.

into effect. He put it to the House whether a measure which seemed calculated to convert a riotous peasantry into a class of industrious farmers and yeomen was not deserving of commendation.[1]

The debate which followed on this and similar motions revealed a variety of opinions on the part of members of both Houses of Parliament. It was feared that many who might take advantage of the assistance of the government, especially the Irish, would be bitter enemies of the government. Would not the void created by emigration be filled at once by paupers from other parishes? What assurance was there that the emigrants would not desert the colony in favor of the United States?[2]

The select committee which was appointed reported that, although it was not prepared with a permanent system of emigration, it recommended an immediate grant of £50,000.

In extensive districts in Ireland, Scotland, and England, the redundant population causes great misery and deteriorates the general condition of the labouring classes; wages are reduced below the minimum necessary for health, and have to be supplemented by parochial rates in England and by charity and plunder in Ireland. . . . The redundant population represses the industry and endangers the peace of the Mother Country; it would encourage the safety and industry of the colonies.

The committee was of the opinion that whatever might be the demands from other quarters, it was vain to hope for any permanent advantage from any system of emigration which did not apply primarily to Ireland, "whose population, unless some other outlet be opened to them, must shortly fill

[1] *Hansard's Parliamentary Debates*, Vol. XIII, pp. 1359-1363.
[2] Ibid. Vol. XVI, pp. 490, 501, 510; Vol. XVIII, pp. 938-966.

up any vacuum created in England or in Scotland, and reduce the labouring classes to a uniform state of degradation and misery."[1]

In England and Scotland the term "Irish wages" was in current use. Its significance lies in the fact that the people were painfully aware that the Irish problem was an English problem. If conditions among the working people of England and Scotland were bad, they were infinitely worse in Ireland. In consequence the low standard of living of the Irishman enabled him to work for wages even lower than those paid to the Englishman. In other words, the laboring man in England and Scotland complained of the competition of "cheap Irish labor" just as the American artisan complains of "cheap foreign labor."

This condition is reflected in the report of the committee appointed by the House of Commons to inquire into the state of the Irish poor. Emigration as a remedial measure for Ireland was in the nature of protection to England and Scotland, by stopping the influx of Irish laborers.[2]

The writings and speeches of Edward Gibbon Wakefield did much to popularize the subject of emigration. In fact, Lord Durham's views were largely those of Wakefield. Both men approached the problem of emigration from the standpoint of the interests of the whole British Empire,—the mother country as well as the colonies. Wakefield regarded emigration as a practical method of relieving the economic pressure in the British Isles and of populating and developing the colonies. The essence of his colonization scheme was to

---

[1] M. I. Adam, *Guide to the Principal Parliamentary Papers relating to the Dominions, 1812–1911*, pp. 149–151.

[2] The inquiry was made in 1830. S. C. Johnson, *A History of Emigration from the United Kingdom*, p. 20.

aid emigration by using the proceeds from the sale of public lands in the colonies to pay the cost of transporting emigrants. By fixing the price of lands at a uniform figure, which Wakefield called the "sufficient price," the competition in the labor market at home would be relieved and the labor necessary for the development of the new country would be supplied. His plan was tried out in the Australian colonies between 1830 and 1850, and while it was not wholly successful, the effect of his able writings on the subject was to interest statesmen in emigration and to convince many that a happy future awaited those who were willing to seek homes beyond the seas.[1]

We have seen how the poor laws operated to stifle the ambition of the laboring classes and to increase the burden of taxation in the parishes. It was to alleviate this that the plan of aiding emigration at the expense of the parishes was resorted to for a term of years. In the report of the Poor Law Commissioners for 1834 it was asserted that the experiment had been generally satisfactory wherever it had been made on a considerable scale. In some parishes the annual parochial expenditure, exclusive of the emigration expenses, had been considerably reduced, and the moral condition of laborers had been decidedly improved. It was complained, however, that emigration carried off the industrious and well-behaved and left the idle and profligate. An occasional emigrant returned to the parish at whose expense he had been transported, because of a longing for his old associations and because in the colony he was thrown on his own resources

---

[1] On this subject see Sir C. P. Lucas, *Lord Durham's Report on the Affairs of North America* (Oxford, 1912), Vol. I, pp. 154 ff.; E. G. Wakefield, *A View of the Art of Colonization* (London, 1849); D. Wakefield (ed.), *The Public Lands a Mine of Wealth* (London, 1841).

without the aid of the parish fund. To prevent this it was suggested that emigrants be directed to the districts in the new country where they would find old acquaintances and familiar customs. It was also hoped that the letters from emigrants in such communities to friends and relatives at home would further stimulate emigration by the optimism which they would radiate.[1]

During the nineteenth century the activity of the government in promoting emigration took several forms. In 1831 the Government Commission on Emigration was formed; in 1840 the Colonial Land and Emigration Department was founded for the purpose of collecting and diffusing information about the colonies, to effect the sales of lands in Australia, and to promote emigration by devoting the proceeds of the sales of public lands to that purpose; the Irish famine gave rise to a select committee to consider means of colonization; the Emigrants' Information Office was opened in 1886; and another select committee was appointed by the House of Commons in 1889.[2]

Because of the great distance and expense, and of peculiar social conditions (caused in part by the deportation of criminals), it was necessary to render greater assistance to induce emigration to Australia than to Canada. But in spite of these measures emigrants preferred the United States to either of these countries.[3] Assisted emigration to Canada indirectly stimulated immigration to the United States, for the reasons which have already been given. Various forms of assistance have been furnished by individuals, philanthropic soci-

[1] *Poor Law Commissioners' Report of 1834*, pp. 351–358.

[2] For some account of these and other activities see S. C. Johnson, *A History of Emigration from the United Kingdom*.

[3] *Journal of the Royal Statistical Society*, Vol. I, pp. 156, 157; Vol. XVIII, p. 229.

eties, emigration societies, religious organizations, and trade unions. The great bulk of immigrants to the United States, however, have come without pecuniary aid or have had their transportation paid by prosperous settlers who preceded them. The poverty of the Irish was such that a considerable number of them could not have made use of the opportunities that America afforded unless they had received money and transportation tickets in this way.

In point of time emigration from the British Isles in the nineteenth century precedes that from the other countries of Europe. The social and economic changes wrought by the industrial revolution were manifest before the beginning of the century, and the accumulation of evils became so great that at the close of the Napoleonic wars emigration came to be regarded as a means of alleviating distress at home and of contributing to the development of the colonies. In subsequent chapters it will be seen that the attitude of the British government toward emigration was far more sympathetic than the attitude of Germany, the Scandinavian countries, and Holland. The peculiar environment of the Irish emigrant was destined to have a profound influence in shaping the life of the Irish-American and his descendants and in determining his attitude toward his adopted country as well as toward the government which had formerly claimed his allegiance. It is significant that the Irish are eager to surrender their allegiance to the British crown in favor of American citizenship, whereas the immigrants from England are low in the naturalization percentages.

CHAPTER III

THE SCANDINAVIANS

The emigrants from Sweden, Norway, and Denmark, commonly grouped together under the designation "Scandinavians," have not reached the numbers of those from the United Kingdom and Germany; but in proportion to the population of their native lands their numbers are truly remarkable.

Sweden's greatest king, Gustavus Adolphus, dreamed of founding a state in the New World; but although his successor established a colony on the Delaware, the dream was never realized. Nevertheless, it is the opinion of a competent Swedish observer that the establishment of Swedish-America is the greatest and most significant accomplishment of the Swedish people. Coming almost entirely from the lower classes, the Scandinavian-Americans have produced comparatively few eminent leaders; but with their qualities of industry, thrift, honesty, love of home, respect for law and order, religious nature, interest in education, and physical stamina they have played a respectable part in the development of American society.

During the last century the so-called "family type" gave a distinct stamp to the Scandinavian migration; but since about 1890 the number of single persons has become relatively larger. This generalization applies more to the Swedes than to the other two branches. In general, persecution and oppression have had little to do with the emigration movement, the desire for material betterment being the main reason. The stream of Danish emigrants is relatively small, not because the population of Denmark is smaller than that of Norway, but because the country will support a denser population and because its favorable situation with reference to England and Germany has made for agricultural prosperity. This circumstance should not cause us to lose sight of the fact that the Danes do not have the adventurous and pioneering instinct of the other Scandinavians.

The Scandinavian tide reached the high-water mark in the early eighties. In the three decades prior to that times were particularly hard, due principally to a series of wretched harvests. A letter from Sweden to a Swedish immigrant, dated 1869, relates that conditions were very bad: taxes high; private banks absorbing "like sponges" all coin and nothing remaining in the hands of the people; beggars over-running the country; and the government running behind and making loans. Another letter, written by a Swedish immigrant in 1867, states that "according to reports, conditions in Sweden must be very unfortunate for the poor and the bulk of the people. I believe they would do better to come to America." A Norwegian immigrant in 1835 writes to the same effect. He says:

I do not believe that any of those who suffer under the oppression of others and who must rear their children under straightened circumstances could do better than to help the latter to come to America. . . . I should like to talk to many persons in Norway for a little while, but we do not wish to live in Norway. We lived there altogether too long.[1]

[1] George M. Stephenson, "Typical 'America Letters,'" in *Yearbook of the Swedish Historical Society of America*, 1921–1922, pp. 53–92; Theodore C. Blegen, "A Typical 'America Letter,'" in *Mississippi Valley Historical Review*, Vol. IX, pp. 68–74.

The migration which has brought over seven hundred thousand Norwegians to America dates from 1825 with the coming of the "sloop party," while the Swedish movement began about 1841 with the settlement of Gustaf Unonius and his small party at Pine Lake, Wisconsin.[1] In general, the underlying causes are similar. Hard times, crop failures, difficulty of securing loans, money stringency, low wages, men out of work, the demand for laborers and housemaids in America, a certain dissatisfaction with Church and State, the propaganda of states and of emigration agencies, letters from enthusiastic immigrants, an unfair social system—all contributed to the same end. The "America fever"—a popular term in Sweden and Norway—swept parish after parish. Going to America was not an "industry"; it was a contagious disease.

The size of American farms was a revelation to the Norwegian and Swede. It was incredible but for the fact that his former neighbor, known for his truthfulness, had written that he was in possession of one. Emigration from Sweden was greatest from places where the division of land was greatest. A competent Swedish student of emigration believes that if railway building had begun twenty years sooner it would have stemmed the tide. However that may be, the slow development of canals and railways, built without system and without branch lines, made it still more difficult for the farmer to eke out a comfortable living on his small and often stony farm.[2]

Before 1900 the predominant interest of the Scandinavian Peninsula was agriculture. In Sweden the agricultural population was composed of three classes, *bönder*, *torpare*,

[1] Theodore C. Blegen, "Cleng Peerson and Norwegian Immigration," in *Mississippi Valley Historical Review*, Vol. VII, pp. 303–331.
[2] See Gustav Sundbärg, *Tankar i Utvandringsfrågan*. Stockholm, 1913.

and day laborers; in Norway, *bönder*, *husmaend*, and day laborers. In most matters these respective classes were in similar circumstances. The first class, the freeholders, owned their lands, and, while not as a rule wealthy, were in fairly good circumstances. The system of primogeniture, however, was a cause of considerable dissatisfaction. The earlier emigrants from both countries were largely of this class. The second group, the large dependent class whom we may term "cotters," rented or leased land from the freeholders in return for which they gave a certain number of days' labor and paid rent in kind. The cotter cultivated his small plot of ground and owned a cow or two, a horse, a pig, and a few chickens. His movements were not restricted and he could purchase land if he was able to save enough from his scanty earnings. The changes in methods of farming and in social life created dissatisfaction among both classes. After the break-up of the old system the personal relationship was lost; the freeholder's position no longer carried with it the former respect and reverence, and the cotter lost the patriarchal care that once was his. What the latter gained in some respects was lost in others. The day laborers on farms were relatively few.

Not to leave an erroneous impression, it should be said that the social relations between classes never reached the point of hostility observable in many other countries. With a fairly democratic government, especially in Norway, with illiteracy almost unknown, with great respect for persons in authority, and with a corresponding fondness for social distinctions and titles, it was rather easy to rise in the social scale.[1] An American consul in Sweden reported to his gov-

[1] J. Guinchard (ed.), *Sweden. Historical and Statistical Handbook* (2d ed.), Vol. I, p. 155. Stockholm, 1914.

ernment in 1882 that the Swedish emigrant, as compared with emigrants from other countries, was physically more robust, and was temperate in his habits and apparently well to do.

Without idealizing the Scandinavian emigrant, it may be said that he, probably more than the average emigrant, combined with the adventurous instinct the desire to improve his material condition. Whole districts were seized with the desire to go to America; rustics who had never wandered farther than a day's journey from their cottages wanted to be just like their old neighbors,—to see America. Their small parcels of land seemed even smaller when they read in an "America letter" that Ole Olson, formerly a humble cotter, was the owner of a 160-acre Minnesota farm. To make matters still worse, perhaps Ole had returned for a visit, wearing American clothes and with American money jingling in his pockets at every step. In some cases returned emigrants had received free transportation from steamship companies on condition that they would induce a group of emigrants to take passage on the company's liners.

Political and social discontent taking the form of armed rebellion never disturbed Norway and Sweden in the nineteenth century. The histories of these countries are barren of uprisings like those of 1830 and 1848 in Germany and France. From early times the people were partakers in government, although, in Sweden especially, the privileged classes were in control. The Swedish *Riksdag* down to 1866 was composed of four chambers, one for each class: nobles, clergy, burgesses, and peasants. Each house cast one vote, a majority vote being sufficient to pass all measures except an amendment to the constitution.

Lutheranism has placed a distinct stamp on Scandinavian character. In the past religion has played an important part in the life of the people. Travelers noted the presence of the Bible in the homes and the daily worship at the family altar. The Lutheran church in all lands has sought to educate the youth; but it has a rigid and exacting creed which has frequently led to the development of religious movements outside. The clergy, recruited principally from the nobles and better class, often lacked profound religious convictions, often neglected their duties, and were not overly careful of their personal conduct. Many sermons lacked fire and were tainted with rationalism. Crusaders against vice and intemperance received little encouragement from pastors and even encountered active opposition.

At the time emigration from Sweden was gaining momentum—in the forties and fifties—various streams of dissent were uniting in such force that alarm was felt in conservative quarters. Religious persecution has driven comparatively few Swedish emigrants to America; but from the circumstance that a considerable number were dissatisfied with the state church and that letters from America praised the religious freedom in that country, the aristocracy, clergy, and officeholders were hostile to everything that smacked of America. In a conversation with an English traveler in 1857, a Swedish pastor expressed the opinion that Sweden was not ready for freedom of conscience and that there was little piety in America. "Oh, the sects! the sects!—that is the disgrace of America. . . . What can Christ's Church be worth, when it is broken up into so many little parties, each quarreling with one another?"[1]

In the early stages of the emigration movement there was a disposition among the upper classes to attribute it to the

[1] Charles L. Brace, *The Norse-Folk; or, a Visit to the Homes of Norway and Sweden*, p. 273. New York, 1857.

influence of the *läsare*, or "readers," so called because of their practice of meeting together—at first secretly—to read the Bible. This religious movement took its beginning in opposition to the adoption of the *Catechism* and *Churchbook*, in 1810 and 1811, respectively. An American traveler, Bayard Taylor,[1] found no end to the desire of these people for knowledge about his country.

They overwhelmed us with questions about our country, its government, laws, climate, products and geographical extent. . . . They all complained about the burdens which fall upon a poor man in Sweden, in the shape of government taxes, tithes, and the obligation of supporting a portion of the army, who are distributed among them. . . .

A man residing near Karlskrona was most bitter in denouncing the *läsare*:

Many hundreds from my village [are leaving for America]. Fools! they could do much better at home. Sweden wants every one now. But it is the cursed *läsare*. . . . They turn every one upside down. They make disturbances, break the law and then . . . they must be punished; and so they go to carry on their accursed doings in America. Damn them![2]

An interesting religious movement which led directly to the emigration of several thousand Swedes between 1840 and 1860 centers in the personality and teachings of Eric Janson, who likewise was dissatisfied with the Lutheran church but who, unlike the *läsare*, separated from the state church and founded a church of his own. He denounced the "hireling clergy," and at a public meeting in 1844 burned some of the religious books dear to them. As a consequence of this and

---

[1] *Northern Travel: Summer and Winter Pictures of Sweden, Denmark and Lapland*, pp. 429, 430. New York, 1858.
[2] Brace, *The Norse-Folk*, pp. 406, 407.

of other activities the law of 1726 against dissenters was invoked, and Janson was imprisoned. After a period of persecution the leader and his followers decided to leave their native land in favor of a country where they could establish the New Jerusalem without interference from the authorities. Their colony in Henry County, Illinois, was named Bishop Hill, and contributes an interesting chapter to the history of communistic societies in the United States.[1]

Theodore C. Blegen writes:

The history of Norway is relatively free from religious persecution. Abundant evidence proves, however, that in the first four decades of the nineteenth century dissent and separatism were rather harshly dealt with by the government and the established church. Hans Nielsen Hauge, the leader of a laymen's movement in protest against the "rationalism and secularization then prevalent among the clergy of Norway," was imprisoned from 1804 to 1814.[2]

It is significant that the "sloop folk" of 1825 were Quakers of Stavanger, although the fact that they were humble and poor made it economically advantageous to emigrate. In 1843 a royal commission appointed to investigate the emigration problem reported:

Even though the first sprouts of the migrations must be sought to a certain extent in imperfections in the law, which have produced dissatisfaction among certain individuals, their growth in recent times is the result of other causes, especially of the common need, affecting the great majority of the emigrants, of seeking a less difficult existence in a new country.

[1] M. A. Mikkelsen, "The Bishop Hill Colony. A Religious Communistic Settlement in Henry County, Illinois," in *Johns Hopkins University Studies in History and Political Science*, Vol. X (1892).

[2] This account is based on the scholarly article by Mr. Blegen on "Cleng Peerson and Norwegian Immigration," in *Mississippi Valley Historical Review*, Vol. VII, pp. 303–331.

Religious conditions in Sweden are reflected in the life of the Swedish-Americans. As Sweden is the most aristocratic of the Scandinavian countries, so are her clergy the most hierarchical. Because of her high-church tendencies, she has not looked with favor on revival movements. This attitude of intolerance and even persecution has caused many Swedes, both in the homeland and in America, to affiliate with the more liberal churches, such as the Mission Friends, Methodists, and Baptists, or to sever all connection with organized Christianity. Some of the more recent immigrants are openly hostile to Christianity.[1] The experience with a state church has also made them hostile to church government which suggests any connection between church and state. The organization of the Scandinavian churches in this country is thoroughly democratic, the episcopacy of the mother church having been displaced by the congregational form of government.

The governments of the Scandinavian countries looked with disfavor upon the emigration of the flower of the peasant population, but it was in Sweden that the opposition was most manifest. This opposition came from the landowners, the clergy, and the government officials.[2] Almost without exception the newspapers in Sweden painted America in the blackest colors, giving publicity to every disappointment that could be culled from letters from emigrants. The emigrants charged that the press was subsidized by the interests who desired to keep the common people in subjection and who profited by their labor. At the beginning of the present century the National Society against Emigration was formed

[1] See John O. Evjen, "The Scandinavians and the Book of Concord," in *Lutheran Quarterly*, April, 1906.

[2] See George M. Stephenson, "Some Footnotes to the History of Swedish Immigration from about 1855 to about 1865," in *Yearbook of the Swedish Historical Society of America*, 1921–1922, pp. 33 ff.

and aided and encouraged by the government. The activity of this organization was concerned with propaganda to counteract the "America letters" by fostering loyalty to the country and furnishing information about opportunities at home, to induce Swedish-Americans to return, and to assist people in acquiring homes of their own. The "own your own home" movement was perhaps the most important phase of the society's work. Under the auspices of the government and the society many data bearing on the emigration problem have been gathered and published.[1]

In no country of Europe have the "America letters," emigrant guides, emigration agents, and newspapers from America played a more active part than in the Scandinavian countries. Perhaps the most interesting of the guides is the booklet of thirty-nine pages written by Ole Rynning, a Norwegian immigrant residing at Beaver Creek, Illinois, about seventy miles south of Chicago. In the preface, dated February 13, 1838, he addressed his countrymen as follows:

I have now been in America eight months, and in this time I have had an opportunity to learn much in regard to which I vainly sought to procure information before I left Norway. I felt at that time how unpleasant it is for those who wish to emigrate to America to be without a trustworthy and fairly detailed account of the country. I learned also how great the ignorance of the people is, and what false and preposterous reports were believed as full truth. . . .

The contents of the book give a fairly good idea of the things that were agitating the minds of prospective emigrants and the gross misunderstanding of America. In what general

[1] See, for example, Gustav Sundbärg, *Tankar i Utvandringsfrågan* (Stockholm, 1913) ; Adrian Molin, *Svensk Egnahemspolitik. Några Synpunkter och Förslag* (Stockholm, 1909).

direction from Norway is America situated, and how far away is it? How did the country first become known? What in general is the nature of the country, and for what reason do so many people go there, and expect to make a living? Is it not to be feared that the land will soon be overpopulated? Is it true that the government is going to prohibit more people from coming? In what part of the country have the Norwegians settled? What is the most convenient and cheapest way to reach them? What is the nature of the land where the Norwegians have settled? What does good land cost? What are the prices of cattle and of provisions? How high are wages? What kind of religion is to be found in America? Is there any kind of order or government in the land, or can everyone do as he pleases? What provisions are made for the education of children, and for the care of poor people? What language is spoken in America? Is it difficult to learn? Is there considerable danger from disease in America? Is there reason to fear wild animals and the Indians? For what kind of people is it advisable to emigrate to America, and for whom is it not advisable? What particular dangers is one likely to encounter on the ocean? Is it true that those who are brought to America are sold as slaves? Guiding advice is given for those who wish to go to America: how they should hire a ship; how they should exchange their money; what time of the year and what route are the most convenient; what they ought to take with them.[1]

The letter of a returned emigrant written from Sweden in 1868 testifies to the ubiquity of emigration agents:

At the stations in Sweden we were grievously beset by lieutenants of emigration agents, and in Göteborg the situation was deplorable,

---

[1] Ole Rynning's "True Account of America" is translated in full by Theodore C. Blegen in *Minnesota History Bulletin*, Vol. II, pp. 211–269.

to put it mildly. . . . I want to warn everybody who intends to emigrate not to take any stock in these agents, who talk and make promises as though they were angels of light, but do not know the least thing about what they promise.[1]

The newspapers bristled with advertisements of steamship, emigration, and land companies; and it availed little for the editor in another column to warn his readers against the snares of the unscrupulous. A highly respected minister in the province of Norrland in reply to those who insisted that ministers ought to issue warnings against emigration said that, while he had done so in the past, he refused to do so in the future for the following reasons: (1) He was set down a liar by prospective emigrants and by those who did not intend to emigrate when he cited facts published in the newspapers, because the letters from America told of good fortune and satisfaction and advised emigration. (2) Conditions in Sweden were such that it was not to be wondered at that people wanted to emigrate. (3) The activities of agents and persons residing in Sweden who were actively interested in emigration nullified his efforts. (4) The tide could not be stemmed until a considerable number of emigrants returned and testified that they had been duped.[2]

The conditions and events which have been surveyed pertain more especially to the early or formative years of Scandinavian emigration, for with the beginning of the present century Norway and Sweden had inaugurated a series of reforms which have brought them in the van of the most progressive and enlightened nations. Had these steps been taken a half century earlier the history of Scandinavian emigration

---

[1] George M. Stephenson, "Hemlandet Letters," in *Yearbook of the Swedish Historical Society of America*," 1922–1923, p. 146.

[2] *Gefleposten*, a newspaper in Sweden, cited in *Hemlandet*, July 30, 1867.

would have been written in very different fashion. As it was, the efforts of the ruling classes by untruthful accounts of America to frighten the peasants out of emigrating were only pouring oil on fire. The pietistic and puritanical strain in the American-Scandinavian population is a legacy from the early emigrants who were repelled by the worldliness and unsympathetic attitude of the state-church clergy.

CHAPTER IV

THE GERMANS

More things have been said in diverse ways about the German element in our population than about any other immigrant stock. It has been said that of all the elements which have come during the past century the Germans have on the whole represented the highest type. This sentiment represents perhaps the prevailing opinion prior to the World War. During the hectic years of the war, when pens were dipped in gall and tongues were unbridled and perspectives were distorted, many worthy memories of the past were forgotten. Epithets were bandied about with reckless abandon, the Germans sinning as much as they were sinned against.

In point of numbers the German immigration in the nineteenth century exceeds that of any other stock, in the decade of the eighties no less than 1,452,870 coming to our shores. Up to 1850 the German immigrants were outnumbered by the Irish, but in every subsequent decade to the close of the century the Germans were the most numerous.[1]

The German immigration includes a great variety of types, to be attributed doubtless to the wide differences between portions of Germany and to the peculiar history of the country. Thinking in terms of the German Empire, it is easy to forget the particularistic tendencies of the old Empire and

[1] Albert B. Faust, *The German Element in the United States, with special Reference to its Political, Moral, Social, and Educational Influence*, Vol. I, pp. 573 ff. Boston, 1909.

Confederation, which shattered the dream of a Stein and retarded the work of a Bismarck. An intensive study of German emigration would include a consideration of the geographical features of the country, the political history of each division, the variety of its races, and the diversity of intellectual and economic life. The Prussian and the Saxon, the Catholic and the Protestant, the peasant and the factory worker, may be as unlike as the laborer in a New England factory and the Iowa farmer.[1]

The history of German immigration may be divided into three periods. The immigrants who came in the colonial period did not leave an impress on American society to the extent that the later immigrants did. From 1776 to 1812, although the stream was not entirely dried up, it was not rapidly fed, a fact that explains why the Germans lost many characteristics which had been imported from across the water. In the second period, from 1815 to 1852, political refugees and intellectual men lent a distinctive flavor to the movement. Many were high-spirited young people, inspired by fresh ideals which they had failed to realize in the Old World. Numerically this period is of less importance than the ones which precede and follow. In the exodus after 1852, which assumed the proportions of a stampede, economic causes overshadowed all others. The immigrants were agriculturists, small tradesmen, mechanics, and common laborers. A characteristic common to the three periods is the migration of family groups, as in the case of the Scandinavians. In the last thirty years single persons have come in largeɪ proportions.

---

[1] W. H. Dawson, *The Evolution of Modern Germany*, chap. ii, 1914. The German settlements in America had the characteristics of the region of Germany from which the immigrants came.

In the study of the background of the migration in the colonial period religious and political persecution assumes considerable importance. It is sufficient to remind the student of history of the misery which followed in the wake of the Thirty Years' War, the War of the Palatinate, the War of the Spanish Succession, and the War of the Austrian Succession. In some parts religious persecution of the worst sort existed, particularly in the Palatinate. In fact, so many fled from that region that in America the term "Palatines" was applied without discrimination to German immigrants. From 1720 to 1750 the colonial population was recruited by Moravians, Mennonites, Dunkards, Lutherans, and Reformed Germans, many of whom were redemptioners.[1]

One of the most interesting of the early movements of emigration occurred in the Rhenish Palatinate in 1709. William Penn traveled in the Palatinate and preached to a people who had many things in common with the Quakers. The Mennonites dressed simply, were "conscientious objectors" to war, refused to take judicial oaths, had no paid ministry, and did not believe in infant baptism. After Penn returned to England and obtained the grant of the province which came to be called Pennsylvania, he prepared literature setting forth the advantages of the province, and it was circulated among the prospective emigrants. The great rush of emigrants was in 1709, following the devastation wrought by the War of the Spanish Succession, the very severe winter, and the unfounded rumor that Queen Anne of England would transport free of charge those who desired to go to America. By October about thirteen thousand ragged and miserable

---

[1] The most satisfactory general account of the causes of German immigration is Faust's two-volume work, cited above. Lucy F. Bittinger's *The Germans in Colonial Times* (Philadelphia, 1901) is an interesting little volume.

Germans found themselves in London and furnished a curious sight for the citizens of that city. England cared for and disposed of them as best she could. Some were sent to Ireland, but the greater number found their way to America. The nineteenth century witnessed a wonderful transformation in Germany. At the beginning of the century four great intellectual leaders stand out: Kant, Fichte, Goethe, and Schiller. For a time these men exercised a controlling influence on the German people and brought them out of the slough of despond after the humiliation of their country during the Napoleonic wars. Aided by such men as Stein and Niebuhr, a strong feeling of nationalism and patriotism was developed in direct opposition to the domination of Metternich, the evil genius of constitutional and political development. "Metternichmus," as the Germans called it, made the political life of the people impossible.

In opposition to the reactionary régime clubs were formed to keep alive the liberal spirit. They were not political organizations primarily; their declared objects were the fostering of high moral ideas, the stimulating of patriotism, and the engendering of the scientific spirit. University students and professors took a leading part in the liberal movement, the University of Jena being one of the most important centers of liberalism. Although the radicalism of the *Deutsche Burschenschaften*, as the student organizations were called, can easily be overemphasized, it is undoubtedly true that at some of the meetings sentiments were expressed by enthusiastic and somewhat intoxicated speakers that unduly excited the already overwrought nerves of the reactionaries. An incident which attracted considerable attention occurred at Eisenach, Luther's birthplace, in October, 1817, when students kindled a bonfire and burned certain books and regalia sacred to the powers that be, in imitation of Luther's burning of the papal bull and canon law. A more serious affair, followed by more serious consequences, was the stabbing of a suspected Russian spy by a member of a *Burschenschaft*, in March, 1819. The governments of Austria and Prussia now coöperated to investigate liberal activities, and for ten years most oppressive measures were brought to bear on those who were suspect or suspected of being suspect. What the present day terms "smelling-committees" spied on university professors and others. These measures brought discontent especially in the southern states,—Baden, Württemberg, Bavaria, Hesse-Darmstadt, and the Rhineland,—and caused many to flee to Switzerland, France, the Netherlands, and especially to England and the United States. Compared to the emigration which followed the revolutions of 1830 and 1848, the numbers were few, and they were absorbed rapidly into the population of America.[1]

Under these discouraging conditions many turned their thoughts to America as a land where their ideals might be realized. Some even dreamed of establishing a German state in the West where the German language would be on an equal basis with English in legislative bodies, in courts, and in schools. A number of the educated German immigrants complained of the absence of high ideals in American life—in politics and religion—and of the lack of appreciation of the true worth of German character and culture. The movement to establish a bilingual state touched only a few of the cultivated immigrants, the bulk of them caring or knowing little or nothing about it.[2]

[1] Carl Schurz, *Reminiscences*, Vol. I.
[2] Kate Everest, "How Wisconsin came by its Large German Element," in Wisconsin State Historical Society, Collections, Vol. XII, pp. 302 ff.

In 1824 Gottfried Duden arrived at St. Louis, Missouri, and later became a farmer in that state. Duden was a highly intelligent man, with a classical education and with considerable experience. He wrote letters and pamphlets giving a glowing description of the new country, which were circulated in Germany and made a deep impression. Duden was well and favorably known, and his statements carried great weight. Many did not read his writings carefully and were misled; and when they met with disappointments in the New World, they saddled the blame on Duden. In answer to his accusers Duden published his "Self-accusation because of his American Report of Travel, as a Warning against Future Indiscreet Emigration," in which he asserts that he intended his work to be read by intelligent human beings and regrets that he did not write in hieroglyphics. Duden's report consists of (1) a collection of letters, (2) a treatise concerning the political condition of the North American free states, and (3) an advisory supplement for emigrating German farmers and for those contemplating commercial undertakings. In one of the letters he wrote:

I am convinced, that if several families, say ten or twenty, who are on friendly terms with one another, should spend a year here in the peaceful situation, such as the American is able to provide for himself so quickly in the midst of an unpeopled forest, they would never yearn again to return to Europe, to visit, yes, but never to stay.

He also expressed the hope that a little city could be founded for the purpose of making it a center of German culture in America, a nucleus of a rejuvenated Germania, a second Fatherland. He hoped that a lively interest in the project would develop and spread in Germany. He had no fear that the Americans would oppose this enterprise, for they had always given German immigrants a hearty welcome and courteous treatment.[1]

The writings of Duden augmented the movement to organize colonization societies and were the direct cause of the formation of the *Giessener Auswanderungs-Gesellschaft* in 1833, with Giessen, in the grand duchy of Hessen, as the center. The original plan of this emigration society was to found a colony in Arkansas, with an administration modeled after the German system. Later Missouri was substituted for Arkansas. Settlements similar to that of the Giessen colony were called "Latin settlements" by the Americans. The "Latin farmers" were not successful in their unaccustomed work and sooner or later abandoned their farms.

Following the revolution of 1830 came more suspects and arrests and still more colonization societies, but the revolution of 1848 inaugurated even more important movements. A number of the "forty-eighters" were ultraradicals, ardent republicans, and against all forms of monarchies. "Liberty" was their watchword. Some of them, like Carl Schurz, came here with a price on their heads. They were literary men, journalists, lawyers, and physicians, whose aggressive character and critical attitude brought forth much hostile criticism from Americans.[2]

The German-Americans are more evenly distributed over the country than are the immigrants from other countries of Europe; but in this period certain centers of German population were established,—St. Louis, Belleville (Illinois),

[1] For an account of the work and influence of Duden, see Kargau, "Missouri's German Immigration," in Missouri Historical Collections, Vol. II, pp. 23 ff., and his translations of Duden's letters, in *Missouri Historical Review*, Vols. XII, XIII, and XIV.

[2] Ernest Bruncken, "German Political Refugees," in *Deutsch-Amerikanische Geschichtsblätter*, October, 1903, pp. 44 ff.

Cleveland, Cincinnati, Milwaukee. According to the census of 1880 Wisconsin had a larger percentage of German-born residents than any other state.

The forces operating to attract immigrants to Wisconsin are typical of those which played a part to a greater or lesser degree in the case of other communities or sections: (1) favorable situation with reference to communication and markets; (2) liberal qualifications for the suffrage, the constitution of 1848 requiring a residence of only one year; (3) lower taxes than in certain adjoining states which had embarked on disastrous internal-improvement enterprises and had accumulated heavy debts; (4) an abundance of unoccupied lands which could be acquired on easy terms; (5) German activities in advertising the state and the advantages of residing in communities where German churches, schools, and societies were established; (6) the appointment of a state commissioner of immigration under a law passed in 1852; (7) the propaganda of railway companies.[1]

A history of German immigration which attempts to give an exhaustive discussion of the causes for the unprecedented exodus since 1850 would require many volumes. All that can be done here is to suggest in general the factors which stand out above others.

A comparison of the population of Germany with that of other countries which have furnished the "old immigrants" does not make the number of German immigrants seem phenomenal. As in the case of the Scandinavian movement, the numbers would probably have been much greater except

[1] See an interesting and scholarly article by Joseph Schafer, "The Yankee and Teuton in Wisconsin," in *Wisconsin Magazine of History*, Vol. VI, pp. 125-145. The author draws on a wealth of material and explains the preference of the Germans and Yankees in selecting land and the conditions which governed settlement.

for the fact that the governments tried as far as possible to keep the people at home by increasing the stringency of the laws controlling emigration and diverting it to the German colonies. But the reports that came to Germany from America in the form of letters from immigrants, books written by enthusiastic German-Americans, and the propaganda by states, societies, and corporations were certain to reap a rich harvest. The American consul at Aix-la-Chapelle wrote that the consulate was continually receiving papers, pamphlets, and other documents about immigration to the United States. Generally this material was accompanied by letters written by the secretary of some immigration society, in which the consular office was requested to place it where it would do the most good. The consul wrote:

After a careful examination of these publications a patriotic American would conclude that, so far as the majority of them are concerned, the question in reality is, where can they be placed so as to do the least harm to the United States.[1]

Most of them came from organizations interested in securing immigration to Southern and Western states, exaggerating conditions in their own states and belittling others. In 1872 ten thousand copies of a *Special Report on Immigration*, consisting of over two hundred pages of information about prices and rentals of land, staple products, access to market, kinds of labor in demand in Western and Southern states, and many other items, was printed in the German language at the expense of the Federal government and circulated in Europe.[2] This document was in great demand and was frequently men-

[1] *United States Consular Reports*, Vol. VI, pp. 123–125.
[2] *House Executive Documents*, 42d Cong., 2d Sess., No. 1; ibid. 43d Cong., 1st Sess., No. 287. This document was also translated into French and Scandinavian.

tioned in consular reports. Coming from the Federal government, the information was considered reliable and carried much weight.

Undoubtedly the German immigrants were in greater demand than those of any other nationality. Their sturdy character, law-abiding instincts, habits of industry, painstaking zeal, honesty, and intelligence made them desirable additions to any agricultural and industrial community. In the early nineties in reply to a questionnaire sent to the governors of states by the Immigration Restriction League, fourteen states expressed a desire for Germans; twelve, Scandinavians; seven, English and Scotch; six, "Irish or other English-speaking peoples"; three, French; two, Swiss; and one, Hollanders and Belgians.[1]

The swelling tide of German immigrants coincided with a feverish development of American enterprise: railroad construction, opening of Western lands, and industrial expansion. The enactment of the homestead law in 1862, granting one hundred and sixty acres of public land practically free on condition of settlement and cultivation, was a tremendous inducement to the land-hungry German who eked out a precarious living by intensive cultivation and the practice of utmost economy. During the fifteen or more years that the homestead measure had been before Congress many a German citizen was watching the legislative situation across the Atlantic as eagerly as an ambitious American. When the bill passed the House of Representatives in February, 1859, the news was received in Germany with many manifestations of joy, and extensive preparations were made for removal to the republic where land was free; but hopes were dashed when it was learned later that the interests

[1] *Senate Reports,* 54th Cong., 1st Sess., No. 290.

antagonistic to the measure had succeeded in defeating it in the Senate.[1] One may guess with certainty that the German-American was not slow to acquaint his friends and relatives in the old country of the election of Abraham Lincoln, the candidate of the Republican party, which had incorporated a homestead plank in its platform as a bid for German votes.

Prior to the World War it was fashionable to praise the wonderful progress of the German Empire along economic and social lines. With no thought of disparaging these achievements, the fact remains that during the last century at least America was a far more attractive place for the farmer and artisan than any country of Europe. A comparison of wages and hours of work in America and Germany shows a heavy advantage in favor of the former. A comparison of agricultural conditions is even more decisive. During the time of greatest industrial and commercial development the German farmer experienced a shortage of labor, increasing cost of production, and a decline in the prices of his products. The heaviest fall was from 1880 to 1889, the years of greatest immigration. With the beginning of the present century the decline of German immigration may be attributed to causes similar to those which produced a falling off from Scandinavia. Free lands were nearly exhausted and land values were up. In short, America was no longer the America of the forties, fifties, sixties, seventies, and eighties; and Germany was no longer the land of Metternich and Bismarck.

Although the German government never tried out colonization schemes like those which operated in Great Britain, earnest efforts to divert emigration to colonies under the

[1] *Chicago Press and Tribune* (weekly), April 28, 1859.

German flag were made. The American consul at Sonne-
berg in 1886 wrote:

It is amusing to see with what eagerness the colonies are written
up and the United States written down. Lately they have been
comparing the German emigration to the United States of this year
with that of the three preceding years, and rejoicing that the figures
show a steady decline during these years. That, according to their
statements, 2500 Germans in New York City were out of employment was not long ago the reason urgently assigned for Germans
not going to the United States. But the annual report of the German Society of New York City, showing the table of excellent
wages obtained by German workmen, is carefully left out. In the
last few weeks they have published the total amount of injury to
life and property in the United States by wind-storms during last
year; therefore it would be better to risk the dangers of African
fever. And so on.[1]

By virtue of the fact that the oppressive measures of the
German and Austrian governments drove into exile a number
of educated and aggressive men who speedily became leaders
among their countrymen in America, the German element,
even before the Civil War, became an important factor in
American politics. The Irish influence prior to 1860 was more
largely negative, whereas the German was more positive.

The inauguration of a restrictive immigration policy by
the United States in 1917 has not materially altered the
character of German immigration. Almost without exception
the Germans can qualify for admission under the literacy
test; and the quota base in the percentage laws was designed
to favor the countries of northern and western Europe.

[1] *House Executive Documents*, 49th Cong., 2d Sess., No. 157, p. 230. See
translation of "German Official Views on Colonial and on American Immigration," printed in a paper established in the interests of colonial emigration, in *House Miscellaneous Documents*, 52d Cong., 1st Sess., Vol. XVI,
pp. 315–319.

CHAPTER V

THE DUTCH

The heroic struggle of the Dutch against the Spaniards and incidents and personalities associated with the founding of the Dutch settlements in colonial times are familiar to every school child. This, together with the pictures of life in Holland, has made us feel that the Dutch are a people very different from the rest of mankind, whereas the truth of the matter is that they are very human, shrewd, and not infrequently mercenary. In other words, they share the characteristics of other immigrants.

That the Dutch were not colonizers as the English were is seen in the expedients employed to attract immigrants to New Netherlands. By a charter of freedom and exemptions large tracts along the Hudson River were granted to Dutch burghers who undertook to procure a certain number of persons to cultivate the land. There was not the same incentive to migrate from Holland that we find in England under the Stuarts. The government took little interest in America, offering no protection from the Indians; the Dutch West India Company was interested solely in the fur trade and in the profits of it; the unfortunate wars with the English resulted disastrously; and there was no religious or political persecution.

A graph showing the emigration from the Netherlands in the nineteenth century would reveal tendencies similar to those of the German and Scandinavian migrations. From

1841 to 1902, inclusive, more than 135,000 people arrived
from the Netherlands. The decade of the eighties brought
no less than 53,000. In the next five years about 25,000
came; thereafter the numbers decline sharply. In 1900
Michigan had the largest Dutch-born population (30,406);
Illinois ranked next (21,916); New Jersey, New York, Iowa,
and Wisconsin, with numbers ranging from 10,000 to 6000,
follow in order.

In considering the causes of migration from Holland we
shall in the main repeat the causes operating in other countries studied, with religious and political discontent playing
a rather relatively important rôle. It is sufficient to say that
the primary causes were economic. The Dutchman, like the
Scandinavian, came to get a better living. The Dutch are
not a migrating people. They are shrewd, hard-headed, cal-
culating, and industrious, as conditions in their settlements
abundantly testify, attracted to America by letters and pamphlets which emphasized the superior opportunities in the
New World.

The impulse for emigration after 1840 grew originally out
of conditions that developed after the establishment of the
kingdom of Holland under the House of Orange, following
the deposition of Napoleon. The new king, William I, pur-
posed to restore the established church to its former position.
Ecclesiastical property was transferred to the state, and the
clergy received their salaries from the state. The church
government was placed in the hands of a general synod,
whose delegates were to be selected under royal control. The
abuses inherent in a state church soon became manifest, and
dissent arose. The dissenters were excommunicated and
subjected to legal and social persecution and discrimination.
This situation, coupled with the facts that employment was

scarce,—many living on the verge of poverty,—and that taxes, a legacy of the war debt contracted during the Napoleonic wars, were high, led many to turn to emigration as a way out.

Although the Congress of Vienna had stripped Holland of her best colonies, Java seemed a possible home for emigrants. But the great distance from the mother country, the unsuitable climate, the uncertain conditions, and the fear of repressive legislation under Dutch rule were formidable obstacles.

Emigration and the future home of emigrants were discussed in a number of pamphlets, written mainly by separatist ministers, of whom Henry P. Scholte and Albertus C. Van Raalte were the most prominent. Scholte was especially favorable to America, dwelling on the economic opportunities, religious freedom, and the fact that there was no restriction on education. The leaders, being of a religious turn of mind, attempted to exclude from the emigrant groups those whom they considered undesirable. Atheists, skeptics, Catholics, and the profane, immoral, and intemperate were not wanted. In selecting sites for settlement they favored places where their religion could be exercised and perpetuated.

In the summer, autumn, and winter of 1846 meetings were held to discuss emigration and to make arrangements for the journey. In September of that year the first installment of emigrants left Holland from Rotterdam under the leadership of Van Raalte. Some time before their departure an appeal in the form of a pamphlet had been sent to America addressed to "Brethren in the Faith in America," asking assistance and direction in the selection of a future home. The appeal was not in vain, for on the landing of the small party a cordial welcome was accorded by ministers and members of the Dutch Reformed Church. Van Raalte traveled extensively in search of a suitable site for settlement and everywhere was treated with the utmost kindness. At Detroit, Michigan, where he established his headquarters, a conference of prominent men was called, at which resolutions were adopted, praising the Dutch for their determination to desert a country for the sake of political and religious liberty, extending a cordial invitation to settle in Michigan, and appointing a committee to coöperate with the immigrants in finding homes. The governor of the state urged the legislature to do its part in making the state attractive. After weighing the advantages of other states, Van Raalte decided upon the Black River valley in Michigan because of its rich soil, timberland, location near a river, the favorable terms on which land could be purchased, and the future possibilities of the region. Dutch immigration to Michigan increased rapidly after the initial settlement. Van Raalte's influence carried great weight. In a long and remarkable letter to his brother-in-law in Holland, later printed in pamphlet form under the title "Holland in America, or the Dutch Colony in the State of Michigan," he made a clever and effective argument in behalf of that state, at the same time casting some rather gratuitous aspersions on certain sister states.

At the time of the Dutch migration into Michigan under the leadership and inspiration of Van Raalte, Henry P. Scholte, a sturdy character, was the Moses of a similar movement into Iowa, where a settlement was founded at Pella. This interesting story has never been told better than in the words of the founder himself, printed and circulated in Holland, where they were read with great interest. We shall draw liberally on this account.[1]

[1] "A Voice from Pella," translated by Jacob Van der Zee, in *Iowa Journal of History and Politics*, Vol. IX, pp. 529–574.

The rumors of his coming to the United States had preceded him, and hardly had he arrived when he was stormed with offers of land so tempting that he was on his guard to escape the snares of unscrupulous land speculators. Armed with letters from the American minister to Holland and from influential friends in America, he had no difficulty in obtaining information. The cordial treatment that he received at the hands of government officials at Washington was in striking contrast with his experiences in his native land. Printed documents and a set of maps of the various states indicating the unsold government lands were presented to him.

Pressure was put on him to direct his colony to Michigan, but he deemed that section too far north, lacking in roads and sufficient prairie land. To the farmer who had already spent a part of his life in the level hayfields and lands of Holland, the unusual battle with trees and constant views of stumps in the midst of meadows and cultivated fields could not be agreeable, he thought.

He investigated the best means of inland transportation and was thus enabled to come into touch with a class of persons whom people were accustomed to call kidnappers and deceivers, who stormed each incoming ship like hungry wolves. They attempted to gain the immigrants' confidence by telling them that all other people were liars. Each transportation office had men of this type in its employ.

These kidnappers have become so accustomed during recent years to see incoming ships filled with half-starved Irishmen or ill-smelling Germans that the rumor of the coming of so many Hollanders, who were bringing some money and a fairly cleanly appearance with them, goaded their zeal anew to give chase after what people here have already quite generally learned to call "willempjes." Among the ship's assailants who were interested in

the oncoming "willempjes" were also some Hollanders, Jews as well
as Gentiles, who were acquainted with the relatives and circumstances of some of whose coming they had heard, obviously obliged
by allies equally concerned in Holland. One can form no idea of
this branch of industry at the seaports and especially at New York;
we should almost be able to read the hearts of these men if one
wishes to be secure from paying toll in some form or another to this
host of unofficial officers.

Scholte writes of the cordiality with which the Americans
welcomed the Dutch and believes that in general they have
too lofty opinions of them. They are represented as re-
sembling the God-fearing Pilgrims, whose coming to a land
of civil and political liberty was one of God's blessings.

The privilege of preaching in his native tongue was in
striking contrast with the treatment accorded Scholte in
Holland, where he was despised, misunderstood, and tram-
pled upon. In response to a petition from the Hollanders
the legislature of Iowa enacted a law giving the right of suffrage to those who had declared their intention of becoming
citizens. This liberal action convinced Scholte that if Holland did not change her policy, thousands of Hollanders
would find room for homes in the New World under a benevolent government.

I am grieved to note that the government of Holland has not
yet forsaken its fatal course, and that the newspapers in support of
the government are not ashamed to print articles which place immigrants to America in a false light. Christians have not refrained
from adding their mite also to create a wrong impression. . . . Here
every person is respected and treated according to his merits; there
are no spies for a suspicious government: the rulers know that this
would not profit them because a subsequent election might at once
deprive them of the chance to lord it over the people by putting
others in their places.

Addressing the wealthy people in his native land, Scholte tells them that it is their duty to help the poor and needy and oppressed. If their own land and colonies cannot offer them work and freedom and Christian instruction, they should render assistance that will make it possible for the unfortunates to prosper among their countrymen in America. In order to supply his bodily wants in this country, an industrious man requires very little more than the money to pay his passage. If, however, the older generation is spread among English-speaking people, their spiritual needs will be sacrificed to material comfort. For this reason Scholte advises settlement in a colony where their mother tongue is spoken and the word of God is preached in a familiar language.

The writings of Scholte and Van Raalte rank in importance with Ole Rynning's *True Account* in stimulating immigration and determining settlement.

The story of the early Dutch settlements is the history of typical frontier communities. Daughter colonies were founded as immigration increased. In 1870 Henry Hospers, a member of the Pella colony, was commissioned by the Board of Immigration of Iowa to go to Holland. Hospers traveled extensively, established an office, and through newspaper advertising and pamphlets informed the people of opportunities in Iowa. Letters seeking information poured into his office. After his return to Iowa he published a newspaper at a new colony that he had founded in Sioux County. In 1875 a book dealing with economic conditions in America and especially in Iowa, written by a Dutch resident of that state, was published in Holland. The author's purpose was partly to counteract the overoptimistic accounts of America circulated by railroad and steamship companies and the malicious misrepresentations by enemies of emigration.

CHAPTER VI

THE NEW IMMIGRATION: INTRODUCTORY

That the immigrants from northern and western Europe are desirable and those from eastern and southern Europe are undesirable has become a trite saying. It is customary to point out that the Nordic races are more akin to the native Americans in appearance, in spirit, and in their attitude toward American institutions and therefore assimilate more easily than the so-called Latin and Slavic and other peoples. The Slavs, Italians, Greeks, and Jews, it is said, have not had that training in self-government which enables them to become useful and intelligent American citizens. That the new immigration is first and last a money-seeking enterprise, a cold-blooded proposition, is cited as a further objection. The old immigrants came to get a better living, but they established permanent homes and appreciated the opportunities America afforded. The "bird of passage" retains his loyalty to his native land and sojourns in this country only until he has accumulated an amount of money sufficient to enable him to return and live in greater comfort. His native environment has made him suspicious of government; and this circumstance, we are told, has made him susceptible to the intrigues of the agitator.

Without attempting to pass judgment, it may be said that comparisons between the old immigrant and the new are unfair to both. Just as the popular opinion of the older immigrant has undergone change with changing circumstances, a revision of opinion regarding later comers is probable. It is unprofitable to compare a racial stock which has been a part of American life for over a half century with a people whose stay with us spans only a few years. It must also be considered that the America of the middle of the last century was a part of a world which later experienced revolutions which were never dreamed of in that day. The question of the desirability of immigration in the present century is a matter entirely apart from the qualities of any racial group. The student of immigration will do well to bear this in mind.

It is not the province of this book to enter into the field of scientific investigation and theory and to pass judgment on the merits of the controversy raging between the "Nordics" and the "non-Nordics." It is sufficient to say that the student of immigration will do well to suspend judgment until "all the evidence is in." It is true that American institutions, American civilization, and American speech are Anglo-Saxon in their origin and that the Englishman, German, and Scandinavian speedily amalgamate on this side of the ocean; but it is hazardous to assert that the so-called new immigrants are unfitted for American citizenship because of an inferiority inherent in their races. That their habits, characters, customs, and modes of thought are profoundly affected by their environment is a trite saying. This was especially true of the Irish immigrants who came before the Civil War. But whether or not the American environment will transform the Italian, Slav, and Jew as it has transformed the Irishman cannot be proved by history. The historian studies the past; if the present is explained by the past, that is no affair of his.

It is rather difficult to explain why emigration from southern and eastern Europe was delayed until the last quarter of the nineteenth century, after hordes of emigrants had deserted the northern and western portions of the Continent. Generally speaking, the effects of the industrial, agricultural, social, and political revolutions were not so noticeable in the earlier years of the century in the countries of southern and eastern Europe as they were in the countries of the old immigration. When the forces retarding the older movement in America and Europe got under way, immigration agents swarmed into the virgin fields of Italy, Austria-Hungary, Russia, and the Balkan states. The stories of opportunities in America were believed as readily as they had been in other countries; and steamship companies were not tardy in accommodating themselves to the swelling throngs who clamored for passage. The following chapters take some account of the more important movements; but these movements are so recent that perspective is difficult to attain. As in the case of the older migration, after the lapse of years there will be an accumulation of documents which will enable the historian to write with a surer hand.

CHAPTER VII

THE ITALIANS

During the present century Italy displaced Germany as the great migrating nation; but owing to the fact that so many Italian emigrants return to their native land, the loss of population is not so serious. Italy is one of the few governments which have encouraged emigration, protecting the emigrants on the voyage and keeping a motherly eye on them in the lands where they are sojourning,—for emigration from Italy is not confined to America. For many years Italians have migrated—perhaps for only a season—to other countries of Europe and to South America, notably Argentina and Brazil.

While Italy's population is not nearly so dense as that of certain other countries, her population increased from somewhat less than 27,000,000 in 1871 to over 34,000,000 in 1905. Unfortunately the natural resources of the country are not rich enough to take care of the increasing population; and especially is this true of southern Italy, where the climate, soil, deforestation, and a pernicious land system have made it exceedingly difficult for the peasant to eke out an existence. During the early period of emigration many farms were run by large leaseholders who took a heavy toll of the profits. Furthermore, obsolete methods of agriculture can be traced indirectly to absentee landlords, who not only despise the peasants and laborers socially but fail to return the profits to the lands in the form of improvements.

Malaria in a virulent form is a scourge of southern Italy and stands forth as one of the principal causes of emigration. The disease breeds in the swamps and stagnant pools, causing the peasant to live miles away from his land on the higher hills. This condition not only causes the farmer to consume considerable time in coming to and going from his work, but in his absence field robbers take toll of his harvest. Another hindrance to the peace of mind of the peasant is the frequency of earthquakes, which not only are destructive of capital but have a terrifying effect upon the mind.

Emigration has well-nigh depopulated certain sections of Calabria and Basilicata. In the latter province, where only about one tenth of the land is cultivable, fields are abandoned and very few opportunities for earning a livelihood are found. Except in the north, Italy is very poor in live stock. Now Italy is not the only country that does not produce enough to nourish its population; but this circumstance is most serious there by reason of the fact that it does not raise or manufacture other products for export sufficient to make up for the deficit. It is a country of specialized agriculture. A protective-tariff policy to build up industries has been tried, but it has been of little benefit to the south and almost exclusively to the advantage of the north. It has operated to close the doors of other countries to Italian exports in retaliation. America no longer furnishes an important market for Italian fruit.

Professor Foerster writes:

History has been kinder to the populations of North Italy than to those of the South. In these circumstances an account of the causes of emigration from the North cannot show such profound economic disorders and maladjustments and such extremities of poverty as were described for the South.[1]

[1] R. F. Foerster, *The Italian Emigration of our Times.* Cambridge, 1919.

Notwithstanding this generalization, Mr. Foerster cites facts and conditions which prove conclusively that the returns to the men and women who toil with their hands are scanty in comparison with the remuneration which may be obtained by migration to the United States and other countries. Extensive tracts of unproductive soil, deforestation, droughts, subdivision of land, absentee proprietors, and backward methods of production have blighted hopes and aspirations.

Taken as a whole, the means of communication in Italy are poor. There are railroads, but they operate under difficulties, not the least of which is the scarcity of fuel. The scarcity of coal has placed Italy at a disadvantage also in competing with the manufactures of other countries.

It is a platitude that the taxing power of a government depends upon the ability of its subjects to pay. Italy has aspired to play the part of a first-class power, acquiring a colonial empire and maintaining a large military establishment. The rôle of a colonial and military power is expensive, and governments with far richer natural resources than Italy is blessed with have encountered strong opposition to the enormous taxes necessary to finance their programs. The Italians are taxed to death. Under this burden industry suffers and the cost of living rises.

With these conditions prevailing, it is natural that emigration should have attracted the attention of statesmen and leaders. Many have reached the conclusion that emigration is the only remedy for the evils inherent in the conditions which have been briefly described. Italy has been deluged with articles, monographs, and statistics published by the government and individuals.

Until rather recent times Italian emigration legislation was scanty. In 1888 a general law was enacted, the tendency of

The law of 1912 recognizes the undeniable fact that in America and other countries immigrants who do not manifest a disposition to become naturalized are targets for suspicion and subject to certain inconveniences and loss of opportunities in some lines of employment. The law holds that naturalized Italians are not exempt from military service; that the son of an Italian emigrant is an Italian citizen unless on attaining his majority he renounces his allegiance; and that those who have lost their citizenship may regain it by rendering military service or by accepting employment under the government, by renouncing foreign citizenship and taking up residence in Italy, or by residing for two years in Italy.

Italian immigration to America as we know it today began about 1880, although from 1860 to 1880 the numbers had swelled to rather large proportions. From 1900 to 1916 the movement was at its height. During the years of Italian participation in the World War naturally every son of Italy was needed at home. After the armistice, however, Italy faced a most serious situation; the country tottered on the brink of revolution. With her people on war rations because of the critical food shortage, and thousands of industrial and agricultural workers on strike or in revolt, emigration loomed up as a safety valve. In the Chamber of Deputies the premier stated that emigration was inevitable, and it was proposed to organize the surplus population for migration on a large scale. At this time thousands of emigrants found the doors to America closed to them by the enactment by Congress in 1917 of a law requiring a literacy test and supplemented by the percentage laws after 1921. The Italian emigrants to America were largely from the south, where the percentage of illiteracy is very much greater than in the north. Just as German emigrants watched the proceedings of Congress on the various homestead bills, the threatened passage of a literacy-test bill by Congress during the present century was closely observed by interested parties in Italy. Measures were proposed and some actually taken to provide schools in those parts which furnished large numbers of American emigrants.

At the present time the Italian Commissioner-General of Emigration has outlined the following program: (1) cultural and professional preparation of the emigrant in the homeland; (2) study of foreign markets and search for new outlets for labor; (3) moral and hygienic assistance and careful oversight during the voyage and after; (4) plans for colonization enterprises, furnishing men for large public works abroad; (5) direction of labor to suitable countries; (6) international agreements with governments and labor contracts with private concerns.

It may be that Argentina and Brazil will be the future mecca of Italian emigrants. These countries for years have received many Italians and have attracted considerable attention in Italy. The agricultural opportunities are said to be favorable, emigrants, according to statistics, acquiring farms after a short apprenticeship as day laborers. Italian immigrants far exceed arrivals from other lands; in consequence Italians have the opportunity of becoming a powerful element in the population as the Germans did in the United States in the nineteenth century. Italy, therefore, has the opportunity of establishing commercial relations with those countries through blood relationship.

Not only do Argentina and Brazil welcome the Italians but they extend cordial invitations. For instance, in 1921 the Buenos Aires Association of Labor, which is an employers' organization, proposed to send a delegation to Europe to inquire into the means of organizing immigration to Argentina on systematic lines. Italians were desired above all others. About the same time Brazil and Italy concluded an agreement respecting the immigration of agricultural laborers. The agreement prescribes equality of treatment in compensation for industrial accidents to Brazilian and Italian workers in either of the two countries. It recognizes the full validity of individual or collective employment contracts concluded in Italy for execution in Brazil. The two governments made provision for special agreements concerning conditions of employment of Italian workers. The Brazilian government promised to institute strict inspection of labor and to protect and place immigrants, in order that contracts may be carried out.[1]

Since the enactment of the American percentage laws, which seriously affected Italian emigration, the Italian shipping companies have suffered great financial loss. In order to diminish this hardship, the Italian Commissioner-General of Emigration has given a monopoly of the transport of Italian emigrants to Italian shipping. Emigrants are forbidden to embark at a foreign port, and the visa of passports is made conditional on the presentation of a certificate signed by the emigration inspector stating that the holder will embark on an Italian vessel at an Italian port.

The Italian government and Italians in the United States are decidedly hostile to the recent immigration policy of the American government. They feel keenly the sting of racial discrimination. They resent the attitude that the people of a country which has given birth to Dante, Petrarch, Michelangelo, Columbus, Mazzini, Cavour, Garibaldi, Marconi, and Caruso are inferior to the Germans, English, Irish, Scandina-

[1] *International Labour Review*, January, 1922, p. 123; February, 1922, pp. 307, 308.

vians, and Dutch. They also question the ethical right of the
United States to prohibit the migration of people from a less
favored land to a land of sparse population and teeming
riches. The drastic restrictionists in the United States claim
that if this view were accepted the country would become "an
international boarding-house," with Uncle Sam playing the
rôle of Santa Claus.

In 1924 the Italian government formally protested against
the enactment of the pending immigration bill in the House,
which reduced Italy's annual quota to about four thousand.
This heavy curtailment of emigration has not only affected
the employment situation in the countries of the new immigration, but, by reducing the cash remittances of emigrants
to their native lands, has caused rather severe financial consequences there. It has been estimated roughly that for a
number of years preceding the World War the amount of
such remittances to Italy averaged about $100,000,000 an-
nually. Rumania was frank enough to make the reduction
of emigrant remittances to that country one of the grounds
of protest against the bill of 1924.

Whatever may be the future of Italian emigration, the
traveler in Italy in years to come will probably not witness
a repetition of conditions pictured in the words of an investigator in the employ of the American Department of State
in 1890.

But the agents of the steamship lines, who cover Italy as the
locusts covered Egypt, are busy as ever. They paint the charms
of big wages in the United States; they often induce the poor peasant to sell his cow and move on to the United States. There is a
good deal of emigration that is assisted by rhetoric as well as by
logic. The flowers of rhetoric easily woo hunger. . . . There are
castles in Spain even for the Calabrian. In this business the com-

mission money of clouds of emigrant agents is the chief inspiration. The ship would starve without steerage list; there is a large profit in handling large numbers, and some thousands of drummers for emigrants swarm over Italy, and their fruit is in the 5000 Italians who in one week of the recent spring cut loose from the Italian peasantry to try chances in the United States. Many more applied in the spring of 1890 than the ships could carry, though they were crammed like sardines in all the decks and in tiers three deep, as my eyes have witnessed—ships which I presume emptied their swarming cargoes on our shores, but which should never have been allowed to leave any port of a civilized state, or, once having left, to touch the civilization of any other state.[1]

It would appear that the extreme restrictive policy of the United States was inaugurated on the eve of a great exodus of Italians to this country,—that the emigrants of the nineteenth century were but the advance guard of a still greater host. In fact, it was freely admitted by the advocates of restriction that the Italian "birds of passage" would be stopped by the meshes of the new law.

[1] F. L. Dingley, "European Immigration," in Special Consular Reports, printed in *House Miscellaneous Documents*, 52d Cong., 1st Sess., Vol. XVI, pp. 211–240.

CHAPTER VIII

THE JEWS

The story of that great migration which has given to the United States about one fourth of the Jewish population of the world is one of the most tragic in history. New York City, containing a Jewish population of more than a million and a half, or one half the number of that race in the entire country, has more Jews than were ever before concentrated in any one place since the beginning of time.[1] In the period from 1881 to 1910 there entered the United States 1,562,800 Jews: 1,119,059 came from Russia, 281,150 from Austria-Hungary, and 67,057 from Rumania. Taking into account the fact that the great bulk of the Jewish emigrants from the United Kingdom and Canada use those countries as halfway houses, over 95 per cent of the American Jews have come from Russia, Austria-Hungary, and Rumania. In these countries the conditions under which the Jews live are strikingly similar. Like the negroes of America they do not enter into the fabric of society. With the Jews, however, you have a race superior in some respects to the oppressors,—superior in the sense that they have reached a higher degree of literacy.

It is a striking fact that under oppression and persecution the Jews retain their characteristics and tend to lose them when the oppression and persecution are relaxed. Here is a people, without a country for centuries, scattered all over the

[1] It is not to be inferred that all the Jews in New York are immigrants; the number includes the American-born.

world, living under most adverse circumstances, increasing in numbers and retaining a love for the things that made them "the chosen people."

When we think of present-day Jewish emigration, the country that immediately comes to mind is Russia, the country which prior to 1918 harbored almost one half of the Jewish people; but the Jewry of America is the product of three successive waves of migration.

First in point of time are the Spanish Jews, the descendants of the race who were exiled from the Iberian Peninsula in the last years of the fifteenth century and who came by way of Central and South America. The second—the German wave —came principally from southern Germany in the years between 1830 and 1870, resulting from the distress following the Napoleonic wars and the revolutionary disturbances of 1830 and 1848. Strictly orthodox, these Jews were German in language, education, and dress. In round numbers the American Jewish population in 1880, established mainly by these two movements, was 230,000. The exodus from Russia began in 1881 and drew on a population of 8,000,000. The causes for this outpouring, which has only one parallel in Jewish history—the uprooting of the multitude from Palestine in the time of Jesus Christ—will be the subject of this chapter.

Russia annexed its Jewish problem when it took the lion's share of the spoils in the partition of Poland between Russia, Prussia, and Austria in the last quarter of the eighteenth century. In order to understand the Jewish situation in Russia at the time of the exodus, we must take a rapid survey of Polish history.

During the Middle Ages and the first century of the modern age Poland became a great empire, occupying a vast area on the map of Europe. It was during these years that Poland became first in Jewish population. Where the earliest Jews in Poland came from is a matter of uncertainty; they may have migrated from the lower Danube. The later migration, beginning toward the end of the twelfth century, came from western Europe, Germany in particular, and gained in volume during the fifteenth and sixteenth centuries. The student of European history will recall that in these centuries the people were crusading against the infidel Turk and that the population of several countries was decimated by the Black Death. The hand of the Christian was laid heavily on the Jew as a result of these events, and the lot of the Jew was not enviable. For instance, toward the end of the thirteenth century about sixteen thousand were expelled from England. With the close of the fifteenth and the beginning of the sixteenth century another great wave of immigration poured into Poland as a consequence of persecution and expulsion. Many of these immigrants came from Bohemia; and this element became the controlling factor in the life of the Polish Jews.

Why did the Jews go to Poland? Because in the Middle Ages Poland was the most liberal government in Europe in its treatment of the Jews. Down to 1572 the Polish kingship was hereditary; but there was always a contest between the king and the powerful nobility. In order to counteract the influence of the nobles, the king invited the Jews to his dominion. In the other countries of Europe whatever rights and privileges the Jews possessed were granted by the rulers, who compelled them to pay dearly; but their rights were greatly restricted. They were allowed to live only in certain designated districts, often compelled to wear a distinctive dress, and excluded from many occupations. As money lenders, a class despised as cordially as were the publicans in Palestine, they were held up as extortioners by the Christians, who were prohibited by law from lending money on interest. The fact that they were not Christians gave rise to all sorts of stories about them: that they sacrificed Christian boys in their religious rites; that they "clipped" the coins; that they followed a different code of morals in dealing with Christians from that followed among the people of their own race. In 1264 the duke of Poland granted a charter to the Jews, which was confirmed by his successors and later extended to the whole kingdom, by which they were given property rights and religious toleration. The rulers profited financially by their liberality, because the Jews brought in capital and were able to pay handsomely when called upon. In fact in all lands the Jewish population was a sponge to be squeezed when the rulers needed money.

The Polish kings had to overcome the hostility of the church and the nobility to their Jewish policy. The church adopted restrictions against the Jews on the ground that they were a menace to Christianity. The clergy prohibited social intercourse with them and proposed to segregate them in ghettos and to distinguish them by a special headgear, in order that a Christian might recognize at sight an "unbaptized dog." The nobles hated them because they were under the protection of the king, and the peasants came to hate them because they were the tax farmers and the middlemen who took heavy toll on what they bought from them and sold to them. When in 1572 Poland became an elective monarchy, the nobles were in the ascendancy; and the Jews came under their domination. Their restrictions became so severe that the Jews had to transfer their activities from towns to rural districts; but as they were prohibited from engaging in agriculture, they became the commercial men and were regarded as parasites by those who made their living by cultivating the soil.

With the transfer of the bulk of the Jewish population in Poland to Russia began the series of events which precipitated the exodus to America in the last quarter of the nineteenth century. Prior to 1772, the date of the first partition, Russia had excluded the Jews; but now at one fell swoop the Czar added a large population of Jews to his dominions and thereby annexed the great Jewish problem. It has been said that whereas the Polish kings were the founders of Jewish rights, the Russian czars were the founders of Jewish rightlessness; and that while in Poland opposition to the Jews arose among the people and pushed its way upwards to the throne, in Russia the opposition originated on the throne and trickled down to the people.

A short time after the annexation of Polish territory the Russian government shut up the vast territory of Russia from the Jews and confined them to the original Polish territory, thus establishing what came to be known as the Jewish pale of settlement. From this time on the Jews were restricted more and more, both as to territory and privileges.

During the reign of Nicholas I (1825–1855) the policies which resulted in the wholesale migration of the Jews began in real earnest. More and more the economic and territorial latitude of the Jews was contracted. They were drafted into the army, not at the age of eighteen, as were the other subjects of the Czar, but at the age of twelve; but the required twenty-five years of service was reckoned from the eighteenth year of the conscript. The purpose of this was, of course, to take the Jews away from the pale of settlement and from the influence of their religion and education. The decree of 1853 gave every Jew permission to capture any one of his coreligionists who might be found without a passport and present him as a substitute for himself or any member of his family liable for military service.

Alexander II (1855–1881) began his reign as a liberal but became a reactionary. Toward the close of his rule the pogroms which have disgraced Russia and certain other countries of Europe were inaugurated. The pogroms are usually occasioned by a Jewish or Christian festival and are precipitated by a rather trivial event, as, for instance, a quarrel or fight between a Christian and a Jew. Sometimes whole villages or cities are wiped out by these massacres. The assassination of Alexander II in March, 1881, gave fresh impulse to the persecution of the Jews. Whoever may have been guilty of the crime, the event was turned to the advantage of the Jew-haters. The press, aided by government officials, aroused the populace to such an extent that pogroms broke out simultaneously in many places. At Warsaw, in December, the massacre lasted three days. As the result of these occurrences the migration of Jews began *en masse* in 1881, and America was looked upon as the promised land.

Some time before these events the government of the United States had manifested an interest in the Jewish problem, partly because Jews of American citizenship had suffered humiliation and hardships in Russia and partly because the American people looked with sympathy upon the plight of the Jewish subjects of the Czar. In response to representations and inquiries from the American government the Russian government was always studiously courteous but careful not to commit itself to any change of policy, placing the blame for their condition on the Jews themselves. For example, according to a report of a member of a commission for the improvement of the life of the Hebrews in Russia, transmitted to our government by the American minister in Leningrad in 1875, the demand for an extension of the rights of residence did not come so much from the Hebrews themselves as from the local representatives of the government in the provinces where the Hebrew population was massed together, and their representatives were less inspired by the thought of improving the condition of the Hebrews than by the desire to alleviate the sad condition of the native population. According to them the large number of Hebrews, not finding sufficient means for supporting themselves by honest means, were compelled to earn their bread by exploiting the Christian population or by having recourse to all kinds of underhanded practices. The officials insisted that the Jews, being preëminently a mercantile class in an agricultural country, exploited the productive Christian peasant population.

The existence of middlemen is frequently an evil, but how much more so when these middlemen constitute a caste having nothing in common with the rest of the population either by origin, religion or language, a caste which desires to know nothing in the world except their fellow-believers, a caste petrified in their born isolation, often following fanatical leaders, and regarding the laws of the country in which they live as only externally binding on them, avoiding compliance with them by all possible means, and always in every manner acting together.

In other countries where Jews had liberties, continued the report, the greater civilization and intelligence enabled Christians to protect themselves, but even in Vienna the Hebrews had got into their hands all the banking houses, all the newspaper press, and the large part of the real estate of the city.[1]

[1] *House Executive Documents*, 51st Cong., 1st Sess., No. 470, pp. 25–28. The article "The Jews in Roumania," in the *Century Magazine* (Vol. XLIX, pp. 780–783), by the queen of Rumania ("Carmen Sylva"), sets forth the identical objections.

In April, 1880, the American Secretary of State, responding to a petition from the Union of American Hebrew Congregations, directed our minister at Leningrad to express the views of our government "in a manner which will subserve the interests of religious freedom." The following year our government protested against the pogroms which followed the assassination of the Czar. Speeches in Congress and throughout the country voiced the indignation of the American people and convinced the victims across the water that in one country at least the Jew found sympathy and could expect fair treatment. At a large protest meeting in New York in February, 1882, when the first Russian refugees began to arrive, one of the speakers exclaimed:

Let them come! I would to heaven it were in our power to take the whole three million Jews in Russia. The valley of the Mississippi alone could throw her strong arms around them, and draw them all to her opulent bosom, and bless them with homes of comfort, prosperity, and happiness.[1]

In 1890 the House of Representatives adopted a resolution requesting the president to communicate to the House any information respecting the enforcement of proscriptive edicts against Jews and whether American citizens had because of their religion been expelled from Russia or forbidden ordinary privileges. At about the same time the American minister made a formal protest to the Russian government, stating that the matter was not purely internal, since it affected the interests of the United States. At the time of the terrible Kishinev massacre in 1903 the American Secretary of State issued a ringing protest, and in 1910 Congress voted to abrogate our treaty with Russia out of protest against the treatment Jewish-American citizens were accorded in Russia.

[1] S. M. Dubnov, *The Jews of Russia and Poland*, Vol. II, pp. 292 ff.

How effective the American protests were it is difficult to say; but before all the world our government was acclaimed as the champion of the oppressed, and this most certainly did not fall on deaf Jewish ears. The Russian government let it be known that it would not prevent the emigration of the Jews, although it was anxious to remain on good terms with America. In 1880, in an interview with the American minister, the Russian foreign minister stated that his government had found the Jewish problem very vexatious and dangerous and that its experiences with Jewish subjects had shown them to be a bad class of society; that in late years they had been active participants in revolutionary conspiracies and plots against the life of the emperor and had shown a restless and disloyal inclination; that the tendency had been to treat American Jews leniently because of their small number, but owing to the large number of German and Austrian Jews on the border it was difficult to repeal or relax the laws. The foreign minister inquired if the Americans, in similar manner, were not seeking to exclude or regulate the Chinese immigrants and denying them rights extended to other inhabitants.[1]

Instead of throwing obstacles in the way of Jewish emigration, the Russian government positively encouraged it. The "temporary rules" of May, 1882, forbade Jews henceforth to settle anew outside of the towns and townlets, suspended the completion of instruments of purchase of real property and merchandise in the name of Jews outside of the towns and townlets, and forbade Jews to carry on business on Sundays and Christian holidays. These "rules" dislodged the Jews from nine tenths of the territory formerly open to them and denied them the privilege of doing business on the days

[1] *House Executive Documents*, 51st Cong., 1st Sess., No. 470, pp. 43, 44.

when the non-Jewish business man reaped the greatest harvest. Jews were expelled by wholesale from important centers of population. In the same decade serious restrictions were placed on Jewish physicians and lawyers, and the number of Jews admitted to schools in proportion to the Christian school population was drastically curtailed. Parents, brothers, and near relatives were heavily fined for evasions of military service. This latter measure probably greatly stimulated emigration, because whole families left rather than remain to pay the fine for the one who emigrated.[1]

Beginning in 1881 a large number of emigration societies were organized, and "Emigration to America" became the watchword. Once under way, the emigration to America was accelerated by glowing "America letters" and remittances from across the water. In the early nineties a German-Jewish capitalist, Baron Maurice de Hirsch, determined to contribute hi, fortune to the establishment of a colony of his people i 1 Argentina. He believed it possible to transport 3,250,000 Jews from Russia to the new colony within a period of twenty-five years; but the scheme was a failure. America was destined to be the promised land.

With the accession of Nicholas II (1894–1917) a weak tool of the bureaucracy occupied the throne of the czars. His reign was pregnant with disasters to Russia, to the Jews, and to himself. In 1903 occurred the terrible massacre of the Jews at Kishinev, which called forth protests from the American government and press, as well as from an enlightened public opinion throughout the civilized world. During the Russo-Japanese War (1904–1905) an imperial ukase promised Jews who served in the army a general right of residence within

[1] S. M. Dubnov, *The Jews of Russia and Poland*, Vol. II, pp. 318–356.

and without the pale of settlement, but instead of alleviating
their distress the war brought riots and massacres. The
promise of the government was not kept.

Then came the World War. During these horrible years
the Jews were fighting under every flag, and the pale was the
scene of conditions which only the imagery of the Apocalypse
can describe. At the outbreak of the war the Jewish leaders
exhorted their people to be loyal to Russia. In August, 1915,
the council of ministers issued a decree permitting Jews in
the area affected by the war to move into the interior of
Russia. This measure was primarily military, but it was also
designed to gain for Russia the good will of other nations.
The logic of events—the Bolshevik revolution—decided that
by this measure the pale of settlement was permanently
abolished. Thus while the emancipation of the Jews in western Europe was a slow process, the Russian emancipation was
accomplished at one stroke, a turn of events which some
Jewish leaders say is not without grave peril to the future of
their people, pointing out that it may result in detachment
from Judaism and Jewish interests.

When the armies overran Poland the Jews knew not
whither to turn for sympathy. The Russians played off the
Poles against the Jews, the Germans played off the Poles
against the Jews, and the Poles played off the Russians
against the Jews. The Russian military authorities attributed
their military disasters to the Jews, accusing them of being
spies, poisoning wells, and all sorts of crimes. The Yiddish
speech and press were suppressed, and telephone conversa-
tions in Yiddish were prohibited. The Jewish refugees who
fled before the advance of the Russian army into Bukowina
and sought refuge in Rumania were treated with savage

brutality by the Rumanians. In July, 1915, the Rumanian government expelled all Jews from the Austrian border, and they were forced to leave without their belongings.[1]

The signing of the armistice and the treaty of peace did not put an end to the anti-Semitic outbreaks. In the Ukraine in 1919 and 1920 approximately one hundred and twenty thousand men, women, and children were killed, whole villages were wiped out, and the entire Jewish population of southern Russia was reduced to the brink of starvation.[2] The publication of the alleged *Protocols of the Learned Elders at Zion*, a document which purported to reveal the designs of Jews for the subjugation of Christendom, is symptomatic of the anti-Semitism which swept over Europe and America at the close of the war.

With the end of the World War the dream of a revived Polish state was realized, and again the Jews found themselves subjects of Polish sovereignty. One provision of the Polish treaty aroused indignation among the Poles, namely, that "in view of the historical development of the Jewish question and the great animosity aroused by it, special protection is necessary for the Jews of Poland." It is but natural that the Poles after over a century's striving for a national state should resent this guaranty from the outside of protection to racial, linguistic, and religious minorities.

In view of the disorders and tense situation in Poland, commissions were appointed under the authority of the American and British governments to investigate Jewish matters in that state in 1919. While there is some disagreement in

[1] American Jewish Committee, *The Jews in the Eastern War Zone* (New York, 1916).

[2] For an interesting and perhaps somewhat prejudiced account of these events, see Elias Heifetz, *The Slaughter of the Jews in the Ukraine in 1919.* New York, 1921.

the four reports submitted by members of these commissions, they are in substantial agreement in viewing the situation in the large.[1] Without attempting to fix the responsibility for the conditions and events following the armistice, it is evident that out of this complicated situation many differences were bound to arise, and for many years to come the circumstances which produced the great exodus which began in 1881 will operate to stimulate emigration in the future. According to Henry Morgenthau, a member of the American mission, "at the end of the Great War the chaotic and unnatural state of affairs in which Poland found itself gave good ground for a condition of social unrest, which, together with the world-stimulated tendency toward national self-determination, accentuated the feeling between Jewish and non-Jewish elements. The chauvinistic reaction created by the sudden acquisition of a long-coveted freedom ripened the public mind for anti-Semitic or anti-alien sentiment, which was strongly agitated by the press and by politicians."

In the belief that the Jewish inhabitants were politically hostile to the Polish state Jewish merchants were boycotted; Jews were stopped by soldiers and had their beards either torn out or cut off; homes were raided; Yiddish newspapers were suppressed; and murders were committed.

It is not the province of the historian to prophesy; but in conclusion it may be permitted to quote the words of Captain Wright, a member of the British mission:

But the situation of the Jews will hardly be a happier one. Every morning an ordinary Jewish gentleman—in Warsaw very like what he is in London—reads papers that cover his race with contumely.

[1] *The Jews in Poland. Official Reports of the American and British Investigating Missions.* A pamphlet published by the National Polish Committee of America, Chicago, Illinois.

He and his women folk never deal with Poles except to be treated with insolence, and his children come back from school with their ears ringing with abuse. Every independent Polish institution is as determined to oust the Jews, the national enemy, as in England, we, during the war, were to oust the Germans. Jewish professors, however able, have been turned out of universities; Jewish doctors, however famous, from hospitals. Every university, by some means or other, exerts itself to keep down its Jewish undergraduates to a minimum. Tramway companies will not have Jewish employes, and so on throughout the whole range of Jewish life.

In surveying the background of Jewish emigration political, social, and religious persecution stand out boldly, but at bottom the situation is economic. It is because of their race and religion that the Jews are deprived of the opportunities they cultivate so eagerly and assiduously in America. In America they meet with intolerance and discrimination, but they prosper; and the law knows no discrimination between Jew and Gentile.

CHAPTER IX

THE SLAVS

Although the Slavs are among the most numerous of the so-called new immigrants—being exceeded only by the Italians —they are very imperfectly understood by Americans because they come from so many different countries and are designated by so many different names. The department of immigration classifies them in the order of importance as follows: Poles, Slovaks, Croatians or Slovenians, Ruthenians or Russniak, Moravians and Bohemians, Bulgarians and Serbians and Montenegrins, Russians, and Dalmatians and Bosnians and Herzegovinians. The changes in the map of Europe since the signing of the armistice are bewildering to the student of immigration who pores over the documents dealing with Slavic immigration published prior to the World War. We shall save ourselves some confusion if we regard the situation with the pre-war map of Europe before us. Over 90 per cent of the Slavs have come from the old Austro-Hungarian Monarchy and the old Russian Empire, with the former far in the lead. We shall, therefore, be concerned mainly with the peoples and conditions of that political Tower of Babel: in other words, our background is Austria-Hungary to 1914.

It is commonly asserted that the comparatively small part played by the Slavs in history in proportion to their numbers is due to lack of aggressiveness and lack of cohesion. Whatever may be the limitations inherent in the race, if such there be, this circumstance can probably be partly explained by their unfortunate geographical situation and partly by differences in religion. The ancient kingdom of Poland occupied a large area, but it lacked natural boundaries. When the advance of the Turk was checked by the Polish king John Sobieski in 1685, the troubles of the Slavs were by no means ended. Their differences with other races are attested by many Czech proverbs: "Do not believe a Hungarian unless he has three eyes in his forehead." "Peace with the Germans is like that between a wolf and a lamb." Kept in subjection by Magyar, German, and Turk, the Slavs have not had the training in self-government that we find among the Teutonic peoples. Unlike the Americans, they do not conceive of government as a part of themselves.

Within Austria-Hungary were included all the Slavic peoples except the Bulgarians and the Russians, and within no other political division of Europe was found such a great variety of geographical features and climate. In the northwest were the Germans; in the east, the Slavs and the Magyars; and along the Mediterranean coast and in the southeast, the Italians and the Rumanians. The west was largely Roman Catholic; the east contained Greek Catholics, Protestants, and Jews.

The Austro-Hungarian Monarchy was the result of the *Ausgleich*, or agreement, of 1867, a compact between the Germans in Austria and the Magyars in Hungary, both minority races who kept the Slavs in subjection by sowing discord among the various branches—not a particularly difficult undertaking. While the causes of emigration spring from a complicated set of circumstances, as in other countries political and social dissatisfaction is certainly an important contributory cause.

The great bulk of the emigrants were peasants. When serfdom was abolished in 1848, the peasant became a free proprietor, gradually paying the state for his land. But serfdom was not obliterated in a day; the remnants remained both economically and psychologically. Agriculture was in a backward state, owing to the absence of improved methods and excessive subdivision of land. The cottagers who cultivated small plots of land and supplemented their earnings by hiring out to landholders or worked at trades; the laborers who lived in cottages belonging to their employers, who paid wages partly in cash and partly in kind; and the farm hands who were hired by the year and were boarded by the employers—all were in poor circumstances. The rise of modern industry deprived them of their "sidelines," as it did in England. The future held little in store; the children deserved something better than poverty. Why not emigrate?

The desire to go to America was further stimulated by heavy taxes, military service,—especially irksome in a land where loyalty is displaced by the yoke of subjection,—political unrest, "America letters," returned emigrants, and agents of steamship companies.

No more than in Sweden and Germany did the ruling classes in Austria and Hungary look with favor on emigration, and the usual means of discouraging it, already familiar to us by our study of other countries, were employed. In Hungary, for example, the stream took its beginning in the seventies. The government tried to check it in 1881 by a law directed at the agents of steamship companies. During the last two decades of the last century the number of emigrants averaged from 20,000 to 30,000 annually; but at the turn of the century there was a sharp upward trend, reaching

120,000 in 1903. The law of 1903 prohibited public speeches and advertisements recommending emigration, stationed police on the frontier to detect unlawful emigration, and provided for the creation of a fund to assist emigrants to return. The following were forbidden to emigrate: parents who had not made provision for those left behind; male minors who did not have the consent of parents; female minors unaccompanied by trustworthy persons; persons with insufficient means; criminals and the mentally deficient.[1]

Bohemian emigration falls within three periods. The first, from 1620 to 1648, the time of the Thirty Years' War, saw the downfall of Bohemian independence and the defeat of Protestantism. With political and religious freedom crushed and the process of Germanization begun, America became the refuge for political and religious exiles. The second period began in 1735, when the same general causes operated. The nineteenth-century movement dates from about 1848, when the promise of a free Bohemia was shattered by Austrian troops. The desire for political independence in Bohemia, which asserted itself in that year, has been strong since the writings of John Huss in the first years of the fifteenth century crystallized the Bohemian language. The tradition of Huss in religion has also lived on in opposition to Roman Catholicism as known in Austria. In a people high in point of literacy as the Bohemians are, traditions are difficult to stamp out. A fresh impulse to emigration followed the Austro-Prussian War of 1866 and the removal of certain legal obstacles.

[1] "The Hungarian Emigration Law," by Baron Louis de Sevay (royal commissioner of emigration), in *North American Review*, Vol. CLXXXII, pp. 115–122. The article is a defense of the government's policy. See report of the American consul at Budapest, 1886, in *House Executive Documents*, 49th Cong., 2d Sess., No. 157.

The bulk of emigrants came from the southern and agricultural districts, but the industrial transition caused the movement to assume a more urban tinge. The Bohemians in America can point with pride to several distinguished names in American history.

While the Bohemians have been the victims of Germanization, the people associated with them in the present Czechoslovakian republic, the Slovaks, have been the victims of Magyarization. As with the Bohemians, however, the roots of Slovak emigration are found in the economic situation. These interesting people inhabit a country poor in resources, situated along the southern slopes of the Carpathian Mountains. Although closely related to the Bohemians in language and blood, they show a higher percentage of illiteracy. They began emigrating sporadically about 1873, and about 1880 the stream became constant. The fact that an unusual number of emigrants were day laborers and servant girls who intended to remain in America only until they could accumulate a certain amount of money would indicate that political dissatisfaction was secondary; but having breathed the free air of America they had little desire to return to their native land, where all things Slovak were anathema to the ruling Magyars.

The Slovenians, a group living in Carniola and Carinthia, have no written language and have been Germanized to a considerable extent. They are an energetic, thrifty people who have probably acquired these qualities in their efforts to eke out a living in a mountainous country unfavorable to agriculture. In Carniola, which furnishes most of the American Slovenians, the remittances inclosed in "America letters" were so numerous that an investigation of the causes of emigration was ordered by the governor.

The Serbo-Croatians, like the Slovenians, are a South Slav group. The causes for their emigration may be summarized as follows: dissatisfaction with Hungary; great stretches of barren and rugged soil; long and severe winters; fierce struggles with the Turks; primitive conditions; lack of capital, industries, and means of transportation.

The Slavic emigration from the Adriatic coast of Austria-Hungary is hardly a stream; it is rather a series of individual departures which, in the aggregate, has reached respectable proportions. With these people, as with the emigrants from Montenegro, Serbia, and Bulgaria, the percentage of illiteracy is very high. They are victims of natural conditions, who in spite of handicaps become uniformly prosperous in America.

The Poles, of whom there are about 25,000,000 in Europe and America, are generally supposed to be numerous and strong enough to be able to take care of themselves in spite of their precarious political situation in Europe. And in reality, if the whole territory of Poland belonged to one of the three great powers which participated in the disruption of the republic, the strength and energy of the Polish people would probably be sufficient to regain the political independence of the country. But the task, which would be comparatively easy when dealing with one power, becomes impossible when opposed by the combined forces of three such military powers as Russia, Germany and Austria. . . . The Polish people as a whole refuse to be denationalized and consider themselves still a nation. . . . The great German poet, Schiller, says: "Whoever wants to understand the song of a poet must go and see his native land." With just as much right we maintain that in order to understand thoroughly what liberty is and what her practices are, one must come and see her in her native land. The sight of so many different nationalities living happily and peacefully together under the banner and laws of a great and free republic . . . will be a revelation to many a Polish patriot, scientist, author and artist who knows such things only from hearsay or from books.

The extracts given above from a letter to an American newspaper written by the editor of a Polish newspaper published in Chicago[1] explain only partly, but certainly quite accurately, why thousands of "America letters" similar in content to the following were written in the Polish language.

And now I will write you how I am getting along. I am getting along very, very well. I have worked in a factory and I am now working in a hotel. I receive 18 (in our money 32) dollars a month, and that is very good. If you would like it we could bring Wladzio over some day. We eat here every day what we get only for Easter in our country. We are bringing over Helena and brother now. I had $120 and I sent back $90.[2]

One can scarcely wonder that in order to stop emigration letters were opened by government officials, and if they praised America they were not delivered.[3]

Whether he was a subject of Austria, Russia, or Germany, the Pole found it economically and politically advantageous to emigrate to America. The conditions which beset him in the land of his nativity were depressing. The first emigrants in a community heard of America from across the border of Hungary, or from returned Jewish emigrants, or from returned German emigrants. It is the familiar story of a people deprived of a good living, ground down by an upper class which by fair means or foul tried to discredit America, seized by an intense desire to share in the good things so naïvely related in letters from friends and relatives.

Although Polish immigrants were not unknown in America before the Civil War, it was not until after 1870 that the migration became large.

---

[1] *Chicago Record-Herald*, June 28, 1909.
[2] Philip Davis, *Immigration and Americanization*, pp. 741, 742.
[3] Emily G. Balch, *Our Slavic Fellow Citizens*, p. 135.

The causes of the emigration of another Slavic group from Austrian Galicia, the Ruthenians, are similar to those we have considered in reference to the Poles. There has been considerable friction between these peoples, partly because the Ruthenians are Greek Catholics and the Poles are loyal Roman Catholics and partly because the Ruthenians claim that the Poles were given a free hand over them by the Austrian government in order to keep the Poles contented.

Although the number of Slavs in European Russia before 1914 was more than four times as great as the number within Austria-Hungary, from 1899 to 1908 the emigrants from the latter more than twice exceeded those from Russia. The sparse population, absence of racial friction, and vast areas of fertile soil probably account for this.

What effect the dismemberment of Austria-Hungary and the readjustments in the Balkan Peninsula after the World War would have had on emigration to America will never be known, because under the post-war American immigration laws the quotas for the Slavic peoples are relatively insignificant.

PART II. THE IMMIGRANTS IN AMERICA

CHAPTER X

KNOW-NOTHINGISM

The presence of aliens and foreign-born citizens has always furnished problems for the American government and people, but on the whole they have been solved with good judgment and justice. It may be said with positive emphasis that collectively the American people have accorded a welcome to immigrants which bears eloquent testimony to the justice of their institutions and to their stability. Of course there have always been Americans who have harbored misgivings over the influx of hordes of foreigners, unacquainted with our language, customs, and institutions; and misgivings have sometimes given place to hostility, intense and unreasonable. This hostility may be grounded in religious, political, or economic prejudices combined or singly.

There have been times when a section of the country has felt that unrestricted immigration was detrimental to its interests. An analysis of votes on certain measures in Congress related to immigration reveals sectional groupings. In fact it is impossible to understand the history of immigration legislation without keeping clearly in mind the sectional nature of America and laying bare the interplay of various interests.

The newer section—the West—has usually favored immigration. Western optimism, abundant land to be had for the asking or at ridiculously low prices, the crying need for unskilled labor to develop the country, and a society relatively free from conventions have facilitated assimilation. The West in the days of the public lands was truly a no man's land. It belonged to the man, native or foreign, with courage and muscular endurance. The immigrant who settled in the older sections found a more stratified society. Industries have furnished abundant employment for immigrant labor, but an industrial society is not the most fertile soil for the immigrant to take root. Organized labor looks askance at the immigrant who comes with a standard of living below the American standard. The congregation of racial stocks in portions of our cities has caused alarm. For twenty years preceding the Civil War, as we shall see, the South felt that the arrival of every immigrant meant the diminution of the political power of the slavocracy because the newcomers settled in the free states, where land was cheap and accessible and opportunities for employment were abundant. In other words, the Southerners feared the immigrant because he avoided their section and increased the population of sections whose antagonism to the institution of slavery was increasing with the passing of each year. Since the abolition of slavery the South has been plagued with an appalling racial problem and has had no desire to add to the problems of the country by complicating the racial medley still further. In general, the South has favored immigration restriction. A threatened tidal wave of Oriental immigration, real or imaginary, has been a constant worry to the Pacific coast since before the days of the Civil War; and in recent years it has seriously disturbed our relations with China and Japan.

Public opinion with regard to immigration is determined by a complex of events and conditions within the country and without. At the present time America appears to be committed to a drastic policy of immigration restriction, a culmination of a growing skepticism extending over a generation and intensified by a series of problems accompanying and growing out of the World War. In the period from 1840 to 1860, when immigrants from the British Isles and from Germany were pouring in and Scandinavian and Dutch immigration was getting under way, the resulting conditions and problems were strangely similar and dissimilar.

Nativism today is more largely rooted in social, economic, and racial conditions and prejudices, whereas in the former period religious feeling was more intense. Fear that our cherished ideals and institutions were in danger was present then as well as now. Today it is feared that the foreigners will not become citizens; so naturalization statistics are marshaled to prove or to disprove the desirability of certain peoples. The nativist of the forties and fifties feared that immigrants would naturalize too early and too easily. In order to prevent the political activity of people whose environment was very different from that of the American voter, he proposed a long period of residence before citizenship could be acquired.

It may be set down as a fundamental fact that since the adoption of the Federal Constitution American politics have never been free from Know-Nothingism; and the antagonism between native Americans and the foreign-born has been especially noticeable when either element or both have believed their rights to be endangered. For instance, in the administration of John Adams (1797–1801), when several prominent men of foreign birth were in active opposition to the Federalist policy, a naturalization law lengthening the period required for citizenship from five to fourteen years was enacted, and an alien act followed immediately by which the president was clothed with power to order all aliens whom he judged dangerous to the peace and safety of the country to depart from the territory of the United States. At the incoming of the Republicans to power with the inauguration of Thomas Jefferson, the residence requirement for naturalization was fixed at five years, and the alien act expired.

Federalist opposition in New England to the war with Great Britain (1812–1815), prosecuted by a Republican administration, took the form of a convention at Hartford, Connecticut, where, among others, a resolution was adopted proposing an amendment to the Constitution rendering naturalized citizens ineligible to membership in the Senate and House of Representatives and incapable of holding any civil office under the authority of the United States.

The term "hyphenated citizen" had not been coined at that early day, but these measures and proposed measures were directed at citizens and residents alleged to harbor a "divided allegiance."

It was not, however, until the great wave of immigration reached our shores in the two decades before the Civil War that agitation against immigration and the foreign-born assumed such alarming proportions. This spectacular outburst of political nativism was due to a remarkable combination of circumstances, some of which had no connection whatever with immigration.

Statistics are wearisome and frequently misleading, but even a novice in handling figures can read into the immigration statistics of this period a movement pregnant with important consequences, whether for evil or for good.

From 1790 to 1800 approximately 50,000 foreigners came to our shores; 154,000 from 1820 to 1830; 252,000 from 1831 to 1835; 346,000 from 1836 to 1840; 1,713,000 from 1841 to 1850; 379,000 in 1851; 371,000 in 1852; 368,000 in 1853; 428,000 in 1854; 2,378,000 from 1851 to 1860. In 1850 the aggregate immigrant population in the states of New York, Pennsylvania, Ohio, Illinois, Wisconsin, and Massachusetts was 1,075,702; in 1860 it had increased to 2,619,083.[1]

The influx of aliens in this period, as well as later, was more noticeable because of the tendency to concentrate in cities and communities. The Irish congregated in the manufacturing cities of the East. The Germans, possessed of more money, went in large numbers to the West, where they became valuable additions to the agricultural population; but many of them settled in New York, Cincinnati, St. Louis, Philadelphia, Baltimore, Milwaukee, and other cities. In the urban centers hostility to the foreign-born was much greater than in the rural districts. Naturally economic competition was stronger in the cities. Serious outbreaks occurred between native and foreign laborers. Many immigrants lived in the poorer sections of the cities in squalor and filth, the breeding places of crime and vice. In New York State in 1850, of 59,855 paupers who at a yearly cost of $817,336 were supported by the state, 40,580 were foreign-born. Armed with these and similar statistics from certain other states, agitators aroused their countrymen to the dangers of pauper immigration.

[1] There is considerable discrepancy in immigration statistics. It should also be remembered that until 1820 the government of the United States kept no account of immigrant arrivals, and not until 1907 were departing immigrants recorded. Before the latter date the net gain in population from immigration can only be estimated.

The influx of foreigners showed itself in the hostility of organized labor. Labor leaders charged that capitalists were importing strike-breakers and cheap laborers, men whose abject condition in their native countries made them submissive and peaceful and willing to work from fourteen to sixteen hours per day at low wages. American labor, it was alleged, was degraded. The daughters of New England farmers employed in factories refused to work alongside the immigrants because of the social stigma. The foreigners produced labor leaders who had seen the misery of the working classes of Europe. To prevent their co-workers from sinking into similar circumstances in the adopted land, they urged the organization of labor associations and urged measures which grated harshly on the ears of many Americans. Not until after the decade of the forties were two languages employed in labor-union meetings, but after this as many as ten languages were in use.[1]

Among the Irish and German immigrants were many Roman Catholics. The erection of Catholic churches and the establishment of convents was a most terrifying thing to the intensely Protestant Americans. The possibility of the Pope's colonizing America with Catholics in order to extend his authority over the republic was very real in the minds of many earnest people. To what purpose, they asked, were Catholics flocking into the police forces of our cities, enlisting in military organizations, and storing firearms in the basements of Catholic churches if a day of reckoning between Protestants and Catholics was not near at hand? The Reverend Lyman Beecher, a Congregational minister intensely interested in the educational development of the West, de-

[1] John R. Commons, *History of Labour in the United States*, Vol. I, pp. 412 ff.

livered lectures in many places, exhorting his countrymen to be alive to the dark designs of the reactionary potentates of Europe. The establishment of educational institutions was his method of coping with the outpouring of Catholic and revolutionary Europe on our shores.

Just as the Puritans could not conceive of a system of education which did not include religious instruction, so the Irish and German Catholics and the German and Scandinavian Lutherans established parochial schools in their communities. The Catholics who sent their children to the public schools objected to the reading of the Protestant Bible in their presence. Where the Catholics were strong numerically their activity sometimes took the form of a movement to secure state appropriations for parochial schools. Then many held, as many hold now, that the common school is our most effective nationalizing agency. In the words of a newspaper editorial of the time, the common school "takes the child of the exile of Hungary, of the half-starved emigrant from the Emerald Isle, and of the hardy Norwegian, and places them on the same bench with the offspring of those whose ancestors' bones bleached upon the fields of Lexington. . . . As the child of the foreigner plays with his school fellow, he learns to whistle 'Yankee Doodle' and sing 'Hail Columbia,' and before he leaves the school-desk for the plough, the anvil or the trowel, he is as sturdy a little republican as can be found in the land."[1]

Not only would the parochial school bring the children of the immigrants up in the religion of their native land, but it would perpetuate the language of their fathers. The immigrants naturally looked to their priests and pastors for leadership and guidance, partly because of their office and partly

[1] *Minnesota Chronicle and Register* (St. Paul), September 23, 1850.

because by education and training they were qualified for that distinction. Among the Germans there were laymen who possessed to a marked degree the qualities of leadership, men of education and refinement who were virtual exiles from their native land. The educated immigrants, clergy and laity, were conscious of their cultural inheritance and impressed upon their countrymen the necessity of retaining the good of their native land, sometimes at the expense of familiarizing themselves with the language, customs, and institutions of the adopted country. The critical attitude toward America was deeply resented by the native-born Americans.

The Germans and the Irish, and to some extent the Scandinavians, brought with them ideas about temperance and Sabbath observance very different from those of Puritan New England. The Germans enjoyed their beer, and they joined the Irish in opposing the enactment of the "Maine law," which was agitated in every state of the Union. The immigrants attended *Turnvereine* and picnics on the Sabbath and declared openly that the puritanical Sabbath was an infringement on personal liberty. Moreover, among the Germans and the Irish there was a sprinkling of radicals and atheists who scoffed at religion and ridiculed institutions and principles that were deeply rooted in the American character. The principles of the German Democratic Association may be taken as an example of the radical tendencies which infected a very few, but which were played up by agitators to prove that American institutions were threatened by the infusion of aliens. The association demanded universal manhood suffrage, the election of all officers by the people, the abolition of the presidency, the abolition of senates, the right of the people to recall their representatives at their pleasure, and the right of the people to change the Constitution whenever they like. All lawsuits should be conducted without expense to the parties involved. A department of government should be set up for the purpose of protecting immigrants. The term of residence for acquiring citizenship should be reduced. In regard to foreign relations they demanded the abandonment of neutrality and intervention in behalf of every people struggling for liberty. In matters of religion they insisted on greater personal freedom and liberty of conscience; the repeal of laws of Sabbath observance; the discontinuance of prayers in Congress; the repeal of laws enacting a religious test before taking office; the taxation of church property; and the prohibition of incorporations of all church property in the name of ecclesiastics.[1]

The liberal naturalization laws which have been in force, with a brief interruption, during our entire history have been justified by the results; but, like all liberal measures, they have been abused. The evils of foreign-born suffrage were undoubtedly great in the cities of the East, where immigrants were naturalized wholesale and herded to the polls by ward-heelers, native and foreign. The immigrants to some extent considered themselves a separate class, and their prejudices were carefully nursed by demagogues and self-seekers. Urged by foreign-language newspapers and their leaders, the naturalized Americans showed a disposition to exercise the privilege of the ballot box as citizens. On certain issues they voted in a body. Political meetings were held at which foreign languages were used and rather strong statements were uttered. The fact that foreigners, unacquainted with American conditions and speaking a strange language, should presume to dictate to native Americans what course their

[1] J. W. Laurens, *The Crisis, or the Enemies of America Unmasked* (Philadelphia, 1855), pp. 59–71.

government should pursue was sorely trying to citizens who were willing to overlook other evils attributed to immigration.

The unsettled state of Europe, which was rocked by revolutions, affected the political situation in America. It was easy to read into the words of the radicals among the immigrants dangerous consequences. The socialistic experiment, or the alleged experiment, in France which followed the revolution of 1848 appeared to presage similar activities in other countries, including our own. The close of the Crimean War (1854–1856) was expected to precipitate a horde of immigrants.

The influence of the foreign-born shows itself in the political agitation of the time. The political movement against "foreign" influence began as early as the thirties, although, of course, there had been isolated instances before. In 1835 a Native American party was organized in New York City, and although it was unsuccessful at the polls it attracted an encouraging vote. In 1836 the party ran a candidate for mayor, and the following year, by a fusion with the Whigs, it carried the city election.

From 1840 to 1854 there were two main parties,—Whig and Democratic,—but "third parties" sprang up from time to time. At the beginning the Irish, Germans, Dutch, and Scandinavians tended to vote the Democratic ticket. They had heard of Jefferson and Jackson, the patron saints of the Democracy and the champions of the common people, and the name "democratic" seemed to promise more than "whig." Since the Democratic party harbored the bulk of the naturalized voters, the nativists were driven into the rival organization. With many immigrants "whig" and "nativism" were synonymous terms. This circumstance was taken advantage of by the Democrats, who seized every opportunity to pin the stigma of unfriendliness to immigrants on to the Whigs. It is significant that political parties have frequently included naturalization planks in their platforms.

In some respects the political contest of 1840, the "Tippecanoe and Tyler too" campaign, is a landmark in our political history, partly because it popularized the public-land question and was followed by the enactment of an important public-land measure, the Preëmption Law. All things considered, the public-land policy of the United States has been liberal and enlightened, but there were always people who thought that the public domain should be administered primarily in the interest of the settler, giving him a preference over the speculator and man of larger means. The Preëmption Act of 1841 was a step in that direction, but it did not satisfy an ever-increasing number who insisted that Congress should pass a law granting one hundred and sixty acres of land free to the actual settler on condition that he would reside on the homestead, cultivate it, and make improvements. The movement for a homestead law gained momentum during the forties and fifties until in 1862 it was signed by President Lincoln.[1]

The public-land question and immigration were closely connected. The preëmption and homestead measures were attacked as direct bounties to immigrants. Not only was the grant of one hundred and sixty acres of land a strong inducement to immigrate to the United States, but the existence of millions of acres of lands to be had for the asking kept land values down in other states.

[1] On the relation between immigration and the public lands, see *Political History of the Public Lands from 1840 to 1862*, by G. M. Stephenson.

The immigrants were land hungry and kept an eye on the land bills before Congress and the platforms of political parties. The Germans by virtue of their numbers exercised a strong political influence. They formed associations and held meetings in the interest of "land reform." Many homestead petitions presented to Congress were signed exclusively by Germans. Their slogan was "The right of the people to the use of the soil." Radical German papers denounced the capitalists and land speculators and declared that the emancipation of the common people would be effected by reserving the land for actual settlers and limiting the amount of land a man could own or inherit.

A measure of such far-reaching consequences was certain to arouse opposition. A favorite method of attack was to label it "socialistic" and "agrarian," a child of the disordered brains of "unreasonable and half-cracked" imported and domestic radicals. By donating the public lands, it was said, the Federal treasury would be deprived of a fruitful source of revenue. Why tax native Americans for the benefit of foreigners? Why subsidize the paupers, the criminals, and the undesirables of Europe to come here to foment discord? Was not this class legislation? The opponents of the immigrants proposed amendments to homestead bills, limiting their application to native Americans.

On December 5, 1851, Kossuth, the Hungarian revolutionist, arrived at New York, a fugitive from the Austrian government. "I come here," he said, "to invoke the aid of the great American republic to protect my people, peaceably, if they may, by the moral influence of their declarations, but forcibly if they must. . . ." The editor of the *St. Anthony* (Minnesota) *Express*[1] wrote:

[1] January 24, 1852.

The arrival of Louis Kossuth upon our shores may be regarded as one of the most important events of the present century. It has shaken the foundation stones on which our government rests. . . . The question before the American People is—*Shall there be an armed intervention by our government in European affairs?*

The revolutionist received most cordial receptions wherever he appeared; and on the whole he conducted himself with poise and good judgment. In addressing an assembly of Germans in New York, however, he departed from his rule to refrain from expressing opinions on political questions by advising his auditors to turn against the administration and elect a party favorable to the cause of foreign nations struggling for freedom. Like the Minnesota editor, many Americans saw in the visit of Kossuth another example of the disturbing influence of foreigners and charged that the affair was timed to influence the coming presidential campaign. Said a United States senator[1]:

I do not know whether it is socialism from France, or whether it is Kossuthism from Hungary and Italy; but I say that, from the infusion of foreign material, or from the idiosyncrasies of our own people, they have become so inflamed and restive of power that if they were so concentrated in this country, and could make a revolution here as in France or in England, by getting possession of the capital, our inflammable, revolutionary, discontented, dissatisfied people would go far beyond filibusterism or anything of that sort and would strike for the overthrow of the government itself.

One of the difficult problems for the government of the United States to solve has been to determine to what measure of protection naturalized citizens or persons who have declared their intention of becoming citizens are entitled. There

[1] John B. Thompson of Kentucky, April 19, 1854. *Congressional Globe*, 33d Cong., 1st Sess., p. 948.

have been many instances of citizens, or alleged citizens, both naturalized and native, who have resided abroad for many years claiming the protection of our government without discharging the duties of citizenship. A diplomatic agent of the American government at the beginning of the present century reported that he knew of cases where the applicant for naturalization had never resided in the United States more than six months. Applicants have come to the United States for the sole purpose of becoming naturalized for mercenary reasons, immediately returning to their native land. He had knowledge of one instance where a naturalized citizen had resided for over fifty years in the land of his nativity without ever returning to his adopted country and without the ability to speak a word of English.[1]

An event which received considerable newspaper space in 1853 was the case of Martin Koszta, a Hungarian revolutionist who escaped to the United States and declared his intention of becoming a citizen. After residing in this country for nearly two years, business matters caused him to go to Smyrna, Turkey, where he claimed the protection of the American consul. The Austrian consul-general sought permission from the Turkish government to arrest him as a fugitive from Austrian justice. Failing in this, he had him kidnaped and taken on board an Austrian man of war. Just at this time an American warship commanded by Captain Ingraham put in the harbor. The American commander, apprised of the circumstances, demanded Koszta's release and backed up the demand by a show of force. Hostilities were averted by placing the revolutionist under the jurisdiction of the French consul-general. The Austrian government dispatched a stiff note to the American government, demanding

[1] *House Documents*, 57th Cong., 2d Sess., No. 1, pp. 386–388.

that Ingraham's conduct be disavowed and that the person in question be delivered up. Secretary of State Marcy replied in a note which took strong ground in opposition to Austria's contention. Marcy recognized Koszta's right to the protection of the American government; that although he had not yet become naturalized, he had established his domicile in the United States. "Whenever," wrote the secretary, "by the operation of the law of nations, an individual becomes clothed with our national character, be he a native-born or naturalized citizen, an exile driven from his early home by political oppression, or an emigrant enticed from it by the hopes of a better fortune for himself and posterity, he can claim the protection of this government, and it may respond to that claim without being obliged to explain its conduct to any foreign power; for it is its duty to make its nationality respected by other nations and respectable in every quarter of the globe."[1]

The tone of Marcy's note appealed to the patriotism of the American people, who liked to think of their country as the home of the oppressed of other countries; but to some it was only another instance of a politician's truckling to foreigners and an example of the dangerous problems attendant upon immigration.

The fear of Catholic influence in American affairs which disturbed the slumbers of ardent patriots was heightened by the visit of Bedini, a representative of the papacy, who visited America in 1854 to settle a controversy with respect to church property in New York State. Not only that, but the appearance of the prelate in certain cities was the signal for demonstrations of hostility on the part of immigrants as well, who were possessed of the idea that the Catholic Church

[1] J. F. Rhodes, *History of the United States*, Vol. I, pp. 416–419.

was instrumental in suppressing liberal movements in their native lands. These disorders were seized upon by people who had no sympathy with Catholicism to show that foreigners were abusing the hospitality of America. An influential New York newspaper, commenting on the conduct of the Germans at Cincinnati when Bedini visited that city, expressed the opinion that the Germans and Irish who create disorder ought to be expelled from the country.[1]

The German immigrants came here with an inborn hostility to the institution of slavery. Not only were they opposed to the extension of slavery into territory where the institution did not exist, but many were in favor of its abolition in the states where it already existed. The country was already torn by the slavery agitation when the stream of immigration gained volume, and the Germans immediately ranged themselves on the side of freedom. The Kansas-Nebraska Bill, which was enacted into law in 1854, repealed the Missouri Compromise and opened the territories to slavery. The tremendous controversy which raged around this momentous measure is familiar to every student of American history. The German-language newspapers, with few exceptions, condemned the bill, and hundreds of petitions protesting against its passage bore German signatures. The author of the measure, Senator Douglas, was hanged in effigy. This was more than the representatives of the slave states could bear. "Have you not seen, sir," exclaimed Stephen Adams, a senator from Mississippi, "within the last few months, petitions presented here and laid upon your table, remonstrating in the name of foreigners, against the action of this body. Not content with that, have you not learned through the public newspapers, that a mob of foreigners, under the style of foreigners, as-

[1] *New York Herald*, February 1, 1854.

sembled together, and hanged in effigy an honorable member of this body? . . . What do we need of further immigration from other countries? We have a sufficient population to protect us against all the world. We have a sufficient population to settle every portion of our country which it is necessary to settle."[1]

With this background we are able to understand that extraordinary outburst of nativism in the forties and fifties which precipitated the Know-Nothing party. In 1850 was organized in New York the Supreme Order of the Star-Spangled Banner, also known as the Sons of the Sires of '76. This organization came to be known as the Know-Nothing order. It was an oath-bound secret fraternity composed of a national council, with state and local councils. Members were admitted only after a searching examination and an elaborate ritual. A candidate had to be descended from at least two generations of American ancestors. Neither he nor his wife nor any of his ancestors for two generations could have been members of the Roman Catholic Church. The candidate had to be vouched for by a select committee of the council. Obviously there could be no trace of salt-water odor in a Know-Nothing lodge. When a member was asked about the order, he invariably replied "I don't know" or "I know nothing." From this it came that the members were dubbed "Know-Nothings," although they called themselves members of the Native American party. Their purpose was to put none but native Americans in office, men who were acceptable to the councils.

The situation was peculiarly favorable to the formation of a "third party." The Whig party, torn by dissensions, had been in a feeble state since the Compromise of 1850, and it

[1]*Congressional Globe*, 33d Cong., 1st Sess., pp. 944, 945.

never recovered from the deathblow of the Kansas-Nebraska Bill. So in a sense the Know-Nothing party was the successor of, or rather the substitute for, the Whig party. In some instances the antislavery people secured control of the Know-Nothing lodges by reason of the fact that until the appearance of the Republican party there was no political party to which this element could turn. The Democratic party also lost many followers because of dissatisfaction with its slavery planks.

In the beginning of its meteoric career the principles of the Know-Nothing party were secret, but before long they became public property. It advocated the repeal of all naturalization laws, none but native Americans for office, a pure American common-school system, war to the hilt on Romanism, opposition to the formation of military companies composed of foreigners, hostility to all papal influences, more stringent and effective immigration laws, the sending back of all foreign paupers on our shores, and, summing everything up, "our country, our whole country, and nothing but our country."[1]

The Know-Nothings won some startling successes at the polls, either by putting forth tickets of their own or by indorsing certain candidates of other parties. In 1854 they polled 122,282 votes and elected forty members to the state legislature in New York. In Massachusetts the same year a Know-Nothing governor was elected by a majority of 54,000 over his nearest competitor, and practically every member elected to the legislature bore the Know-Nothing stamp. Pennsylvania elected a Whig-American governor and some

[1] The principles of the Know-Nothings were printed in the *American Crusader*, published at Boston. See *Congressional Globe*, 33d Cong., 1st Sess., p. 1708.

members of the legislative body. A few Know-Nothings were elected to Congress from these states.

The elections of the following year were even more startling and certainly boded good for the future of the new party. Six Know-Nothing governors were elected, in Rhode Island, New Hampshire, Connecticut, Massachusetts, California, and Kentucky. In Texas, New York, and Maryland, where there were no gubernatorial contests, Know-Nothing state tickets triumphed. Five state legislatures were controlled by the Know-Nothings, in Rhode Island, Connecticut, Massachusetts, California, and Kentucky; and in New Hampshire, Maryland, and Tennessee the legislatures were controlled by the fusion of Whigs and Know-Nothings. The legislatures of New York, Virginia, Georgia, and Louisiana had strong minority Know-Nothing delegates. In addition Know-Nothing candidates were elected to Congress and to municipal offices.

But the victories for nativism were more apparent than real. In some states the fusion with the Whigs made the Know-Nothing party almost identical with the old Whig party. The victory in Massachusetts in 1854 was partly due to the fact that the Free Soil element, which could not vote the Democratic ticket, cast a protest vote for the Know-Nothing candidates. In some instances local conditions having no relation to nativism contributed to the result. The integrity of a national nativist party depended upon the ability of its leaders to keep the slavery question in the background, but the tragic events following the enactment of the Kansas-Nebraska Act rendered this impossible. As the supreme struggle between freedom and slavery came closer, there was relatively little interest in national legislation except as it had a bearing upon slavery. The newborn Republican party, which came into the field as a protest against the extension of slavery, attracted the antislavery people, many of whom had refused to vote for Democrats and Whigs. They found vent for their political dissatisfaction by supporting the Know-Nothings.

The year that gave the Know-Nothing party its greatest success also sealed its doom. As a rule the men who guided the destiny of the party were self-seekers, ambitious for political office, little known and little experienced in public affairs. The distintegration of the old parties played into their hands, and their success was more largely due to good fortune than to political skill. For a time men of diverse parties and incompatible views found shelter in the Know-Nothing camp, enjoying its hospitality so long as it suited their purposes. But new forces were asserting themselves. In the spring of 1855 the Democrats in Virginia under the leadership of Henry A. Wise, the candidate for governor, won a signal victory over the order after an exciting campaign, which attracted the attention of the entire country. The news of the Know-Nothing defeat spread like wildfire, and the triumphant march of the party was broken.

A few days after the Virginia Waterloo the slavery issue, which had figured largely in that contest, disrupted the national Know-Nothing council assembled at Philadelphia in June. The antislavery delegates seceded and issued an address to the country in favor of the restoration of the Missouri Compromise, the protection of free settlers in Kansas and Nebraska, religious freedom, the open Bible, free schools, and free labor, and against the deportation of convicts and paupers by foreign countries to the United States.

The presidential campaign of 1856 revealed the hopeless future of the Know-Nothing party. The platform was a catchall designed to attract voters of every stripe. The nativist planks were equivocal and not at all satisfactory to the orthodox. The platform declared that Americans must rule America; that no state or territory could admit to the suffrage or to political office any except native citizens unless previously naturalized under Federal law; that a twenty-one years' residence for naturalization should be required; and that there should be no union of church and state, no interference with religion, and no test oaths for office. In nominating Millard Fillmore for the presidency a mild nativist was preferred over a candidate who was willing to fight the good fight as the Know-Nothing leaders saw it in days of success. In the election Fillmore ran a poor third, Buchanan, the Democratic candidate, carrying off the honors, with John C. Frémont, the nominee of the newly organized Republican party, second in the popular and electoral votes.

The Know-Nothing party has never been placed in the proper perspective by historians who have written on the antebellum period of American history. Undoubtedly the feeling against foreigners was very strong in certain states and among certain people; but the success of the party at the polls was made possible by the fact that thousands voted the ticket as a protest against the policies and leadership of the Democratic and Whig parties. The Know-Nothing party was a bridge by which the old-line party men could get away from their parties and avoid the distasteful necessity of voting for their old political opponents.

The fundamental weakness of the party is further attested by its barren legislative achievements. In the Know-Nothing legislature in Massachusetts in 1855 no measures of importance were enacted. Not even the United States senator Henry Wilson, who was elected by this body, was a dyed-in-the-wool Know-Nothing. He was essentially a Free-Soiler and proved it by his course in the Senate.[1] Considerable oratory was spilled in Congress over the proposition to lengthen the residence requirement for naturalization to twenty-one years, but the measure never mustered a majority in either House.

But for the slavery issue Know-Nothingism might have proved a very popular issue. In Massachusetts, New York, Pennsylvania, and certain other Eastern states the feeling against foreigners was strong. These states were strongly Protestant. Catholic immigrants, mainly from Ireland, settled in the Eastern cities. Friction resulted, hostility toward the aliens was fanned by nativist societies, and riots and disorders followed. The slave states experienced nothing like this, but the influx of aliens increased the political power of the free states, which threatened the existence of the institution of slavery. Speaking on the bill to amend the naturalization laws in 1856, Stephen Adams, senator from Mississippi, pointed out that according to the census of 1850 the House of Representatives at that time had twenty-four members representing the foreign population—twenty from the North and four from the South; that in the decade of the forties the North had gained twelve representatives through immigration. "It will be seen," he said, "that but for immigration, the South would have gained five members upon the North, and we would have been gaining our lost political strength, in place of the North gaining upon us. . . . If immigration should be the same for the next five years, by the same apportionment the North will gain upon the South twenty-four additional members from immigration alone; and fifteen

---

[1] George H. Haynes, "A Know-Nothing Legislature," in the Report of the American Historical Association for 1896, pp. 177–187.

years from this day . . . the North will have a majority of more than two to one in the other branch of Congress; and the prospect now is that it will have a similar majority in this body." Mr. Adams pointed out that the immigrants came here prejudiced against the institution of slavery and feared for the future of the South if the immigrants were allowed to vote their convictions.[1]

The optimistic and developing West extended a welcoming hand to the immigrants. They populated the farms and contributed to the prosperity of that section. The evils of a congested foreign population were almost entirely absent. The West demanded a homestead law which would be a direct inducement to everyone, natives and foreigners, to migrate to the vast public domain. The Know-Nothing party was openly hostile to that measure, and for this reason attracted relatively few votes in the newer portions of the country. No party could carry a national election without capturing the Northwest, and the Know-Nothings surrendered any claim to political success in that section by opposing the homestead measure.

The ritual and secrecy of the Know-Nothing lodges were novel and attractive to certain people for a time, but the novelty of the thing wore off. The more level-headed people saw the inconsistency of the party. They believed that the Know-Nothings were as un-American and clannish as the immigrants were said to be. And so the political movement which threatened to overwhelm the old parties succumbed to common sense and to a new set of circumstances.

[1] *Congressional Globe*, 34th Cong., 1st Sess., pp. 1409–1414.

CHAPTER XI

THE IMMIGRANTS IN POLITICS, 1840–1860

Generally speaking, the political history of the United States shows that two parties have been pitted against each other in political campaigns and that "third parties" have seldom counted in the electoral vote. The American political system has not been productive of "coalitions" and "mosaic ministries" in the European sense. This is not to say, however, that American politics has not been profoundly affected by "blocs" and sectional combinations.

With the increase of immigration the foreign-born voters and their immediate descendants constituted a "special interest." In some states and communities they held the balance of power, and politicians in making up party slates and writing party platforms were compelled to take account of this fact. In the two decades preceding the election of Abraham Lincoln the immigrants became increasingly influential in politics, and special efforts were made by political leaders to capture the German and Irish vote. The immigrants, as we have observed, naturally gravitated to the Democratic party—the party of Jefferson and Jackson and the rival organization of the nativistic Whigs.

In the election of 1844, when Polk and Dallas, the Democratic candidates, triumphed over the Whig nominees, Clay and Frelinghuysen, it was the opinion of certain Whig leaders that the naturalized vote went against them. In appealing to the immigrants the Democrats denounced Clay as the enemy of the Preëmption Act and Frelinghuysen as a nativist. Fillmore wrote to Clay that the abolitionists and foreign Catholics in New York State had defeated him. According to another correspondent:

> Foreigners who have "no lot or inheritance" in the matter have robbed us of our inheritance. . . . Ireland has reconquered the country which England lost. . . . In Baltimore alone in the short space of two months 1,000 naturalized. Out of this number nine-tenths voted the locofoco ticket.[1]

The war with Mexico which occurred in the Polk administration brought the slavery issue before the country in the form of the Wilmot Proviso: that slavery should be prohibited in any territory about to be acquired from Mexico. Both the old parties split on this question, and a third party, the Free Soil party, with a platform opposing the extension of slavery, made its appearance. Its slogan was "Free soil and free farms," a principle which attracted a goodly number of Germans, although as yet the great majority remained loyal to the Democratic party. The Compromise of 1850 had apparently settled the slavery question; so the election of 1852 was a rather colorless affair which resulted in the overwhelming election of the Democratic candidate, Franklin Pierce. But the calm was only before the storm.

The year 1854 was pregnant with great political events. Two great legislative measures of far-reaching importance came before Congress,—the Kansas-Nebraska Bill and the Homestead Bill,—and both vitally affected the fortunes of the immigrants. The former bill, by repealing the Missouri Compromise, opened the territories to slavery; and the latter opened the vast public domain in the states and territories to

[1] W. L. Barre, *The Life and Public Services of Millard Fillmore*, pp. 294 ff.

the settler on most liberal terms. The two measures were directly antagonistic. It was not to be expected that the slave power would throw away the fruits of victory gained by the passage of the Kansas-Nebraska Bill by failing to prevent at all costs the enactment of a law which would give the pioneers from the free states and from Europe a bounty of one hundred and sixty acres of land, a tract entirely inadequate for the Southern slaveholder. The attitude of the South toward these two bills determined to no small degree the political alignment of the immigrants.

The South was never willing to admit that slavery was a moral question. The Constitution specifically recognized the legality of slavery, and the slaveholders felt that any attempt to interfere with their property rights was unconstitutional; that Federal and state laws interfering with the movement or existence of their property were unjust and contrary to the spirit and letter of the Constitution. They became increasingly angry with agitators, alien and native-born, who attacked slavery and made out the South to be morally inferior to them.

The population of the slave states was increasing, but not nearly at the rate of the free states. The large plantation system made for scattered population and froze out the small planter or farmer, who could not compete with the large-scale farmer. In the forty or more years preceding the Civil War there was a heavy emigration from the South, and what was the South's loss was a gain to the West. The South could offer no inducements to European immigrants. The absence of factories and public lands and the presence of slave labor were serious handicaps. The propaganda of Northern states and Northern interests could not be counteracted by the South.

The Know-Nothing press played into the hands of the South by opposing the Homestead Bill. It asserted that if the bill passed we should have all the paupers of Europe flocking to our shores to participate in the distribution of the public lands. The homestead policy would make America an asylum for the "lazzaroni" and vagabond population of the world, and the title of American citizenship would cease to command respect.[1] A Democratic paper published at Charleston was alarmed at the spectacle of trains from New York "solely freighted with Germans and their plunder, *in transitu* for the extreme Northwest," with a thousand foreigners aboard. According to this paper the Germans, with their ignorance of our institutions, had vitiated the principles of the Democratic party.

Whole towns and counties are settled by these people, while they are scattered more or less in every portion of the North, in numbers sufficient to control the elections. The Homestead Bill is a grand scheme to settle the Northwest and create new States.[2]

The fact that the Homestead Bill was identified with free soilism and abolitionism was patent. The same paper continues:

We make bold to say that it is the most dangerous abolition bill which has ever been directly pressed in Congress. How many individuals are there in the South who can and will take advantage of the bonus to emigrate to the frontier, because, perchance, 160 acres of land invite them?

The Know-Nothing party and nativism were popular not only in the South but in New England and the East as well; but after the enactment of the Kansas-Nebraska Law in 1854

[1] *Baltimore Clipper*, March 7, 1854.
[2] *Charleston Mercury* (tri-weekly), March 17, 1860.

there was a tendency to overlook the faults, or alleged faults, of the Germans and to remember that they were opposed to the extension of slavery. The Eastern states had no "peculiar institution" whose permanence was threatened by foreign immigration or by the migration of population to the West. The immigrants became the factory workers and increased population, in spite of a heavy exodus of native-born citizens, and a prosperous West furnished a market for the products of Eastern factories.

The West had its heart set on a liberal homestead law. This exuberant and optimistic section had little fear of the immigrant. In the shirt-sleeve society of the West the immigrant was estimated more nearly at his worth. There were no better farmers anywhere than the Germans, Scandinavians, and Dutch. They were industrious, law-abiding, and appreciative of the opportunities America afforded them.

When the Kansas-Nebraska Bill reached the Senate, opposition in the South to the immigrants took the form of an amendment, introduced by Clayton of Delaware, which provided that only citizens of the United States should have the right of suffrage and of holding office in the territory. The amendment was adopted by a close vote, with one exception all the affirmative votes being from the slave states and all the negatives from the free states.[1] The Clayton amendment figured largely in the German newspapers, whose editors asserted that by its adoption the hostility of the South to the foreign-born was proved. More and more, slavery extension and opposition to the immigrants became associated.

In the House of Representatives the only hope of defeating the Homestead Bill was to take advantage of the Know-Nothing sentiment by proposing an amendment to limit its

[1] Rhodes, *History of the United States*, Vol. I, p. 476.

application to native Americans, a proposition which was rejected. But in the Senate the South was in control. Clayton introduced an amendment to strike out the provision to give rights to foreigners who declared their intention to become citizens. This amendment, which was adopted, and a later motion by Chase of Ohio to reinstate the provision, which was rejected, produced an acrimonious sectional debate. Senator Seward of New York maintained that if foreigners were excluded from the benefits of the bill, American citizens would go on the public lands and aliens would remain on the Atlantic coast, with the result that agricultural labor in the East would be paid excessively high wages.[1] John B. Thompson, a Whig senator from Kentucky, was opposed to acquiring territory and giving it to "these foreigners and emigrants, who come here, and lazy fellows and loafers in our midst. . . . We will give it to the foreigners, and then we will get up a German interest, having its center at Cincinnati and Louisville, and other places over the Union. . . . We will build up a foreign power that shall control the whole American people. . . . The first thing you see these president-aspirants do . . . is to start out a demagoging; and, sir, he draws himself up; he is not an American at all; his father was an Irishman, and his mother a Dutchman [laughter]. That is the beginning of it. Then though he has no respect for religion . . . the next thing we hear he is making the sign of the cross to catch Catholics [laughter]; and then, sir, to top off the thing, he offers all the land to these men, just as the wicked one of old offered to our Savior the kingdoms of the world, if he would fall down and worship him, when the old scoundrel had not an inch of terra firma in all creation to put his foot upon [great laughter]."[2] Clay of Alabama feared

[1] *Congressional Globe*, 33d Cong., 1st Sess., pp. 1808, 1809. [2] Ibid. pp. 945-949.

that the adoption of Chase's amendment would result in the growing up of a Know-Nothing party in the Southern states. He pointed out that those states had been freer from all species of radicalism than any other section of the Union, and but for the pure conservative principles and the true American feeling of the South, the radical, meddlesome spirit of the North would have involved the country in a foreign war.[1] Dodge of Iowa voiced the feeling of the West:

> The poor German emigrant who lands at New Orleans, or New York, and works his way three thousand miles up the Mississippi with his family, and goes into Nebraska, or Kansas, or Minnesota, to make your roads and fight your battles, is the man who is identified with you in every way; and for him I want a homestead, and I trust I shall get it.[2]

In 1854 the South defeated the Homestead Bill and prevented the passage of a bill until 1860, when it was killed by the veto of President Buchanan, whose policies were in accord with the slave section.

Historians are in agreement that the passage of the Kansas-Nebraska Bill precipitated a political realignment. A distinguished scholar has called it the most momentous measure that ever passed Congress before the Civil War.[3] A new party, the present Republican organization, came into existence, definitely pledged against the extension of slavery into new territory. From this time there were two major parties opposed to each other: the Democratic, in which the strength of slave power was concentrated with its stronghold in the South, and the Republican, the party with practically all its supporters in the North.

[1] *Congressional Globe*, 33d Cong., 1st Sess., p. 1705.
[2] Ibid. p. 753.
[3] Rhodes, *History of the United States*, Vol. I, pp. 490, 491.

In the presidential canvass of 1856 the slavery issue over-shadowed all others. James Buchanan, "a Northern man with Southern principles," was elected on the Democratic ticket; but in this, its first national contest, the Republican party polled an extraordinarily large vote. One of the alarming things revealed in the election figures was the rapidly increasing number of Germans who were deserting the Democratic standard. As the political lines between slavery and freedom became prominent the Germans, who because of their numbers wielded considerable power, more and more cast their lot with the parties committed against the extension of slavery. The political strategy in the four years preceding the all-important election of 1860 consisted in dangling tempting bait before the immigrants in order to entice them into the rival political camps.[1]

The "decisive issue" in the election of 1860 was, of course, slavery; but there were many voters, native and foreign-born, who applied different tests to the candidates and parties. There were four parties in the field, but only two figured seriously with the bulk of voters in the free states. The Republicans nominated the frontier Illinois lawyer, Abraham Lincoln, who had gained national prominence through his debates with another distinguished citizen of Illinois, Stephen A. Douglas, who now, as the nominee of the Northern wing of the Democratic party, was his strongest opponent for the presidency. Both parties realized that national success could not be gained without carrying the Northwest. In this growing section the foreign-born held the balance of political power. Their numbers in certain other

[1] George M. Stephenson, "Nativism in the Forties and Fifties, with special Reference to the Mississippi Valley," in *Mississippi Valley Historical Review*, Vol. IX, pp. 185–202.

states were large enough to enable them to demand a price for their much-desired support.

At this time the Irish, who were concentrated largely in the cities and towns of the East, were incurably Democratic. Their leaders were convinced that their fortunes were safer in Democratic hands than in Republican. The Germans, Scandinavians, and Dutch naturally belonged in the Republican party, because they were opposed to the extension of slavery and because the South was opposed to the Homestead Bill. But the Germans especially were hesitant about joining the younger party before they were convinced that it had purged itself of Know-Nothingism. The demise of the Know-Nothing party left its adherents without political shelter. In the North the bulk of them drifted into the Republican camp. Republican neophytes of Know-Nothing complexion proposed measures in legislative bodies and conventions strongly suggestive of nativism. For instance, the Republican legislature of Massachusetts—a state with an intensely Protestant native population and an intensely Catholic Irish-born population—as late as 1859 adopted by an overwhelming majority an amendment to the state constitution providing that no person of foreign birth should be entitled to vote or should be eligible to office unless he had resided within the jurisdiction of the United States for two years subsequent to his naturalization. Very naturally the Democrats were not tardy in calling the attention of the foreign-born voters to the fact that a party sponsoring this measure could hardly honestly claim to be friendly to immigrants.

Moreover, the puritanical element was strong in Republican councils. Leading Republicans took a firm stand in favor of laws requiring a strict observance of the Sabbath and laws regulating or prohibiting the manufacture and sale of liquor. These measures were directly contrary to the German idea of personal liberty. The deep pietistic strain in the early Scandinavian and Dutch immigrants caused them rather to favor the Republican party because of its puritanism. But to the Germans the names Republican and Know-Nothing were synonymous. *Sociale Republik*, a German-language labor paper published in New York, was strongly antislavery, but as late as 1858 it roundly condemned the Republican party for combining with the Know-Nothings and declared that the time had come for German-Americans to assert their rights. The editor disclaimed all intention of the Germans to nominate a candidate of their own for the presidency, but declared that they would support the man who would come closest to espousing their cause. If no candidate would look with favor on their cause, then they would withhold their votes. At German mass meetings resolutions censuring the Republican party were adopted, declaring that it claimed to be the party of freedom but in practice discriminated against immigrants, making fine promises before elections but forgetting them soon after.

The editors of foreign-language papers, ably assisted by Democratic politicians, pried into the records of Republican candidates for evidence of flirtations with Know-Nothingism. Open letters were addressed to aspiring politicians demanding that they state their views on questions vital to immigrants. In 1859 Abraham Lincoln replied to such a letter to the eminent satisfaction of the parties concerned. With his political astuteness Lincoln sensed the danger of allowing conditions peculiar to a state or locality, as in the case of Massachusetts, to jeopardize the success of the party in the coming presidential contest. He would antagonize neither the immigrants nor the nativists.

There were Republican leaders, especially in the West, where nativism had never flourished as it had in the older states, who were alive to the dangers in the situation and waged unceasing warfare against the fusion or threatened fusion with Know-Nothingism. They ridiculed the fears and sneered at the "Americanism" of the Know-Nothings. One speaker pictured "American Protestantism stealing the very livery of the Jesuits and raising the war-cry against Rome." "It should not strain at the gnat of American Catholicism, whilst it swallows down at one gulp the huge camel of American slavery." He waxed sarcastic over American-Protestant slaveholders in the South seeking to "Americanize" and Christianize Catholics. He defended the immigrants as good citizens or possessing the properties of good citizenship, denying that they alone were characterized by drunkenness, profanation of the Sabbath, ruffianism, and illiteracy.[1]

Spurred on by the knowledge that the Republicans were angling for their votes, the Germans played the game. In states where the German element was considerable, like Iowa, Illinois, Minnesota, and Wisconsin, Germans were recognized in making up party slates and choosing delegates to conventions. On the eve of the assembling of the Republican convention at Chicago in May, 1860, representative Germans met in that city. They demanded that the Republican platform contain planks condemning measures hostile to adopted citizens and favoring a liberal homestead law and positive opposition to the extension of slavery. Although no candidate for the presidential nomination was recommended, the German press leaned toward William H. Seward of New York, whose record as governor of New York and United States senator had gained him the favor of the immigrants.

[1] George W. Julian, *Speeches on Political Questions*, pp. 109, 126.

Carl Schurz of Wisconsin, who had been active in politics and had proved himself an effective campaign speaker, presented the German cause to the convention and stated that he represented three hundred thousand German votes. The Republican convention adopted a platform containing the "Dutch plank," as it was called by the Democrats. In the campaign especial efforts were made to capture the foreign vote. Carl Schurz, a member of the national committee, had charge of the "foreign department." He engaged prominent German, Scandinavian, and Dutch speakers to address their countrymen in their native tongue. They belittled the "nativistic" element in the Republican party, claiming that the party had always been friendly to the immigrants. The Massachusetts two-year amendment was explained away on the ground that it was directed against the Irish Catholics and that it in no way reflected the sentiments of Republicans toward Protestant immigrants or the sentiment of Republicans in other states. Copies of Republican homestead bills printed in foreign languages were circulated, and pains were taken to point out that they were more liberal in their benefits than the bills introduced by Democrats. The Democratic party, it was said, was controlled by the South and had shown its hostility to immigrants by obstructing the passage of several bills and had defeated a bill that very year through the veto of President Buchanan, who was said to be a weak tool of Southern politicians. Moreover, the immigrants were reminded that the Douglas platform was silent on the homestead question.

The Republican tactics were entirely successful. Carl Schurz reported that the Germans were coming to the Republicans by hundreds and thousands. From Philadelphia he wrote:

The old "Pennsylvania Dutch" follow me like children, although they can only half understand me. The Democrats are furious, and wherever I have spoken they telegraph like mad in all directions for German speakers to neutralize the effect of my speeches.

In some places entire German Democratic clubs went over to the Republicans. In July (1860) the *New Ulm* (Minnesota) *Pionier* gave a list of seventy-three German papers throughout the country that were supporting the Republican ticket. Twenty-two were dailies, five semi-weeklies or tri-weeklies, and forty-six weeklies. The rest of the German papers were grouped as follows: thirty-five for Douglas; fifteen for Breckinridge, the nominee of the Southern wing of the Democratic party; ten for Bell, the candidate of the Constitutional Union party; one ultra-radical; and ten which had not taken a definite position. Henry P. Scholte, the founder and leader of the large Dutch settlement at Pella, Iowa, joined the Republican ranks in 1859. Shortly after his arrival in this country he affiliated with the Democratic party because of its liberal attitude toward immigrants in contrast to the Whig party and because he was opposed to a strongly centralized government. He was hostile to the institution of slavery, but, like many others, could not stomach the methods of the extreme abolitionists. He was opposed to the passage of the Kansas-Nebraska Bill in 1854, but refused to vote for the Republican candidates in 1856 because of his belief that the party was in the hands of Know-Nothings and abolitionists. The trend of events in Kansas and the Lecompton policy of the Buchanan administration were too much for him, and he turned his back on the party. His change of faith made known through his paper, the *Pella Gazette*, undoubtedly had a tremendous influence with his countrymen not only in Pella but in the large Dutch settlements in Michigan,[1] where he was favorably known.

The Norwegians and Swedes, comparatively few in number prior to 1860, showed partiality toward the Republican cause from the very beginning. As we have observed, the "Maine law" and other puritanical measures had no terrors for them. Their two influential papers, *Hemlandet*, a Swedish paper published at Galesburg and Chicago, Illinois, and *Emigranten*, a Norwegian paper of Madison, Wisconsin, consistently defended the Republicans and denounced the proslavery policies of the Democrats. It may confidently be said that the Scandinavian who refused to vote for Abraham Lincoln in 1860 was a rare specimen. On the other hand, Republican oratory was wasted on the Irish. Concentrated largely in the cities of the East, where they were under the spell of their leaders and naturally repelled by the composition of the Republican party in those states, they felt that their interests rested with the Democracy.

The Democrats appealed in vain to the Germans, Scandinavians, and Dutch. The Republicans having cleared their skirts of Know-Nothingism by condemning the Massachusetts two-year amendment in state platforms and by adopting the "Dutch plank" and a homestead plank in their national platform, no amount of Democratic oratory could erase the record of that party in Congress after the passage of the Kansas-Nebraska Bill.

The Republicans carried the Northwest, a prize for which both parties contended most ardently, because without that section victory was impossible. So close was the vote that a

[1] F. I. Herriott, "Republican Presidential Preliminaries in Iowa, 1857–1860," in *Annals of Iowa*, third series, Vol. IX, pp. 241–283.

change of one vote in twenty would have given those states to Douglas. Here the foreign vote was decisive. A trustworthy student of American history has reached the conclusion that the election of Lincoln and the fate of the Union was determined not by native Americans but by German, Scandinavian, and Dutch voters, who knew least about American history and institutions.[1] No wonder that the Lincoln administration recognized the political power of the foreign-born in appointments to the civil and military service of the government.

The agitation against the foreign-born was eclipsed by the antislavery agitation. The Republican party had made a bid for the votes of the immigrants and won. From that day to this the Germans, Scandinavians, and Dutch have leaned toward the Republican party, but they have shown more political independence than the older American stock, partly because they have not inherited their politics and partly because they have in a sense constituted a special interest. Generally speaking, the Irish have favored the Democratic party. The Democracy has probably "played up" to the Irish more consistently than the rival party, the Republican organization bearing the stamp which was placed upon it in the early days of its existence. For various reasons the foreign policy of that party has been distasteful to the Irish.

The conditions prevailing in the early years of immigration, when the old immigration was in its infancy, determined to a large degree the political tendency of these stocks. Circumstances and events which gave a deceptive measure of success to political nativism have obscured the fact that on the whole America extended a welcoming hand to the immi-

[1] William E. Dodd, "The Fight for the Northwest, 1860," in *American Historical Review*, Vol. XVI, p. 788.

grants. What hostility there was expressed itself largely in political proscription and in efforts to prevent the establishment of institutions which would perpetuate foreign languages, customs, and religions. The need of the kind of labor furnished by the immigrants was so urgent that proposals to restrict immigration were almost entirely absent. Legislation to restrict the coming of foreigners materially was not enacted until more than half a century later. The political rôle of the immigrants in these years, as we have seen, was marked and culminated in the momentous election of Abraham Lincoln.

CHAPTER XII

FROM ENCOURAGEMENT TO REGULATION

When a nation engages in a great war its perspective changes. There is a shifting of emphasis. The Civil War solidified sentiment in the North, the section which harbored the bulk of the immigrants. The thought of saving the Union was uppermost.

The immigrants proved their loyalty to the adopted country by enlisting in the Federal army. Whole regiments were made up of the foreign-born. Some of the leading officers were adopted citizens, men like Carl Schurz, Franz Sigel, Hans Heg, and Hans Mattson, to mention no others. The important German element in the population of Missouri probably prevented that state from seceding from the Union. The immigrants were strongly attached to the Federal government. In their native lands they thought of America in terms of the United States. They knew little of the rivalries and jealousies between the American states, and they had not resided here long enough to form a special attachment to any state. Moreover, their naturalization made them first of all citizens of the United States, and their title to the public lands had been obtained from the Federal government.

The withdrawal of the Southern members from Congress was followed by the enactment of the Homestead Law in May, 1862. This opened the public domain to settlers, native and foreign-born, on liberal terms and facilitated the assimilation of immigrants for many years to come, besides offering a most attractive inducement to immigrate. The absorption of thousands from civil pursuits into the army created a shortage of laborers to till the fields and to man the factories. The construction of the Pacific Railway and the construction and repair of other roads not only furnished employment but made it easier to distribute the immigrants. In 1865 it was estimated that a million and a quarter people had left their peaceful pursuits, that twenty railroads were in process of construction or under contract in the West alone, furnishing employment for 20,000 men, and that the repair of railroads would give employment to an additional 10,000.[1]

It was under these conditions that Congress passed a law encouraging immigration by direct legislation, the only instance of the Federal government's taking direct action to that end, although there are many examples of legislation friendly to immigration.

President Lincoln recommended the enactment of a law encouraging immigration, calling the attention of Congress to the deficiency of laborers in every field of industry, especially in agriculture and in the mines, and to the tens of thousands of persons destitute of remunerative occupation thronging our foreign consulates and offering to emigrate if cheap and essential assistance were offered. The Senate committee on agriculture in 1864 reported favorably on the proposal to establish a bureau of immigration. "The advantages which have accrued heretofore from immigration can scarcely be computed," read the report. "Such is the labor performed by the thrifty immigrant that he cannot enrich himself without contributing his full quota to the increase of the intrinsic greatness of the United States. This is equally true whether he work at mining, farming, or as a day laborer

[1] *House Reports*, 38th Cong., 1st Sess., No. 56.

on one of our railroads." The demand for labor was never greater than at the present, the report continued, and the fields of usefulness were never so varied and promising. The South, having torn down the fabric of its labor system by its own hands, will, when the war shall have ceased, present a wide field for voluntary white labor, and it must look to immigration for its supply.[1] The committee was opposed to offering bounties to encourage immigration. Bounties would influence only the idle, the very poor, and the vicious, it was said, but they would have to be paid to all, thus entailing an expenditure beyond the means of the government. Furthermore, foreign governments would object to the drawing off of their population by a bounty system. According to the committee the only aid the government could render would be to disseminate in Europe information about the United States, to protect immigrants against the imposition of runners, and to facilitate their transportation from New York to their destination.

In the House the President's recommendation was referred to a special committee, which reported a bill that received the President's signature on July 4, 1864.[2]

The law provided for the appointment by the president of a commissioner of immigration to be under the Department of State. All contracts that should be made by immigrants to the United States, in conformity with regulations that might be established by the commissioner, whereby immi-

---

[1] Senate Reports, 38th Cong., 1st Sess., No. 15.

[2] House Reports, 38th Cong., 1st Sess., No. 56. The Republican national convention in June, 1864, adopted a resolution stating that "foreign immigration, which in the past has added so much to the wealth, development of resources, and increase of power to the Nation—the asylum of the oppressed of all nations—should be fostered and encouraged by a liberal and just policy" (Senate Documents, 61st Cong., 3d Sess., No. 1, p. 21).

grants pledged the wages of their labor for a term not exceeding twelve months to repay expenses of immigration, should be valid in law. No immigrant could be compulsorily enrolled for military service unless he should voluntarily renounce allegiance to the country of his birth and declare his intention of becoming a citizen of the United States. An immigration office was to be established in New York in charge of the superintendent of immigration, who should arrange for transportation of immigrants to their destination and protect them from fraud. The bill carried an appropriation of $25,000.[1] The law remained in force until March, 1868, when it was repealed by a clause in the consular and diplomatic act, but the party in power reiterated its views on the desirability of encouraging immigration.

Undoubtedly this bill had considerable pressure from employers of labor back of it. Immediately after its enactment the American Emigrant Company was organized. This was a corporation which imported laborers upon orders from employers, who advanced the expenses of the immigrants and paid a commission to the company. It is said that several thousand immigrants were imported under contracts submitted to immigrants by the swarms of immigration agents in Europe.[2] The need for recruits for the army was also a contributory cause. Foreign soldiers honorably discharged from service were given full rights of citizenship without having taken out first papers. In proximity to Castle Garden two large recruiting tents, with flaming banners offering high bounties for recruits, were set up. Recruiting agents spoke the language of the immigrants and knew how to appeal to

[1] *Senate Documents*, 61st Cong., 3d Sess., No. 21, pp. 19–21.
[2] Emerson D. Fite, *Social and Industrial Conditions in the North during the Civil War*, pp. 189 ff.

them, many of whom were hard pressed for money and responded readily. After the enactment of the draft, or enrollment, law in 1863, a number of immigrants hired out as substitutes for those who were liable for service but found it inconvenient to serve.

Another incident of the Civil War affecting the foreign-born was that of the draft riots in New York City in July, 1863. The disorder was especially severe in the ninth congressional district, constituting the eastern end of the city, where the population was largely Irish, engaged in unskilled labor and living in tenements. Most of them were Democrats, under the influence of Democratic campaign literature and speeches which denounced the Lincoln administration for perpetrating an unnecessary war and sponsoring an unconstitutional draft law. The substitute clause in the law aroused considerable opposition among immigrants, as well as among the laboring classes generally. It was regarded as a scheme to permit the rich to escape military service. The Copperheads and the Peace Democrats held it up as a classic example of the despotic nature of the Republican administration. The fears of the ignorant were also played upon by the circulation of a rumor that it was the determination of the Republicans, when they had put down the Southern slaveholders, to turn around and put down the Roman Catholic religion.[1] Ever since the organization of the Republican party the Democrats had told the immigrants that the Republican "abolitionists" were in a dark conspiracy to elevate the negro at the expense of the foreign-born. The migration of negroes to the North during the Civil War and the fact that they had been used as strike-breakers on railways and docks lent color to the

[1] *Brownson's Quarterly Review*, Vol. XX, pp. 367 ff., 385 ff. (July and October, 1863). The editor of this periodical was a convert to Catholicism.

charge, and the draft riots took the form of an attack upon the negroes as well as upon the government officials whose duty it was to enforce the law. After a really serious situation had developed, the rioters dispersed partly by the coercion of Federal troops and partly on the advice of the Catholic clergy. There were other disturbances, in Pennsylvania, New Jersey, and Wisconsin, mainly among foreigners. The most effective opposition to the prosecution of the war in the North, however, did not come from immigrants but from native-born citizens of Southern birth and extraction.[1]

The repeal of the act of 1864 was the natural result of the close of the war and in no way indicated opposition to immigration. The Homestead Act, the activities of the states, steamship companies, railway and land agencies, letters of immigrants, and the boasting of returned immigrants were encouragement enough. The Republican platform of 1868 favored the encouragement of immigration, and in the same year the committee on foreign affairs in the House of Representatives reported favorably on the passage of a bill for that purpose.[2] "We want people to fill up these States and Territories," said the report; "we want land cultivated, that wealth and plenty may abound; we want the resources of these agricultural states developed. We desire by the legislation which we propose in relation to emigration, to let the toiling and almost starving millions of foreign lands know, that in America there are free homes, where every citizen, be he native or naturalized, is guaranteed protection in his right to life, liberty, and property, according to the principle of the Declaration of Independence. And while it is specially neces-sary, in view of the public burdens now resting upon the

---

[1] For a sober account of the draft riots, see Rhodes, *History of the United States*, Vol. V, pp. 320 ff.   [2] *House Reports*, 40th Cong., 2d Sess., No. 76.

people, that as a nation we should encourage every honorable means which may tend to give relief, it is also an apt and desirable movement to adopt national measures for the encouragement of immigration, in view of the revolution in the sentiments of the people of all nations upon all the great questions of human rights. . . . In harmony, then, with the spirit of the age, having in view the growth, prosperity, greatness, and power of our land, as also the general good of mankind, let us throw open wide the doors of this republic, and invite the earnest and honest people of all nations to come."

The proposed bill, which was not passed, imposed the duty of disseminating information about the United States upon our consuls in foreign countries, especially in the North German Confederacy, Austria, Sweden, and Norway, but only with the authority of those governments. Any state or territory was allowed, through the Secretary of State, to furnish consuls with information, books, pamphlets, documents, etc.

In October, 1870, a convention called by the governors of several states met at Indianapolis to consider means by which immigration to the United States could best be promoted, and memorialized Congress in favor of the establishment by the Federal government of a national bureau of immigration, to be charged with power to protect immigrants en route to the United States and after their arrival.[1]

There is abundant evidence that in these years immigration was ardently desired. In 1871 the Federal government published a "Special Report on Immigration," by Edward Young, chief of the bureau of statistics. This document of two hundred and thirty-one pages contained information for immigrants relative to prices and rentals of land, staple products,

[1] *Senate Miscellaneous Documents*, 42d Cong., 1st Sess., No. 3.

facilities for market, and kinds of labor in demand in Western and Southern states. There were tables showing the average weekly wages paid in several states and sections, the cost of provisions and dry goods, and house rents in manufacturing districts in 1869–1870. Several thousand copies of this report were distributed in Europe. Eight or ten thousand additional copies were purchased and distributed by corporations and private firms. Consuls reported that the document had great influence, emanating as it did from the national government, in which the immigrants placed more confidence than in the state governments.[1]

With the rapidly mounting numbers of immigrants in the seventies it was becoming apparent that the government was failing to discharge its obligations. The earliest phase of Federal immigration regulation was a series of acts directing collectors of customs to receive from all shipmasters a manifest, or list, giving the age, sex, occupation, former residence, and destination of all passengers.[2] But what regulation there was, was largely in the hands of the states concerned. New York levied a head tax and required a manifest from the shipmaster. It had also created a board of commissioners empowered to administer all immigration affairs. Massachusetts had similar legislation. The Federal Supreme Court, by a five-to-four decision in 1849, declared certain state laws unconstitutional on the ground that they violated the right of Congress to regulate commerce; that it was illegal to tax United States commerce for state funds; that a treaty between the United States and Great Britain was infringed; and that since Congress had admitted immigrants free and had intentionally done so, it was presumptuous for the states

[1] *House Executive Documents*, 42d Cong., 1st Sess., No. 1; ibid. 43d Cong., 1st Sess., No. 287. [2] March 2, 1819.

to tax them. A similar decision was rendered in 1875 with reference to certain other state laws. The court recommended Federal legislation.

These decisions left the states without means of inspecting and caring for destitute immigrants. The legislature of New York memorialized Congress, asking for Federal legislation necessary for the protection of immigrants as well as for the security of cities, towns, and counties of the state.[1] There is evidence that convicts were pardoned in foreign countries on condition that they would emigrate to the United States. This matter was taken up with certain European governments, and in 1866 Congress passed a joint resolution protesting against such acts "as unfriendly and inconsistent with the comity of nations."[2]

It is passing strange that the Federal government should have been so tardy in enacting suitable immigration legislation; but even were there no documentary evidence it is not difficult to visualize the tremendous influences pulling in the opposite direction: steamship companies, employers of labor, and all varieties of persons fattening off the gullible immigrants.

The first general Federal immigration law bears the date August 3, 1882. To defray the expenses of regulating immigration and for the care of immigrants it levied a head tax of fifty cents on any passenger not a citizen of the United States coming by steam or sailing vessel from a foreign port to the United States. Foreign convicts (except those convicted for political offenses), lunatics, idiots, and persons likely to become public charges were excluded. This measure was a

[1] *Senate Miscellaneous Documents*, 44th Cong., 1st Sess., No. 96.
[2] *House Executive Documents*, 43d Cong., 1st Sess., No. 253; *Senate Documents*, 61st Cong., 3d Sess., No. 21, p. 22.

compromise with state regulation, in that state boards, contracted for by the Secretary of the Treasury, inspected and protected immigrants and were financed by the head tax. The undesirables were rejected by the state boards and sent back at the shipowners' expense.

The law was a very conservative step in the direction of regulation, and it failed to keep out many who were classed as undesirables. Labor organizations were becoming stronger and more numerous in the seventies and eighties, and their energies were enlisted to prevent the importation of contract labor. Partly in response to this pressure a law of 1885 made it unlawful to prepay the transportation or in any wise assist or encourage the importation of aliens under a contract to perform labor or service of any kind, except skilled workmen in a new industry when they could not be otherwise obtained. The law was defective. Machinery for its enforcement was not set up; it failed to provide for inspection and deportation. It was difficult to prove in court that the law had been violated. Companies sent agents to Europe to advertise and circulate literature, but they were usually careful not to enter into contracts. Steamship companies took out insurance on individuals barred by the law, and the insurance companies considered them good risks, because they could make enough profit on those who got through to pay the fines for those who were caught in the legal meshes. It is said that certain ships contained as many as 25 per cent who were ineligible for admission. The act was amended in 1887 by empowering the Secretary of the Treasury to deport contract laborers. The following year he was given power to return within the year an immigrant landing contrary to law, at the expense of the person previously contracting for his services if he came from adjoining territory; if otherwise, at the expense of the owner of the vessel. There was little cordial coöperation between the Federal inspectors and the state boards; so actually the inspecting was done by Federal officials, although in theory there was double inspection.

In 1888 a select committee of the House of Representatives conducted an investigation the results of which were published under the name of the "Ford Committee Report."[1] The committee held hearings in New York, Boston, Pittsburgh, and Detroit. At Pittsburgh the investigation revealed the fact that over five hundred immigrant paupers and insane had arrived at that city within a period of six months, many of the paupers, according to the report, wearing clothes that bore the branded name of the workhouse of which they had been inmates in Ireland. It was also learned that many undesirables landed at Quebec and entered the United States across the Canadian border. The committee came to the conclusion that the time had come to draw the line, to select the good from the bad, to sift the wheat from the chaff. It pointed to the fact that many anarchists, who were persecuted in Germany and England, were coming to our shores. An investigation by a Senate committee conducted at the same time found similar conditions. Evidence was collected which purported to show the evil influence of cheap foreign labor on American workingmen and that the so-called new immigrants were undesirable material for American citizenship.[2]

The act of March 3, 1891, which followed these investigations, added to the list of excluded persons, so that at this stage the following were inadmissible: idiots, insane, paupers, and persons likely to become public charges, persons suffering from dangerous, contagious, or loathsome diseases, persons

[1] *House Reports*, 50th Cong., 2d Sess., No. 3792.
[2] *Senate Reports*, 51st Cong., 1st Sess., No. 1095.

who had been convicted of felony or other infamous crimes, polygamists, and persons whose passage was paid by others. Persons whose passage was paid for by a friend or a relative in the United States or who had been convicted of political offenses were not included. The contract-labor law was strengthened by making it unlawful to publish advertisements encouraging immigration by promises of employment.

It is worthy of notice that these acts were passed at a time when the country was prosperous; but it was also a time of labor and agricultural unrest, when discontent manifested itself through the Farmers' Alliance and the Populist party. General Weaver, the Populist candidate for the presidency in 1892, is reported to have said that he counted his listeners by the acres instead of by the thousands. It is not without significance that in the two decades prior to 1890 the free lands had been so rapidly exhausted that the Federal census for that year reported the disappearance of the frontier.[1]   In the presidential campaign of 1892 the three leading parties— Republican, Democratic, and Populist—adopted planks favoring further restriction of immigration.

The late eighties and early nineties witnessed the reappearance of Know-Nothingism in the form of the American Protective Association, popularly known as the A.P.A., directed mainly against the Roman Catholic Church. The large numerical increase of Catholics through the immigration from the countries of southern and eastern Europe, and the consequent increased political power of Catholicism, awakened feelings akin to those which the coming of Irish and German Catholics aroused before the Civil War. The A.P.A.'s made large claims about their numbers and influence. They took to themselves the credit for overturning the political machinery

[1] F. J. Turner, *The Frontier in American History*, chap. i.

in a number of states and the election of more than a hundred members of Congress pledged to support their platform.[1] Be that as it may, it is a fact that they received much publicity, and through their "orators" stirred up considerable ill-feeling between Protestants and Catholics. Their organization, however, is important historically not because of what it accomplished or attempted to accomplish but because, like the latter-day Ku Klux Klan, it is a symptom of hostility to certain elements in our population.[2]

It appears that waves of anti-Catholicism sweep over the country periodically. The impulse usually comes from some rather spectacular event, such as the alleged defeat of Mr. Blaine for the presidency in 1884 through Catholic hostility, the Ferrer incident in Spain in 1909, the Roosevelt incident in Rome in 1910, and the activity of the Knights of Columbus during and since the World War. Papers like the *Menace*, the *Rail Splitter*, and the *American Standard*, which appeal to religious prejudice, can usually count on a large circulation, at least for a season. Indiscreet utterances by Catholic leaders sometimes furnish fuel for the fire. In mat-

[1] *Senate Documents*, 61st Cong., 3d Sess., No. 21, pp. 45, 46.

[2] The periodical literature on A. P. A.-ism is voluminous and, of course, highly controversial. The following references will furnish a fair idea of the principles and program of the organization and what its opponents thought of them: Traynor, "The Aims and Methods of the A.P.A.," in *North American Review*, Vol. CLXXXIX, pp. 67–76; Traynor, "The Menace of Romanism," ibid. Vol. CLXI, pp. 129–140; Traynor, "The Policy and Power of the A.P.A.," ibid. Vol. CLXXII, pp. 858–866; McCreary, "The Roman Catholic Church as a Factor in Politics," in *American Journal of Politics*, Vol. IV, pp. 119–131; Robinson, "The threatened Revival of Know-Nothingism," ibid. Vol. V, pp. 504–525; Jenkins, "The A.P.A. Conspirators," in *Catholic World*, Vol. LVII, pp. 685–693; Young, "The Coming Contest—with a Retrospect," ibid. Vol. LVIII, pp. 457–472; Young, "The Coming Contest—Have Catholics a Protestant Enemy?" ibid. Vol. LVIII, pp. 694–708; Lathrop, "Catholic Loyalty. A Reply to the President of the A.P.A. and to Bishop Doane," in *North American Review*, Vol. CLIX, pp. 218–224.

ters of this kind it is difficult to get at the facts. Certain it is that religion has played a rôle, and sometimes an important one, in American politics, although we have escaped religious *blocs* in the European sense in our legislative bodies. Charges have been made on the floor of Congress that anti-Catholicism is back of the agitation to restrict immigration in the last thirty years.

The creed adopted by the supreme council of the A.P.A. at Des Moines, Iowa, in 1894 contained the following:[1]

Prohibition of the importation of pauper labor and the restriction of all immigration to persons who can show their honest intention of becoming self-supporting citizens. Change in the naturalization laws by repealing the act authorizing the naturalization of minors without previous declaration of intention. Prerequisites for citizenship and suffrage to include the ability to speak the language of the land and a continuous residence of seven years after declaration. A protest against the lax enforcement of naturalization laws. Exclusion of teachers in the public schools who are subjects of an "un-American ecclesiastical institution." Opposition to state aid to parochial schools. Rather sharp criticism was directed against the Catholic Church.

The organization of the Immigration Restriction League in 1894 is another indication that sentiment in favor of cutting down the number of immigrants was increasing. This organization sent letters to the governors of states inquiring whether or not immigrants were desired in their respective states, and if so, what races were preferred. Replies were received from twenty-six states. Eight desired no more immigrants. Germans and Scandinavians were in the greatest demand, fourteen states expressing a desire for the former

[1] *Chicago Tribune*, May 6, 1894.

and twelve for the latter. In general the old immigrants were preferred.[1] It should be remembered that this inquiry was conducted during the years of a severe agricultural and industrial depression following the panic of 1893. Farmers were burning corn for fuel, prices of wheat and oats were insufficient to pay the cost of cultivation, and factories were idle. William J. Bryan, the Democratic candidate for the presidency in 1896, voicing the discontent of the farmer and laboring man, attracted hosts of followers and for a time appeared to have excellent prospects for election.

At the annual meeting of the Farmers' National Congress of America at Parkersburg, West Virginia, in November, 1894, delegates representing thirty-six states, appointed by the governors, were present. It was the sentiment of the convention that the immigration of the past years had trespassed upon the interests of American laborers and that the immigration laws were either inadequate or inefficiently enforced. Congress was memorialized to take suitable action.[2]

At this time three methods of restriction were under consideration by Congress: a capitation tax, consular inspection, and a literacy test. The Senate committee on immigration reported that the head tax was a severe and thorough but somewhat undiscriminating method for which the country was not yet ready. It was also of the opinion that consular inspection was impracticable.[3] A commission appointed in October, 1892, to investigate the expediency of consular inspection urged the following objections: (1) It would cause international complications. (2) It would impose duties upon consuls not recognized by international law. (3) It would

[1] *Senate Reports*, 54th Cong., 1st Sess., No. 290.
[2] *Senate Miscellaneous Documents*, 53d Cong., 2d Sess., No. 35.
[3] *Senate Reports*, 54th Cong., 1st Sess., No. 290.

provide a dual administration of immigration laws by the State and Treasury departments, immigration officials being under the jurisdiction of the latter department and the consular service under the former. (4) It would bring to our shores a lower class of immigrants and prove a hindrance to able-bodied men. (5) American consuls were too few in number to carry the increased duties. (6) Immigrants would have to travel many miles to the residence of the nearest consul, and the consul would have to rely upon their statements or write to the municipal authorities, who might misrepresent the facts in order to get rid of them.[1] The Senate committee was in favor of excluding those who could not read and write, because it would exclude a large portion of the present immigration; that is, people from southern and eastern Europe.

The Senate passed a literacy-test bill on December 17, 1896, by a vote of 52 to 10. The negative votes were all Democratic. The Republican vote in favor was so large that the bill would have passed even if all the Democrats had voted in the negative. The three Populist senators voted with the Republican majority. In the House of Representatives the Republican majority was overwhelming, and the bill passed by a vote of 217 to 36, three fourths of the negative votes being Democratic.

It is interesting to note that since 1897 four bills embodying provisions for a literacy test have passed Congress by large majorities only to encounter presidential vetoes. A Democrat, Grover Cleveland, vetoed the bill of 1897; a Republican, William H. Taft, refused to approve a bill in 1913; and a Democrat, Woodrow Wilson, vetoed bills in 1915 and 1917, the latter becoming a law over the veto. In each case the

[1] *Senate Miscellaneous Documents*, 53d Cong., 2d Sess., No. 253.

veto message urged strong and well-considered objections which undoubtedly represented the author's honest and matured convictions without reference to political expediency. A superficial explanation of this bit of political history may be ventured. Individual congressmen, yielding to pressure from local interests or provincial in their outlook, have voted for these measures, whereas the presidents, with a wider horizon and a deeper insight into the principles and consequences involved, have registered disapproval.

President Cleveland, repudiated by his own party and about to retire from political activity, submitted his veto message the day before he relinquished his presidential duties to William McKinley, March 3, 1897. The bill marks a radical departure from our national policy, said the message. Heretofore we have welcomed all who came here, except those whose moral and physical condition or history threatened danger to our national welfare and safety. A century's stupendous growth, largely due to the assimilation and thrift of millions of sturdy and patriotic adopted citizens, attests the success of this generous and free-handed policy. The restriction is not made on grounds that an excess of population crowds our land, it continued. Referring to the contention that the quality of recent immigration was undesirable, the President asserted that the time was within recent memory when the same thing was said of immigrants who with their descendants are numbered among our best citizens. The congestion of population in our cities was neither general nor permanent and did not demand a reversal of our policy. The prevailing widespread unemployment was attributed to other causes and would pass away with the advent of settled and wholesome financial policies. He did not believe that the literacy test would keep out the diseased, the immoral, and the agitators, because violence and disorder as a rule do not originate with illiterate laborers.[1]

The House passed the bill over the veto, but in the Senate a two-thirds majority could not be mustered, Democrats and Populists swinging over to sustain the chief executive.

No general immigration legislation was enacted until 1903, although rather important changes in the administration of the laws were made. In 1898 Congress created an Industrial Commission with power to investigate questions pertaining to immigration and to suggest legislation. The report of the commission was published in 1901 and contains a wealth of material for the investigator.[2] The recommendations of the commission were embodied in a bill introduced into the House of Representatives, the object being to codify existing legislation and to strengthen it in spots. By a heavy majority the House added a literacy test excluding all persons over fifteen years of age unable to read English or some other language, excepting wives, children under eighteen, and grandparents of admissible immigrants. The Senate eliminated the literacy test and added provisions raising the head tax from $1 to $2 and making it unlawful to assist in the unlawful entry or naturalization of anarchists. The bill was approved by President Roosevelt on March 3, 1903. During his term of office Mr. Roosevelt constantly recommended restrictive legislation. Perhaps no president has been more sympathetic with the immigrants and more popular with them. He was especially popular with the Germans and Scandinavians. No doubt the assassination of President McKinley by a Polish anarchist in 1901 was partly responsible for the provision regarding anarchists.

[1] *Senate Documents*, 54th Cong., 2d Sess., No. 185.
[2] *House Documents*, 57th Cong., 1st Sess., No. 184.

On February 20, 1907, President Roosevelt approved another general immigration law. This raised the head tax to $4 and added the following to the excluded classes: imbeciles, feeble-minded, and prostitutes. It created an immigration commission composed of three senators, three representatives, and three members to be appointed by the president of the United States. The president was empowered to call at his discretion an international conference, or to send commissioners to any foreign country for the purpose of adjusting any matter relating to immigration by international agreement. The executive was also authorized to revoke the passports of aliens when it should appear that such passports were used to enter United States territory to the detriment of labor conditions—a provision pointed at the increasing immigration of Japanese. The act of 1882 was amended to regulate further steerage conditions. A division of distribution in the bureau of immigration was created to keep in touch with proper state officials and to furnish immigrants information about opportunities for employment. A much-needed improvement in the service was the requirement that steamship companies should furnish lists of departing passengers, thus enabling the government in the future to arrive at a more accurate estimate of the net gain or loss in immigration for any year.

In 1910 the law was amended by providing for the punishment and deportation of aliens who in any way profited from immoral practices, and this was followed by the so-called Mann White Slave Act, prohibiting the transportation from one state to another of persons for immoral purposes.

During the closing weeks of Taft's administration (1913) Congress passed another bill, containing a literacy test. In his veto message Mr. Taft said that the bill contained many valuable amendments to the existing immigration law, that it received strong support in Congress, and that it was recommended by an able commission after an extended investigation. But he could not approve it, because it violated a principle that ought to be upheld in dealing with immigration. There was probably no political appeal in the message; it was written after the presidential campaign, when Mr. Taft had been overwhelmingly defeated, carrying only two states, Utah and Vermont. It may be pointed out, however, that the President wrote the message with the character of the campaign conducted by his manager in mind. Taft's platform contained an immigration-restriction plank; Wilson's and Roosevelt's were silent. In appealing to the foreign-born voters Mr. Hilles, the Republican campaign manager, issued the following statement:

The Democratic candidate has not been able to explain away his "Know-Nothing" ideas concerning immigrants. Foreign-born voters really have a vital issue in the campaign. . . . The Dillingham-Burnett bill has been condemned by the German-American Alliance and other associations. Its chief provisions are still indorsed by another element. Dr. Wilson is looked to, if elected, to bring these immigration restrictions into operation with the help of a Democratic congress. . . . President Taft, if reëlected, would positively prevent any such proposed legislation from becoming effective.

Probably in response to this the editors and publishers of one hundred and twenty foreign-language newspapers issued an address advocating the reëlection of Taft. "President Taft," it said, "has shown himself to be a friend of the immigrant, while Woodrow Wilson has publicly condemned all immigrants except the Chinese."[1] The statement about Mr. Wilson probably referred to a comparison of the Chinese

[1] *Congressional Record*, 64th Cong., 1st Sess., pp. 4772, 4773.

with immigrants from southern Europe contained in his historical contributions written some time before he became prominent in politics.

As we have seen, the law of 1907 provided for an immigration commission which conducted the most exhaustive immigration investigation in our history. The results of the commission's activities are published in some forty volumes, usually known under the name of *The Dillingham Report*, after Senator Dillingham of Vermont, the chairman of the commission. Not only did the experts employed by this body conduct their investigations into many phases of American life, but they extended their researches to Europe, seeking out the conditions producing emigration, the character of emigrants, emigration legislation, and many pertinent facts. This report has undoubtedly had a large influence in determining the character of immigration legislation. In recent years, however, there has been a tendency to question those portions of the report dealing with the newer immigrants.[1]

At this point it may be useful to give a brief statement of the changes in the administration system during the period under review. In 1891 the office of superintendent of immigration under the Treasury Department was created, followed in 1894 by the establishment of the bureau of immigration, when the superintendent was designated as the commissioner-general of immigration. In 1903 the Department of Commerce and Labor was created, and the commissioner was placed under the jurisdiction of that department. In 1906

[1] The Dillingham Report is published in *Senate Documents*, 61st Cong. An excellent brief criticism of the report is an article by John P. Gavit, "Americans by Choice," in the *Survey*, Vol. XLVII, pp. 817–821. The *Survey*, Vol. XXV, pp. 517–604, is devoted to the report of the commission, giving articles by men connected with the commission, recommendations, and criticisms.

naturalization, previously under the Treasury Department, was transferred to the office of the commissioner, but in 1912 it was turned over to the bureau of naturalization. With the establishment of the Department of Labor in 1913, matters pertaining to immigration and naturalization were assigned to that department. In the act of 1917, to be considered later, no administrative changes were made.

For a half-century following the Civil War, in spite of a growing sentiment in favor of curtailing the number of European immigrants, legislation was concerned mainly with excluding certain undesirables without reference to race and with perfecting the machinery of administration. Two executive vetoes foiled the attempt of congressional majorities to depart from the traditional open-door policy. The exclusion of orientals by legislation and by international agreement, effected in this period, is reserved for discussion in separate chapters.

CHAPTER XIII

THE LITERACY TEST

The years following the inauguration of Woodrow Wilson on March 4, 1913, are crowded with events which shook the world. Europe is still reeling from the terrible blows that were struck in the fateful years from 1914 to 1919. The mind of America was unsettled. It was a time of testing. The people were divided on fundamental questions, but all were united in believing that a new epoch, for better or worse, was upon us. Legislative bodies were admonished to be watchful of America's interests.

We have reviewed immigration legislation designed to protect the country from the coming of certain classes of undesirables from Europe and the efforts that were made to cut down the rapidly increasing number of immigrants, defeated by the vetoes of Mr. Cleveland and Mr. Taft. In 1914, the year of the outbreak of the World War, the total immigration reached the highest figure it has ever attained, 1,218,480, with the exception of the year 1907, when the figure was 1,285,349. The outpouring of southern and eastern Europe had called forth innumerable magazine articles and newspaper editorials, with dire predictions for the future of America unless the tide was stemmed. The Dillingham Report furnished the text for many an article and speech in Congress echoing the sentiment voiced by the *Nation* some years before immigration had gained the volume and assumed the character of the twentieth century.

We have to make head against the great tide of barbarism which our vast frontier is ever rolling back on us, and at the same time to raise up to the American level the vast horde of immigrants which are every year deposited on our shores without any other preparation for their new life than discontent with their old one.[1]

During the Crimean War (1854–1856) many Americans were uneasy at the thought that the close of the struggle would be followed by a greatly increased volume of immigration, when so many men would be mustered out of service and find difficulty in adjusting themselves to peaceful pursuits. With the outbreak of the World War immigration declined sharply. Of course no one dreamed that the war could last four years or that it would assume such proportions and ferocity and entail such fundamental changes. But it was pretty generally felt that when the time for demobilization arrived, a great exodus would follow. So it may be said that the World War precipitated and hastened restrictive immigration legislation and ushered in a new period in immigration history.

The advocates of restriction fastened upon the literacy test as the most effective method that was likely to pass Congress. The principle had been approved by that body on two former occasions by large majorities, and there was every reason to expect that a majority could be mustered again.

The interests for and against the measure are difficult to determine with accuracy, but in a general way they can be singled out. For reasons that are fairly obvious the recent immigrants were opposed. This is indicated by the fact that the press representing them, and several congressmen from districts which had a large foreign-born element, were in opposition. Of course some congressmen may have voted in

[1] The *Nation*, January 2, 1868.

response to pressure from the employers of immigrants, rather than from a desire to oblige their foreign-born constituents. A considerable number of naturalized citizens and their descendants among the old immigrants—principally among the Irish and the Germans—were opposed. The roll call in the House shows a liberal sprinkling of Irish names, but it must be remembered that a number of these representatives were from industrial centers in the East. Cardinal Gibbons of Baltimore, the most eminent of American Catholic prelates, respected and honored by men of all creeds, threw his influence against the measure. The Scandinavians, partly because the test would exclude few if any from the lands of their fathers and partly because the number of immigrants from those nations was small, were probably friendly to the measure.[1]

The "humanitarians" took the position that literacy is no test of character, using the argument that if Abraham Lincoln's mother had been an immigrant, and if the literacy test had been in force at the time, she would have been refused admission. In reply to this it was stated that people of enterprise and ambition learn to read under almost any conditions, and that Abraham Lincoln learned to read and write under difficulties fully as great as those existing in any country of Europe at the present time; and that therefore the inability to read is *prima facie* evidence that the applicant is unfit for American citizenship.

The steamship and railway companies and the owners of factories and mines used their influence in opposing the bill. The steamship companies profited handsomely by the trans-

---

[1] See results of the referendum conducted by Congressman Schall in the tenth congressional district of Minnesota.—*Congressional Record*, 64th Cong., 1st Sess., p. 4798.

portation of immigrants, and the other corporations added to their profits by exploiting them. Evidence has been produced to show that there are instances of steel and mine employers' collecting a motley assembly of nationalities in order to prevent unity of council and action among their employees. Moreover, many are honest in believing that the immigrants furnish the "mud sills" of society, performing the coarse work without which modern society cannot function; that instead of pulling down the American workingman, the immigrant pushes him into a higher stratum of society.[1]

The Socialists, with their international outlook, opposed the erection of a national barrier. Thinking of the laboring classes, they ignore national boundaries. Their remedy for the evils which beset the worker are not to be cured by preventing his crossing international frontiers, but by the application of principles which would revolutionize industry. Meyer London of New York, the only Socialist in Congress at the time, voted in the negative on the passage of the bill.

Organized labor naturally favored the literacy test. In spite of the fact that a great variety of occupations are represented by organized labor, its attitude toward the immigration problem has usually been in favor of restriction. It is true that in the thirties and forties George Henry Evans, the labor agitator and organizer, believed free lands reserved for the actual cultivator was the salvation of labor rather than restriction; but since the Civil War restriction has usually been the watchword. Samuel Gompers, the late efficient and autocratic president of the American Federation of Labor, pointed out that the new immigrants have been crowding out

[1] Compare the speech of Senator Hammond of South Carolina, March 4, 1858, in which he eulogizes the institution of slavery on similar grounds.— *Congressional Globe*, 35th Cong., 1st Sess., Appendix, pp. 68–71.

the native Americans and the immigrants from northern Europe, and that steamship companies, bankers, dealers in food supplies, and others benefiting from immigrant trade have actually supported through their advertisements Italian daily newspapers in New York and have encouraged the continuance of the steady stream of immigrants regardless of the labor supply. The older immigrants, he explained, spoke English or a kindred language; many of them became farmers at the time the country needed settlers, and those who entered trades did not lower the American standard of living, nor did they create the social problems of the present-day "foreign" colonies.[1] The executive committee at the convention of the American Federation of Labor in 1914 declared that the cessation of the war in Europe would be followed by a flood of immigrants. Europe would do everything possible to retain the best men and to get rid of the disabled and inefficient, thus flooding America with the incapacitated and forcing Americans into competition with these "bits of wreckage." The Federation also favored the exclusion of Japanese by legislation, instead of by the "gentlemen's agreement."[2]

It is undoubtedly true that unrestricted immigration creates difficult problems for organized labor. The ebb and flow of immigrants, the increasing number of "birds of passage" in the present century, prevents their absorption into labor organizations; but it is also true that immigrants form the backbone of some strong unions. The first decade of the present century witnessed the greatest volume of immigration in our history, and the bulk of it came from southern and eastern Europe, yet the tendency was to reduce the length

[1] *Senate Documents*, 63d Cong., 1st Sess., No. 21.
[2] *Report of the Annual Convention of the American Federation of Labor*, 1914, p. 84.

of the workday. Of course this reform might have gone forward more rapidly had it not been for the heavy immigration. Nevertheless, right or wrong, organized labor was the greatest single factor in securing the passage of the literacy-test bills.

Even before the outbreak of the World War probably a majority of native-born Americans were in favor of the literacy test, and after 1914, one may safely say, the tide of public opinion was running strongly. The anti-Catholic feeling had flared up during the presidential campaign of 1912, and the appointment of Joseph P. Tumulty, a Roman Catholic, as secretary to President Wilson had brought forth the usual protests against Catholic domination in politics. Senator James A. Reed of Missouri, speaking on the bill of 1915 in the Senate, charged that anti-Catholicism was back of the measure. Patriotic organizations raised the hue and cry against the foreign-born radicals who fomented such savage movements as the strike in Lawrence, Massachusetts, in 1913–1914, which received a vast amount of publicity in the press of the country. Investigations were conducted which revealed the unsavory conditions existing among immigrant workingmen in industrial centers like Lawrence: immorality and stuffy living-quarters, a single house sometimes housing as many as twenty-five or thirty unmarried men. The measure had the powerful support of the members of the immigration commission, who had spent months in studying conditions in Europe and America. Many of the members were opposed to restriction when they began their work, but they became unanimously in favor when conditions like those at Lawrence were revealed. They urged the literacy test, because no other method could pass Congress at the time and also because, in addition to being restrictive, it was beneficially selective.[1] The measure had considerable support from the descendants of immigrants from northern and western Europe, whose attitude toward the new immigrants was almost identical with that of the descendants of the old American stock.

The South was almost a unit in support of the measure. It was remarked on the floor of Congress that the demand for restriction came from sections of the country to which immigrants were not going. Senator Reed of Missouri in 1915 presented tables in the Senate showing that on the last vote on the literacy test in that body the states possessing the smallest percentage of foreign-born were the strongest advocates of the bill, whereas many of the states having a very high percentage of foreign-born were opposed; that a majority of the states favoring the bill were in point of literacy below the children of immigrants and below the general average of the country as a whole; that the percentage of literacy among the immigrant children was higher than the general average of the country; and that the percentage of literacy among children, one or both of whose parents were immigrants, was far above the general average of the United States. The states which have the lowest percentage of immigrants, said he, are the lowest in literacy. The states that cry "Shut out the illiterate" are themselves the most illiterate.[2] Senator Williams of Mississippi, in reply to Mr. Reed, contended that his tables were misleading and his interpretation fallacious. The literacy of the children of immigrants compared with the literacy of the population of the Southern states, according to the speaker, is explained by the circum-

[1] See letter of Jeremiah W. Jenks to Representative S. D. Fess of Ohio.— *Congressional Record*, 63d Cong., 3d Sess., pp. 3069, 3070.

[2] *Congressional Record*, 63d Cong., 3d Sess., pp. 3000, 3002.

stance that the immigrants gravitate to the cities, where they find educational facilities superior to those of the rural communities. The greater wealth and the consequent larger appropriations for public schools in the states harboring the greater number of immigrants are not due to the presence of the immigrants and their interest in education. On the contrary, immigrants are attracted to those states because their industries offer them employment.

More than any other section the South has been consistently opposed to unrestricted immigration. We have seen that prior to the Civil War that section manifested alarm at the increasing immigration, principally because the immigrants were building up the free states at the political expense of the South. It is true that there were isolated settlements of foreigners, mainly Germans and Scandinavians, before the Civil War, but according to the census of 1900 the entire South, including the old border states, contained only 6 per cent of the foreign population of the United States. The states of Georgia, Alabama, Mississippi, North Carolina, and South Carolina collectively, with a total population of about 13,000,000, harbored a foreign population about equal to that of Vermont, whose population was slightly less than 350,000.[1]

General Carl Schurz, at the behest of President Andrew Johnson, made a tour of inspection of the South at the close of the Civil War. In his report he dwelt at some length on immigration, which he thought would contribute much to the solution of the labor problem of the South. For fifty years the South has had no sympathetic communion with the progressive ideas of the times, he wrote. Like some Asiatic

[1] W. L. Fleming, "Immigration to the Southern States," in *Political Science Quarterly*, Vol. XX, pp. 276–297.

nations, the South was self-satisfied and intolerant of criticism, believing that its civilization was the highest that could be attained. Immigration would develop the South economically because capital would follow. Only the people of the North have capital; but there is so much hostility in the South toward the Yankees that the only solution is for the Federal government to retain control, to give them protection until the Northerners and foreigners are strong enough to protect themselves.[1]

Competent students assert that it took the South at least fifty years to recover from the Civil War. Be that as it may, after 1900 we begin to read about the "new South" which was entering upon an era of industrial and commercial development. Even before the dawn of the present century efforts were made to attract immigrants. Immigration conferences were held, certain states established immigration bureaus and various organizations and individuals published literature advertising the opportunities in Southern states. But with the expansion of industries and the extension of railways the movement assumed a more intensive character. The railways were the most potent factor. On the first and third Tuesdays of each month special home-seekers' rates were offered to enable prospective settlers to visit the South and Southwest. The companies published magazines and employed hundreds of agents. The Italian ambassador to the United States made a tour of the South and Southwest at the expense of the railroads. Provided with the very best accommodations and received royally wherever he stopped, he publicly declared himself most enthusiastic over the opportunities awaiting his countrymen. The steam-

[1] Carl Schurz, *Speeches, Correspondence and Political Papers*, Vol. I, pp. 361–365.

ship companies, ever alert to the possibilities for increased business, coöperated. Many people in the South were becoming increasingly impatient with the negroes, who were leaving the plantations in favor of the cities and manifesting an independence unknown in former years.[1]

This propaganda brought results, but there are several reasons why immigrants prefer to remain in the North. The tradition that the South is hostile to immigrants lingers. Before the Civil War and during the days of reconstruction prospective immigrants were warned against going to the Southern states through letters from immigrants in the North and through foreign-language newspapers. Most unfavorable reports were spread about the climate and general conditions in the South. Northern newspapers and other interests, fearing the competition of Southern factories, have also done their part. The lynching of Italians in New Orleans some thirty years ago was played up in the Italian papers in the United States. There is the tradition also that the laws of the Southern states are very backward in granting protection to the workingman and that child labor in the worst form persists. It may well be questioned if the persons interested in the encouragement of immigration to the South represented any considerable element in the population. It is true that the labor problem has become increasingly serious and that there has been an alarming migration of negroes to the cities and to the North, but the average Southerner was not at all enthusiastic about making additions to the illiterate population. The South got into the game too late to get a share of the immigrants from northern and western Europe, so that from their point of view the character of the immi-

[1] Robert Decourcy Ward, "Immigration to the South," in *Atlantic Monthly*, Vol. XCVI, pp. 611–617.

grants was undesirable. Before the Civil War the South boasted of its pure American population and congratulated itself on the fact that it harbored none of the "rabble" of the Northern cities. Its ballot boxes were not stuffed by the votes of ignorant and radical foreigners. This attitude persists down to the present. In more than one Southern state during the present century political contests have turned on the anti-Catholic issue. Candidates for the offices of governor and United States senator have ridden into office on the tide of religious prejudice. An examination of the votes on the literacy-test bills shows that Southern senators and representatives have registered this hostility to unrestricted immigration.

The literacy-test bill of 1915 passed both Houses of Congress by huge majorities, only seven senators voting in the negative, of whom five were Democrats. It was a time of national excitement; racial feeling was boiling furiously. Newspaper editorials abounded in denunciations of "hyphenated Americans," who were accused of putting loyalty to the land of their birth above loyalty to the land of their adoption. Much was said about the hordes who would descend upon our shores at the close of the war. It must be remembered, however, that a similar bill had passed two years earlier, before the outbreak of war. So it appears that the war was only a contributory cause.

President Wilson's veto message was dated January 28, 1915. The president's objections to the literacy test and, indeed, to the principle of restriction are stated so clearly and forcefully that rather lengthy quotations are justified. The practical idealist is speaking.

In two particulars of vital consequence this bill embodies a radical departure from the traditional and long-established policy of this country, a policy in which our people have conceived the very character of their Government to be expressed, the very mission and spirit of the Nation in respect of its relations to the peoples of the world outside their borders. It seeks to all but close entirely the gates of asylum which have always been open to those who could find nowhere else the right and opportunity of constitutional agitation for what they conceived to be the natural and inalienable rights of men ; and it excludes those to whom the opportunities of elementary education have been denied, without regard to their character, their purposes, or their natural capacity.

Restrictions like these, adopted earlier in our history as a Nation, would very materially have altered the course and cooled the humane ardors of our politics. The right of political asylum has brought to this country many a man of noble character and elevated purpose who was marked as an outlaw in his own less fortunate land, and who has yet become an ornament to our citizenship and to our public councils. The children and compatriots of these illustrious Americans must stand amazed to see the representatives of their Nation now resolved, in the fullness of our national strength and at the maturity of our great institutions, to risk turning such men back from our shores without test of quality or purpose. . . .

The literacy test and the tests and restrictions which accompany it constitute an even more radical change in the policy of the Nation. Hitherto we have generously kept our doors open to all who were not unfitted by reason of disease or incapacity for self-support or such personal records and antecedents as were likely to make them a menace to our peace and order or to the wholesome and essential relationships of life. In this bill it is proposed to turn away from tests of character and of quality and impose tests which exclude and restrict ; for the new tests here embodied are not tests of quality or of character or of personal fitness, but tests of opportunity. Those who come seeking opportunity are not to be admitted unless they have already had one of the chief of the opportunities they seek, the opportunity of education. The object of such provision is restriction, not selection.

Both Mr. Taft and Mr. Wilson expressed regret that they were unable to approve the immigration bills because of opposition to the literacy-test provisions; they were generous in praising the other sections of the proposed measures and recognized the desirability of increasing the efficiency and improving the methods of handling this important branch of the public service. Congress insisted, however, on retaining the literacy provision in a general bill, and on May 1, 1917, a new law became effective over President Wilson's veto. This departure in our immigration policy was decided upon a few days before the close of President Wilson's first term and a few weeks before Congress, by large majorities, declared war on the Imperial German government. Southern members of both Houses were almost a unit in favor of the bill, and some even urged the exclusion of negro immigrants. In the House the vote to recommit the bill with instructions to strike out the literacy test shows that most of those who voted in the affirmative were representatives from the centers of population or men with Irish names.

The act of 1917 increased the head tax to $8, children under sixteen accompanying father or mother being exempt. The following classes of aliens were excluded: idiots, imbeciles, the feeble-minded, the insane, inebriates, paupers, beggars, persons afflicted with tuberculosis or dangerous contagious or loathsome diseases, persons likely to become public charges, criminals, polygamists, anarchists, people who believe in the violent overthrow of government, members of organizations opposed to organized government, prostitutes, contract laborers, assisted immigrants, Asiatics (not including Japanese), and persons over sixteen years of age "physically capable of reading, who cannot read the English language, or some other language or dialect, including Hebrew or Yiddish." The test did not apply to the father or grandfather over fifty-five years of age or a wife, mother, grandmother or unmarried or widowed daughter of any admissible alien, whether such relative could read or not. Neither did it apply to persons fleeing from religious or political persecution, skilled laborers, actors, professional men, and others. The method of applying the test is simple. Having designated the particular language in which he desires to be examined, the alien is required to read not less than thirty nor more than forty words in ordinary use printed on uniform slips.

In the light of subsequent legislation it would appear that the enactment of the literacy-test law of 1917 heralded a new period in the history of immigration. Although one of the merits claimed for the measure was that it was beneficially selective, it is obvious that in purpose it was restrictive. It proved to be the entering wedge for drastic restriction, followed as it was by legislation more extreme than was ever dreamed of when the test was first proposed. The convulsions of Europe and the readjustments and threatened readjustments in America in the post-war days magnified a hundredfold the fears that made the literacy test a legislative reality.

CHAPTER XIV

THE PERCENTAGE PLAN

When the armistice was signed on November 11, 1918, hundreds of thousands of American citizens, men and women, had left their peace-time pursuits and were "doing their bit" to bring the war against the Central Powers to a successful termination. There was a tremendous labor shortage, "nonessential industries" had greatly curtailed their output, and wages were excessively high in certain branches of industry. Immigration had practically ceased. In fact, thousands of the citizens of the allied nations had left the country to fight under the flags of their native lands. In order to alleviate the food shortage in Europe the American people set aside "meatless" and "wheatless" days. Farmers were urged to make every inch of land productive.

It was but natural that these conditions should have been seized upon by interested parties to urge the necessity of increased immigration and the repeal of the literacy test. The president of the Interracial Conference,—a meeting sponsored by various interests opposed to drastic immigration restriction,—which met in New York in April, 1920, stated that America was short four million workers, and that approximately five times as many unskilled male immigrant workers left the United States between November, 1918, and October, 1919, as came during this period. The conference endeavored to learn why America no longer attracted the Greeks, Italians, and Syrians as of old. It was suggested that the immigrants were leaving because of prohibition, because they wished to learn about the fortunes of their relatives during the war, because they wished to see the havoc wrought by the conflict, and in order to convert their American money into the currency of their native lands, which would become a small fortune by the favorable rates of exchange. It was alleged that some corporations were considering the possibility of erecting plants in foreign countries, where labor which had been in the habit of coming to America could be secured. The literacy test was pronounced a failure in keeping out undesirables. Some of the most powerful newspapers agitated the repeal of that provision of the law. Instead of cutting down the number of immigrants the conference urged that the country should welcome and utilize this valuable gift by facilitating distribution, assisting immigrants to secure employment, informing them about the principles of the American government, and protecting them against exploitation.[1]

The sentiments expressed at this conference represented but a small part of the people. The tide of public opinion was running strongly in the opposite direction. Perhaps the country had never before experienced such intense hostility to immigration. The country was hysterical. With the rapidly ebbing war prosperity and the demobilization of the military forces in America and Europe, thousands were seeking in vain for employment. "Something more like a panic than enthusiasm is manifested by our growing army of idle workers, which already numbers two million, according to the American Federation of Labor, over the promise of vast reënforcements from the war-broken countries of Europe," was the assertion of one of the widely read weekly publications in December, 1920.

[1] *Literary Digest*, April 24, 1920, pp. 12, 13.

Through its leaders it entreats Congress to put a two-year ban on all immigration, and insists that "no other question is of such vital importance to the workers" as is that of protection from "the menace of excess of immigration.". . . Nor is labor, we gather from the news and editorial columns of the daily press, the only element of the community that sees cause for alarm in recent official announcements that "at this minute all records (of immigration) are being broken" and that behind the men and women now crowding through our gates at the rate of 125,000 a month are countless others—estimates range from 15,000,000 to 25,000,000— either clamoring for immediate passage or planning to leave their native lands at the earliest opportunity. . . . In addition to citing our already existing unemployment problem as a reason for checking the inrush of foreigners, many editorial observers warn us that a considerable number of the newcomers are revolutionary radicals who add to the ominous forces of social unrest; that the United States has reached a "point of saturation" where it cannot properly assimilate the foreign elements already here; and that failure to recognize this fact may result in the loss of the "American type."[1]

American visitors to Europe, including the commissioner-general of immigration, who studied the problem at its source, predicted a deluge of immigration. As in the days of Know-Nothingism, much was made of the pauperism and criminality among the foreign-born; but the alleged fact that the ranks of the radicals were largely recruited from the immigrants weighed more heavily in the turbulent post-war days. From the beginning the powerful influence of the American Legion was on the side of drastic restriction. It sounded the alarm that American institutions and ideals were in grave danger, and it urged the total prohibition of immigration for a period of five years. Other organizations shared the gloomy predictions of the Legion.

[1] *Literary Digest*, December 18, 1920, p. 7.

During the war and the months immediately following the armistice the United States was a very uncomfortable place for radicals, especially those of foreign birth. Practically every state had enacted legislation to curb their activity. Meetings were broken up by mobs as well as by government agents; radical headquarters were raided, and frequently the raids were carried out in a most brutal manner. Men and women against whom not a shred of evidence of disloyalty could be found were unceremoniously thrown into jail, treated worse than criminals in ordinary times, and branded by newspaper reporters as traitors of the deepest dye. Men and women who ventured to express the opinion that these proceedings were contrary to the spirit of American institutions and to defend the reputations of the accused were sometimes threatened with similar treatment. In the deportation raids of January, 1920, about 10,000 arrests were made and 3289 warrants were issued, of which 2709 were served. Over 900 cases were dismissed for lack of sufficient evidence.[1] Congress talked of impeaching the Assistant Secretary of Labor in the Wilson administration, Louis F. Post, because of alleged failure to exercise his power to deport alien enemies; that is, those who were liable to deportation under the act of October 16, 1918. This act covers aliens who advocate the overthrow of the government by force or violence and those who are members of, or affiliated with, any organization which

[1] Francis F. Kane, "The Communist Deportations," in the *Survey*, April 24, 1920, p. 141. In his book *The Deportations Delirium of Nineteen-twenty: A Personal Narrative of an Historic Official Experience* (Chicago, 1923) Mr. Post defends his policy. In the words of a reviewer the book is "a ringing indictment of both the American government and the American people—the former for acts of heartless oppression . . . and the latter for the indifference with which the most hideous injustices perpetrated by high officials in perfect contempt of constitutional guarantees were regarded."— *New Republic*, February 20, 1924.

entertains a belief in or advocates the use of violence. The
procedure under the law was decidedly objectionable. The
accused was brought before an inspector of the Department
of Labor, the final decision in the case resting with the Secretary of Labor. The accused was deprived of the right of a
jury trial, he was compelled to witness against himself, and
he might be tried with utter disregard of evidence. Mr. Post,
who for a time was Acting Secretary of Labor, proceeded
carefully in the cases brought before him and incurred the
ire of those who detected sympathy with radicalism. With
the subsidence of the war hysteria there is an increasing
tendency to defend the policy of Mr. Post as against the
methods of the department of justice under the attorney
general, A. Mitchell Palmer.

During the last days of 1919 the army transport *Buford*
sailed out of New York Harbor with two hundred and forty-
nine deportees, among whom Emma Goldman and Alexander
Berkman were the most conspicuous. A staid, conservative
New England paper expressed the opinion that the sailing of
the "Soviet Ark," "with its cargo of undesirables," may prove
"as epoch-making as the immortal voyage of Columbus."
Another paper asserted that "they made the unholiest cargo
that ever left our shores."[1]

The Interracial Conference, which included in its ranks
several hundred financial and industrial organizations and
representatives of nearly all the races in America, asserted
that the raids and deportations greatly unsettled the foreign-
born population. "The person of foreign birth participating
in activities which are aimed at the destruction of our government by force is arrested and held for deportation, whereas
an American who may be employed in the same shop with

[1] *Literary Digest*, January 3, 1920, p. 14.

him, who is a member of the same radical organization and a participant in the same ultra-radical activities, is not molested," read the statement. "That is the condition that is making the foreign-born believe that there is one kind of justice for them and another kind for the native residents."

Not only did the Department of Labor come in for censure because of alleged sympathy with radicalism, but even President Wilson himself was attacked. "A very long list of appointees strongly supports such a view," ventured a Boston paper.[1] Commissioner Frederic C. Howe, stationed at Ellis Island, was strongly under suspicion of failing to enforce properly the law respecting the inspection of immigrants.

These instances have been cited to show the temper of the country, inflamed as it was by sensational and highly colored newspaper stories, rather than for the purpose of expressing judgment on the administration or on the immigrants or on the country as a whole. An effort has been made to picture the background for the legislation and proposed legislation which followed in the wake of the war.

In the weeks immediately preceding the convening of Congress in December, 1920, the press of the country literally teemed with editorials, feature articles, and news stories pertaining to immigration. Frederick A. Wallis, immigration commissioner at the port of New York, in syndicated articles estimated that one million immigrants would enter during the fiscal year 1920–1921. "More than ten million are now waiting in various parts of war-stricken Europe," he said, "to swarm to the United States as soon as they can obtain transportation. . . . Congress must look to the situation at once. . . . We need the man of good intentions, but we cannot establish any sort of preferential admission without

[1] *Literary Digest*, December 13, 1919, p. 18.

first amending the constitution of the United States. . . .
There never was a greater farce than the literacy test. It
does not mean that a man will become a good productive
citizen because he can read and write a few words."[1]

During 1919 and 1920 bills were proposed to suspend
immigration from one to fifty years. The upshot of it all
was the passage in the House of Representatives in December, 1920, of a bill to suspend immigration for fourteen
months. The Senate substituted for it a bill to restrict immigration on a percentage basis. In the Dillingham Report of
1910–1911, the percentage method had been suggested as a
possible means of controlling immigration, the suggestion being to limit the immigration from a certain country to a percentage of the average immigration from that country for a
given term of years. The plan was subsequently revised so as
to limit immigration to a fixed percentage of the foreign-born
of each nationality resident in the United States according to
the census of 1910 and in a later act according to the census
of 1890.

The basic principle of this proposal was urged by the National Committee for Constructive Immigration Legislation.
The secretary of this organization, Dr. Sidney L. Gulick, a
missionary to Japan, was sincerely interested in arriving at a
solution of the immigration problem which would at the same
time promote friendly feeling between the United States and
foreign nations and satisfy public opinion in the United
States. The bill proposed by his organization contained the
following provisions: (1) The regulation of all immigration
on a percentage principle, with the application of this principle to each people or mother-tongue group separately but
impartially. (2) The annual admission of from 5 to 15 per

[1] *Minneapolis Journal*, December 5, 1920.

cent (or from 3 to 10 per cent) of those of each people already naturalized, including the American-born children of that people as recorded in the census of 1920. (3) The creation of an immigration commission to determine annually the rate within the specified limits etc. (4) The sending of examining immigration officers to ports from which immigrants largely sail, and the establishment of regulations for steamship companies which bring immigrants to America, to prevent needless hardship in the administration of the laws. (5) The raising of standards of qualifications for citizenship and the extension of the privileges of naturalization to everyone who qualifies. (6) The separation of the citizenship of a wife from that of her husband. (7) The repeal of all laws dealing specifically and differentially with the Chinese. It will be noted that the percentage was based on naturalized immigrants and American-born children, rather than on the number of immigrants according to the census. Undoubtedly the literature and propaganda of this organization popularized the percentage plan and brought it forcefully to the attention of Congress.

Senator Dillingham had introduced percentage bills before the war, and to him must be given a due measure of credit for keeping the plan before the Congress. The Senate bill which was substituted for the House bill in the 1920–1921 session was introduced by Mr. Dillingham. The Senate committee on immigration reported that no emergency existed which warranted prohibiting immigration for fourteen months, and recommended limiting the number of admissible aliens to 5 per cent of resident aliens based on the census of 1910. Mr. Dillingham frankly stated before the Senate that the bill was designed to cut down the number of immigrants from southeastern Europe. As finally passed by the Senate and agreed to by the House after the appointment of a conference committee, the bill restricted immigration on a 3-per-cent basis until June 30, 1922, being thus a temporary settlement. True to his convictions that the doors of opportunity in America ought not to be closed to citizens of other nations, President Wilson failed to sign the bill, which came to him within less than ten days before the final adjournment of Congress on March 4, 1921, and so the bill was killed by a "pocket veto." The literacy test thus remained the sole method of restricting immigration.

According to the statement from the bureau of immigration, the total number of immigrants admitted during the fiscal year ending June 30, 1921, was 805,228, as compared with 430,001 during the preceding fiscal year and an annual average of 1,034,940 for the five years between 1910 and 1914. From these figures it can be seen that immigration was on the increase while these bills were before Congress, but they do not bear out the dire predictions about a tidal wave of immigrants. The bill which failed to gain the approval of President Wilson fixed the maximum immigration between April 1, 1921, and June 30, 1922, at about 355,000.

Shortly after the inauguration of President Harding Congress met in extraordinary session on April 11, 1921. Eleven days later the House of Representatives passed a bill which closely resembled the one which died by the "pocket veto," except for certain changes which enlarged the numbers which might be admitted during the emergency period. The Senate committee rejected the House bill and substituted the bill which had been introduced by Senator Dillingham, this measure being identical with the bill passed by the previous Congress, except for the change in the date it was to become effective. Senator Heflin of Alabama in a fiery speech contended for a far more drastic restriction than was provided in the bill. He denounced the activities of certain foreign-born radicals and pointed to the difference between the former type of immigrants and "some of the miserable horde that is coming now." He feared the day would come when the alien population would outnumber the native stock unless proper legislation were enacted. "They can get us divided on any great issue," he said, "and get their forces in compact, concrete form and hold the balance of power and decide issues that will affect the conduct and life of the United States Government."[1]

Senator Colt of Rhode Island, a state containing a large proportion of foreign-born, interrupted the Alabama senator by a statement to the effect that among those who strove to avoid the draft during the war the percentage of aliens was comparatively low. He did not think that exaggerated statements should be made which the facts did not seem to warrant. In discussing the bill further Mr. Colt referred to the fact that the pending bill "is only a temporary measure providing for an emergency based upon a proposition, which, to my mind, is much exaggerated as shown by statistics, that owing to war conditions abroad there is a flood of immigrants who are seeking to come to this country. The committee tried to take a reasonable view. There were those who wanted 5 per cent or even more. There were those who were in favor of the principle of suspension. . . . Ever since we have had a record of departures, 35 aliens have departed to every 100 who have arrived. So far as the immigration from southern and eastern Europe is concerned, in the year ending June 30, 1920, 122 went home to every 100 who came in."

The Senate bill, in the form of an amendment to the

[1] *Congressional Record*, May 2, 1921.

House bill, passed on May 3. A conference committee was appointed to smooth out the differences between the two Houses, and on May 19, 1921, it was signed by President Harding, to remain in force until June 30, 1922. At the next session of Congress the law, with minor changes which in no way affected the principle of the measure, was extended to June 30, 1924.

In enacting this legislation Congress undoubtedly complied with the wishes of the majority of the people of the United States for a radical restriction of immigration. The bills passed both Houses by huge majorities, in the Senate in 1921 only one negative vote was cast on the bill. The principle of admitting persons fleeing from religious and political persecution was also abandoned, also with the approval of the public.

In making this radical departure from our traditional immigration policy Congress was but registering the post-war fear of alien influence. "Here we have the result not of sober reason nor of a well-matured and thought-out national policy but of fear psychology," writes a student of the latter-day Ku Klux Klan.[1] "The immense popularity of this drastic immigration law with the masses of Americans should throw some light for us upon the readiness with which men listen to the Klan's anti-foreign propaganda."

Organized in 1915, the Ku Klux Klan grew like a weed in 1920, 1921, and 1922. As an organization it probably had small influence over Congress. For the historian its importance lies in the fact that it is a lineal descendant of Know-Nothingism and A.P.A.-ism and striking evidence of the fact

[1] John M. Mecklin, *The Ku Klux Klan: a Study of the American Mind* (New York, 1924), p. 124. This book is an interesting study of the origin, causes, and operation of the Ku Klux Klan. Although popular and rhetorical in its treatment, it aims to be scientific and impartial.

that the latent fear of Catholicism and "foreigners" in the American mind may flare up at any time. Solon compared the people unto the sea, and orators and counselors to the winds; for that the sea would be calm and quiet, if the winds did not trouble it. One may not be a believer in unrestricted immigration and yet believe that in these stormy years the orators and counselors were organizers of the Klan, the anti-Semitic articles in the *Dearborn Independent*, and the sensational "anti-red" editorials and stories in the newspapers. These agitators breathed on the coals of anti-Catholicism and racial hatred, already blazing from the angry blast of wartime propaganda, and the nation was ablaze. Unlike the Know-Nothing movement, but like the A.P.A., the Ku Klux Klan took a strong hold in the Middle West. With Catholics, Jews, and immigrants excluded from its membership, it recruits its ranks from the descendants of the old American stock and of the Protestant "old immigration," who rule the Mississippi Valley and the South. It is also significant that those rabid and miserably edited anti-Catholic sheets, the *Menace* and the *Rail Splitter*, are published in small towns in the Middle West and have hosts of readers in the rural communities in that section.[1]

As to the practical operation of the 3-per-cent law, opinions differ. Undoubtedly some way will always be found to evade the wisest and most carefully drawn statute, and in its enforcement injustice will creep in at times. The law provided that not more than 20 per cent of a country's quota might enter the United States in any one month. Steamships

[1] The attitude of the Ku Klux Klan toward immigration is given in an address delivered on the occasion of Klan day at the state fair of Texas at Dallas, October 24, 1923, by Dr. W. H. Evans, Imperial Wizard, entitled "The Menace of Modern Immigration." The address is printed in pamphlet form.

with a cargo of Poles, for instance, raced into New York Harbor to breast the quota tape in order to land their passengers and relieve the transportation companies of the expense of carrying them back to Europe, as the law provided. In some instances immigration officials, tempering law enforcement with mercy, admitted under bond hundreds of dejected and homesick aliens detained at Ellis Island, because their country's quota had been filled, until the lapse of time made them admissible. Canada, Mexico, and the countries of South and Central America were not included in the quota provisions. Taking advantage of this loophole a number of Europeans, unable to enter the United States directly because their countries' quotas were filled, went to these countries with the hope of gaining entrance by this route after a year's sojourn. The American consulates in those countries reported that several hundred prospective immigrants applied for visas of passports, some of them laboring under the impression that it was merely necessary for them to transship to a steamer bound for an American port.

According to a report of the National Association of Manufacturers and a statement of E. H. Gary, chairman of the board of the United States Steel Corporation, the law produced a shortage of common labor, preventing the employment of many skilled workmen. To remedy this alleged shortage it was proposed to amend the law by fixing the quotas allowed the various nationalities in terms of net immigration. The Secretary of Labor, James J. Davis, was not at all impressed by "the widespread agitation against the immigration law." While admitting the desirability of certain changes in the law, he was not in favor of letting down the bars.[1] Undoubtedly the propaganda conducted by the

[1] *Minneapolis Tribune*, January 2, April 18, and September 2, 1923.

new immigrants, employers of labor, and steamship companies magnified the injustice of the law in individual cases as the most effective way of discrediting the measure before the public. It was natural that the facilities at Ellis Island should have been taxed to the utmost at certain times because of the rush of steamships to land immigrants before the exhaustion of the quota. The real test of the law is, Did it accomplish its purpose of restricting immigration effectively and wisely?[1] The answer depends largely upon the individual point of view. If the time has come to curtail immigration drastically, and Nordic superiority is conceded, the answer is affirmative. But either of these premises is debatable.

According to the report of the commissioner-general of immigration, for the period from July 1, 1921, to February 28, 1922, the quota from the countries of northern and western Europe was 197,555, of which 51,981 were admitted. Subtracting the departures, the net gain from those countries was 36,051. For the rest of the world (excluding Orientals) the quota was 154,373, with 119,606 admitted and 113,243 departures, making the net gain 6363. For the period the total net gain was 42,411. The figures show that the countries of the old immigration did not begin to fill their quotas; but by reason of the small number of departures the net gain was larger than from the countries of the new immigration, which more nearly filled their quotas.

In the interval between the enactment of the temporary 3-per-cent law and its expiration (June 30, 1924), the congressional committees on immigration were occupied with the problem of framing a permanent measure. It was evident

---

[1] An excellent criticism of the law and suggestions for improvement are found in the *Survey*, March 15, 1924, pp. 667–669: "Taking the Queue out of Quota," an interview with W. W. Husband, commissioner-general of immigration.

from the tone of the press and the resolutions adopted by thousands of organizations that there would be no relaxation of restriction. On the contrary, everything pointed to an even more extreme law. In the words of an editorial writer, "the critter's eyes were sot." The majority of the House committee on immigration was in sympathy with the extreme restrictionists, whereas the Senate committee was more liberal.

The bill reported by the House committee was the most comprehensive and drastic immigration bill ever reported. The vital point of the proposed measure was the reduction of the percentage from three to two and the change in the quota base from the census of 1910 to the census of 1890. The principal objection to the 1890 census as a quota basis came from the new immigrants, who voiced their protests through the foreign-language press and through hundreds of their organizations.[1] It also evoked representations from European governments, and especially from Italy. These objections were grounded in the fact that the great volume of immigrants from northern and western Europe came before 1890 and the great volume of immigrants from southern and eastern Europe came after that date. There were only 182,580 foreign-born from Italy in this country in 1890, as compared with 1,343,125 in 1910. The effect of the new basis on Jewish immigration may be seen in the fact that there were only 182,644 foreign-born from Russia in 1890, as compared with 1,184,412 in 1910. On the other hand, the Irish foreign-born decreased by 519,258 between 1890 and 1910 and the foreign-born from Germany decreased by 473,657.

---

[1] For documents and testimony see the hearings before the House and Senate Committees and speeches in Congress.—*Congressional Record* and *House Reports*, 68th Cong., 1st Sess., No. 350.

The Italians, Slavs, and Jews asserted, probably correctly, that this discrimination against the new immigration was rooted in the conception of Nordic superiority, always admitting when pressed that the United States government had the legal right to admit or to deny admittance to any individual or groups of individuals. It was the expediency and the justice of the proposed measure that was questioned. A pro memoria from the Italian embassy stated the objection as follows:

The Italian Government has never questioned the right of any country to dispose of its internal affairs as best suited to the national interests; it therefore would understand the Government of the United States raising or lowering the percentage of immigrants admittable in accordance to the interests of the country as long as this was done by varying the quota percentage used so far; the Johnson bill, however, is not based on such equanimous and impartial principle, but patently aims to favor the immigration of some nations to the detriment of others by changing the census year taken as the basis for the percentage quota.

The eagerness of the newer immigrant stocks to present their protests was probably greatly stimulated by their sensitiveness to the propaganda which had been circulated in behalf of the House bill. It was said that they stand low in intelligence; that their blood mingled with that of the older American stock will result in degeneration; that they are contributing greatly to the increasing insanity, criminality, and radicalism of the country. It must be admitted, however, that some of their leaders showed a surprising ignorance of American psychology. To oppose immigration restriction because it would reduce the immigrants' remittances to their native lands and would have a detrimental effect upon the economic development of those countries was only to invite hostility to all immigration. Moreover, the threat of injecting the racial issue in the coming presidential campaign, by lining up the new immigrants in opposition to candidates who favored the 1890 basis, could only antagonize representatives and senators of both parties and cause them to favor the proposition. "The partisan issue was not raised until what I term a foreign bloc raised its head and held out its votes to the Republican party and to the Democratic party alike, offering its support and votes to the party that would assist them in the defeat of the immigration bill, and threatening the defeat of the other party," said a representative from Ohio.[1] "I submit that the Democrats and the Republicans must unite in forming an 'American bloc' and that neither need yield to the foreign influence."

The extended debate on the bill in the House centered around the quota base, the opponents of the bill favoring the retention of the 1910 census or the establishment of a commission to work out a more equitable system of restriction. The vote on the final passage of the bill (April 12, 1924) was overwhelmingly in favor—323 yeas to 71 nays. The influence of the foreign-born voters is clearly attested by the fact that of the negative votes only three came from states west of the Mississippi River (Nebraska, 1 and Missouri, 2) the remainder being from New York, New Jersey, Massachusetts, Connecticut, Rhode Island, Pennsylvania, Illinois, Michigan, Wisconsin, and Maryland.

When the House bill reached the Senate, that body had before it a bill reported by the committee on immigration which fixed the quota at 2 per cent on the basis of the 1910 census. It developed, however, that the senators from the South and from the Middle West and Far West, irrespective

[1] Cable of Ohio. *Congressional Record*, 68th Cong., 1st Sess., March 1, 1924.

of party, were so strongly in favor of the provision in the House bill that a Republican caucus was called in order to consider the advisability of adopting it.

In the Senate the justice of the House bill was attacked most effectively by Mr. Colt of Rhode Island.

For what reason is it proposed to go back to the census of 1890? The reason is the desire to exclude southern and eastern Europeans. If you are going to do that, do it openly. . . . We have 6,000,000 of southern and eastern Europeans living among us who are just as proud of their race as we are of our race. Nothing so accentuates national prejudice as racial discrimination. It is now proposed to divide our 12,000,000 of alien population into two groups of 6,000,000 each. We are in effect saying to one of these groups of 6,000,000, "We wish you had never come here; you Italians are on a lower level than are the Prussians." Italy replies, "We fought by your side; will you now admit five of our enemies to one loyal Italian?" . . . I tell you, Mr. President, that in this proposition to go back to the census of 1890 as a basis for the quota calculation there is involved the adoption of an immigration law based upon racial discrimination, which is the most dangerous and un-American principle ever propounded in the American Senate.

In reply to the senator from Rhode Island, Mr. Heflin of Alabama voiced the sentiment of the South, from which section not a single representative or senator voted against the bill.

Mr. President, we have now reached the time in the life of the Nation when those who are for America must stand out on the one side and those who are willing to throw the gates of our country open to an indiscriminate horde of unfit foreigners must stand on the other. . . . I want to do, in this legislation, what is to the highest and best interest of my own country. I am not legislating for Italy or for any other foreign country. They have nothing to say upon this subject. . . . My good friend who has just spoken is from Rhode Island, a splendid State in our sisterhood, but there are over 60 per cent of foreign born and their offspring in his

State. Have we enough Americans here to speak the American spirit, to talk the American language, to vote for the benefit of America, to take a positive American stand on this question now? If not, Mr. President, the day is coming when we cannot take it. . . . We are told that New England is against this measure; that New England does not want restricted immigration. Why? Because more than 50 per cent of the population of some of their states is foreign born and the offspring of foreigners.[1]

Senator Sheppard of Texas, a state in which the Ku Klux Klan was very active in politics, raised the hue and cry against that "large element" among the foreign-born "which forms the main source and breeding ground of revolutionary and anarchistic propaganda in this country, such as Bolshevism, I.W.W.-ism, communism, and similar movements countenancing violence and disorder." He lamented the passing of the old pre-Civil-War stock; that this stock had been driven from Eastern industrial centers in such numbers as to change materially the racial complexion of states and communities famous in the struggle for American independence.

The Senate voted to adopt the percentage and quota basis of the House bill, adopting first the amendment to change the quota basis from the census of 1910 to the census of 1890 by a vote of 47 to 32 and then adopting the amendment making the percentage two.[2]

The Senate acted adversely on another proposed radical departure from existing laws. This was the proposal of the Secretary of Labor to include Canada, Mexico, and South and Central America in the quota limitations. This suggestion was prompted by the alleged "bootlegging" of aliens across the Canadian and Mexican borders, about which considerable complaint had been made. The Senate, however,

---

[1] *Congressional Record*, 68th Cong., 1st Sess., April 17, 1924.   [2] Ibid.

feared that the adoption of the amendment would seriously affect relations with our sister states in the Western Hemisphere, although there was some opposition to the influx of Mexicans. The Republican senator from New Mexico, Mr. Bursum, who was probably familiar with the character of immigration from Mexico, did not believe that there was danger of the country's being overrun by Mexicans. He asserted that they were in great demand as laborers on railways, in the cotton fields, and in the beet fields. "Mexico is a very sparsely settled country, much more so than any portion of the United States," he said. "The time is not far distant when Mexico will be a very desirable field for Americans to settle in in order to help develop that wealthy country and its vast resources. Through that sort of policy we can hope to obtain a large measure of benefit, but to close the door against our neighbors, first, it is impracticable and, second, it is offensive."[1]

As finally enacted the immigration law of 1924 provides that the annual quota of any nationality shall be 2 per cent of the number of foreign-born individuals of such nationality resident in continental United States as determined by the census of 1890, the minimum quota being fixed at 100. But an amendment had been inserted in the Senate bill, and was adopted by the conference committee, which entirely changes the quota base after July 1, 1927. This is the so-called "national origins" provision.

Under the 1890 quota base the maximum number of immigrants admissible annually totals about 162,000, whereas under the national-origins provision the maximum is arbitrarily fixed at 150,000. With the minimum quota of any nationality fixed at 100, the annual quota of each nationality

[1] *Congressional Record*, 68th Cong., 1st Sess., April 18, 1924.

for each fiscal year shall be a number which bears the same ratio to 150,000 as the number of inhabitants in continental United States in 1920 having that national origin bears to the number of inhabitants in continental United States in 1920. Without entering into the method of determining the quotas as provided in the law, it may be said that the effect of the new system will be to increase the quota for Great Britain and Ireland and to decrease the quotas for Germany and the other countries of northern and western Europe. It will not materially affect the numbers from southeastern Europe as a whole, although there are variations for individual countries. The effect will probably be to keep the annual immigration to the United States considerably below the maximum of 150,000, because it is doubtful if Great Britain and Ireland, year after year, will fill their quota. The law, therefore, discriminates in favor of immigration from the British Isles.

In presenting the national-origins scheme to the Senate Mr. Reed of Pennsylvania probably stated correctly the purpose back of it. He said:

It seems to me that the method we adopted in our law of 1921 of basing the quotas on the foreign-born who were here in 1910 has this element of unfairness in it: That it disregards entirely those of us who are most interested in keeping American stock up to the highest standard—that is, the people who were born here. Surely it is fair to say that we who are native citizens of America are at least as much interested in America's welfare as are our recent arrivals. Yet our present quota law disregards us entirely in making up the quotas. . . . The present quotas are made up on the basis of the foreign-born residents of the United States, and they disregard entirely the 80 per cent of us who were born in this country. Nobody considers the American born in determining what the quota shall be, and that is where the trouble comes.[1]

[1] *Congressional Record*, 68th Cong., 1st Sess., April 3, 1924.

Mr. Reed admitted that the census bureau will be unable to determine with complete exactness the numbers of the different nationalities, but he was of the opinion that reasonable exactness will be reached.

As we have observed, the law of 1924 is the most comprehensive immigration measure which has ever passed Congress. It improves on the previous law in eliminating the racing across the Atlantic by steamships in order to land immigrants before the quotas of the countries are filled, by providing for the issuance of a limited number of immigration visas for each country. When an immigrant obtains a certificate, he knows that he is within the quota and will not be debarred according to the moment of his arrival at the American port. Fathers and mothers, husbands and wives, of citizens of the United States, unmarried children under twenty-one years of age, and bona-fide farmers, their wives and small children, are with certain limitations given preference within the quotas. Strict precautions are provided against the falsification or forgery or illegal transfer of immigration visas, thus reducing to a minimum the entrance of undesirables.

The immigration act of 1924 thus marks the culmination of an agitation covering a quarter of a century in favor of immigration restriction. The hearings and debates on the bill revealed the fact that a heavy majority of the American people, irrespective of racial origin, accepted the restriction of immigration as a social and political necessity. The disagreement was over the method of attaining that restriction. Whether the Congress was wise in registering the demand of a probable majority of Americans for discrimination against the peoples of southeastern Europe by accepting the 1890 quota base and the national-origins system remains to be seen. The historian dare not venture an opinion as to the correctness of the gloomy forebodings of a well-informed student of immigration written while the bill was pending.

We have a graver nationality question in America today than we ever had in our history. The chief object of the restriction of immigration is to promote assimilation. No flood of unrestricted immigration could have operated so effectively to check the process of assimilation as the Johnson immigration bill. We could have attained the results we were seeking in a way that would not have been offensive to any nationality. . . . Nothing is gained by putting on the statute books a measure which is certain to evoke an increasing volume of bitter discontent. It would be far better to extend the present quota law, with all its inadequacies, until our legislators have had time to work out a measure which will operate to make us a more homogeneous nation, instead of splitting us into a collection of mutually hostile racial stocks.[1]

The operation of the law during the first six months, from July 1 to December 31, 1924, indicates that the purpose to reduce immigration from southern and eastern Europe was attained. The net gain from Great Britain and Ireland was 19,028 and from Germany 19,466. The net loss to southern and eastern Europe exceeded 20,000. The total net gain from Europe was about 19,000. The statistics for the non-quota countries show a net loss of 529 persons from Cuba, the West Indies, and all of South and Central America; from Canada and Newfoundland a net gain of 61,000; and from Mexico a net gain of 10,269.

It appears, therefore, that so long as this act remains in effect our population will be recruited almost entirely by immigrants from northern and western Europe and from the non-quota countries of the Western Hemisphere, including such Europeans as may elude the immigration officers.

[1] *New Republic*, February 27, 1924.

CHAPTER XV

THE IMMIGRANTS IN POLITICS, 1860–1914

In a former chapter we have discussed the political activity of the naturalized voters down to the political campaign of 1860; in the present chapter we shall be concerned with the period beginning with the close of the Civil War to the outbreak of the World War. We must be careful not to exaggerate the influence of the foreign-born and their immediate descendants. We must remember the Hartford Convention of 1814–1815, when certain representatives of New England, "the most American part of America," measured by its population, opposed the war with Great Britain and threatened to throw heavy obstacles in the way of its successful prosecution. We should also be reminded of the administrations of Washington, John Adams, and Jefferson, when people took sides and made political capital out of the foreign policy of the administration. It is certainly true, however, that our immigrants carry with them political, religious, and social baggage. Politically the Irish and Germans are the most important, as they are of first importance numerically. They have come from countries whose governments have played leading rôles in world affairs and they have frequently been in disputes with the government of their adopted country. This is less true of the Scandinavians, Dutch, Italians, Slavs, and Jews, but they must be taken into account.

At the close of the Civil War in 1865 feeling against Great Britain was running high because of her attitude and policy during that struggle. This hostility took the form of agitation to annex Canada to the United States. The relations between the United States and Great Britain were strained still further as a result of Fenian raids across the Canadian border. The Fenian Brotherhood was composed of Americans of Irish birth and descent. Its motto was "Ireland—Free and Independent." The Irish in America and Ireland coöperated in attempting to set up an Irish republic. The British government arrested a number of leaders, among whom were naturalized American citizens. Meetings were held in this country protesting the seizure of American citizens in the British Empire. It was alleged that these seizures were made in disregard of the comity of nations and that American citizens were tried for words spoken and acts committed within the limits of the United States, thereby casting American citizenship to the winds and denying the validity of naturalization.[1]

In attempting to prevent the raids into the territory of a power with which we were at peace, the Federal administration incurred the ire of the Fenians and their sympathizers. The Fenians were bitterly attacked by their enemies as disloyal to the United States. They were accused of plotting with the Copperheads and those who had sympathized with the Confederacy and opposed the prosecution of the war. The most impossible stories were circulated, calculated to appeal to the ignorant and gullible. Rumors were broadcast that there were a quarter of a million Fenians distributed

---

[1] *Declaration of Principles, by the Representatives of the Fenian Brotherhood, in Congress assembled, September 7, 1867, at Cleveland, Ohio. Resolutions addressed to the Senate and House of Representatives, adopted by a large meeting of Citizens of the District of Columbia, January 14, 1868. Address of General John O'Neill, President of the Fenian Brotherhood, etc.* (New York, 1868).

throughout the North, thoroughly armed and equipped, ready at a moment's notice to spring to arms to strike a deathblow to civil and religious liberty on this continent. They were said to be backed up by the entire Copperhead element and an almost united South. The alleged plot was first to seize the state armories and the banking capital of the North, this action to be followed by an indiscriminate slaughter of Protestants and Republicans. For the performance of this diabolical work for the Democratic party they had been promised assistance in conquering Canada, liberating Ireland, and establishing the spiritual reign of the Pope on this continent. This scheme was stated to have been perfected at a secret caucus of Democrats, shortly after the defeat of General McClellan for the presidency in 1864, when he made a visit to Rome. The fruits of this visit were said to be an immense importation of Catholics and "ready-made" Democrats. The Republican members of Congress were warned of the plot to destroy the lives of a sufficient number of Republicans to reduce them to a minority in Congress. To accomplish this, railroad accidents, poisonings, and other devices would be resorted to.[1] The present generation is not privileged to laugh at the absurdity of these stories, for we have had abundant evidence that nothing is too impossible to circulate and find ready believers.

At this time the American government was trying to negotiate a settlement of the Alabama claims against Great Britain, and the administration had to be careful not to stir up either the jingoes or the naturalized voters. "Twisting

[1] "To the Republican Members of the Thirty-ninth Congress," a one-page circular dated at Chicago, November 17, 1866; "To the Governors of the Loyal States," a one-page circular dated at New York, January 26, 1867; *Miner's Journal*, February 22, 1868. The reader will understand, of course, that this material is of slight importance.

the British lion's tail" has always been profitable politically. In spite of what seemed at times insuperable obstacles, in May, 1871, the treaty of Washington was signed. This, one of the most remarkable treaties known, provided for a joint tribunal, which sat at Geneva in 1871–1872, to adjudicate the damages to which the Americans were entitled from the depredations of the Confederate cruisers which were constructed in British shipyards. The tribunal was almost disrupted by the American members' putting in claims for indirect damages; that is, a sum covering the cost of the prolongation of the war alleged to have been caused by the escape of the cruisers. This aroused great anger in England, and that country threatened to withdraw her representatives from the tribunal. The affair had to be handled gingerly by the administration because of the impending presidential election. For fear of offending the naturalized voters, as well as many native voters, President Grant could not afford to have it said that his administration was truckling to Great Britain. Curiously enough, at this time the German vote was friendly to England, Germany and England not being at that time commercial and colonial rivals.[1]

At the time of the Franco-German War in 1870–1871 American sympathy was pretty generally on the side of Germany. It was felt that the war had been provoked by France, who had alienated the friendship of America by the efforts of the Emperor Napoleon III to establish an empire in Mexico, taking advantage of the impotence of the American government during the war between the states. Furthermore, Germany was not as yet a great world-power and had not come into conflict with American ambitions and interests.

[1] See the letter of Goldwin Smith to Max Müller, January 31, 1870, in Arnold Haultain's *A Selection from Goldwin Smith's Correspondence*, p. 26.

The Franco-German War was not fought on sea and did not involve the rights of American citizens, but it is interesting to note that the question of the export of arms and munitions came up for discussion at public meetings and in Congress. In Congress the question arose in connection with a resolution calling for the appointment of a select committee to investigate all sales of ordnance stores made by the government of the United States during the Franco-Prussian War. This resolution was introduced in the early part of 1872 by Senator Sumner of Massachusetts, who was at odds with the Grant administration, probably for the purpose of embarrassing the candidacy of Grant. The opposition to Grant within his own party had taken on the form of the Liberal Republican movement, in which Carl Schurz, a German immigrant of 1852, was perhaps the most conspicuous and able leader. General Schurz at this time was a senator from Missouri. Addressing the Senate on the Sumner resolution, he said that during the war, when it became known that our government was furnishing arms to France, a great commotion sprang up among voters of German nationality. Meetings were held all over the country, resolutions were passed, and he was flooded with an avalanche of letters and addresses and protests. Mr. Schurz stated that he did not discuss the matter in the Senate at the time, because he did not wish to involve our relations with the belligerents, although he did call it to the attention of the Secretary of War. In reply to the allegation of Mr. Morton of Indiana, that he was inciting the Germans against the administration, Mr. Schurz denied that he had ever tried to form a party on the basis of nationality.[1]

[1] *Congressional Globe*, 41st Cong., 3d Sess., pp. 953 ff.; ibid. 42d Cong., 2d Sess., pp. 1040, 1047, 1048, 1132, 1133, and Appendix, pp. 67-74; ibid 43d Cong., 1st Sess., pp. 1774, 1775.

Carl Schurz deserves to be listed among the very finest and most useful men in public life. Of that remarkable group of German immigrants usually called the "forty-eighters" he was perhaps the ablest and most distinguished. Shortly after his arrival in the United States he became active in politics, contributing to the election of Lincoln by his penetrating and logical speeches. Appointed minister to Spain by President Lincoln, he resigned after a few months to become a major general in the Federal army. During the campaign of 1864, when for a time the reëlection of Lincoln appeared to be dubious, his speeches rallied many doubtful voters to the Union cause. In 1869 he was elected to represent Missouri in the Senate, where he became an uncompromising opponent of the radical reconstruction policy and a crusader against the corruption and inefficiency of the Grant administration, making enemies of some of the most powerful men in both the Democratic and Republican parties. A master of English style, he never was able to overcome his German accent; and for this reason he was the target for cheap sneers at his foreign birth. Never for long at home in any political party, he supported the man and his cause regardless of political affiliations. His experiences in his native land with the system of Metternich made him antagonistic to anything that smacked of militarism in his adopted country. He was an ardent anti-expansionist, opposing the proposed purchase of San Domingo in the Grant administration and the acquisition of the Philippine Islands and Hawaii during and after the Spanish-American War.

The opposition to General Grant personally and to the policies of his administration culminated in the Liberal Republican movement in the campaign of 1872. Elected to the Senate by the support of Democrats and Liberal Republicans,

Schurz became a leader in organizing the Liberal Republican party. Disqualified by his foreign birth for the presidency, he sought to effect the nomination of a man with a clean record who could consistently stand on a platform calling for tariff reform, amnesty to former Confederates, civil-service reform, the repudiation of the leadership of the Republican party, and opposition to expansion and lavish land grants to railways. Schurz hoped to win the support of the German voters to this program, but the unfortunate nomination of Horace Greeley, the picturesque and erratic editor of the *New York Tribune,* wrecked this prospect. Greeley had antagonized the Germans by his controversy with Archbishop Hughes of New York over state support for Catholic parochial schools and by his agitation for prohibition. Schurz wrote to Greeley that his conversation with prominent Germans and reading of editorials in German papers had convinced him that the Germans would not support him. During the campaign the regular Republicans appealed to the naturalized voters by circulating literature in their mother tongue, defending the policy of the administration with reference to the sale of arms during the Franco-German War and picturing the Republican party as the friend of the immigrant. In recording the fact that Greeley's candidacy was annihilated at the polls, it is not meant to infer that this was accomplished by the Irish and the Germans; these facts are cited as one instance among many where the immigrants figured prominently in politics.[1]

In the campaign of 1876 Mr. Schurz supported Hayes, the Republican candidate, against Tilden, the Democratic nominee. Schurz became a member of President Hayes's cabinet,

[1] See Schurz, *Speeches, Correspondence and Political Papers* and the pamphlets of the campaign of 1872.

accepting the secretaryship of the interior, and his influence weighed heavily in the administration.

The religious issue figured prominently in the presidential contest of 1884. The Democrats nominated Grover Cleveland, who had a good record as governor of New York; but he had, from the standpoint of one element of voters, a vulnerable spot, having vetoed a bill granting state aid to sectarian schools. The Republican candidate, James G. Blaine, although a Presbyterian, had a Catholic mother and a sister who was mother superior in an Indiana convent. As against his Democratic opponent Mr. Blaine could expect the support of many voters who disapproved of the governor's veto; but this support was lost, probably by accident. During the closing days of the canvass Mr. Blaine received a delegation of Protestant clergymen. In the course of his address the spokesman, the Reverend Samuel D. Burchard, made the following statement: "We are Republicans, and we do not propose to leave our party and identify ourselves with the party of Rum, Romanism, and Rebellion." For some reason, variously explained, Mr. Blaine did not repudiate this statement. The inevitable appeared in the Democratic press, which played up the fact that the Republican candidate had allowed the slur on his mother's religion to go unrebuked. The election, as it proved, hinged on the vote of New York, which went Democratic by a close margin, and it may be that the large Catholic vote elected Mr. Cleveland.

The new administration was called upon to adjust certain matters pending with Great Britain. In the campaign of 1888 the Republicans, in order to win Irish votes, charged that Cleveland lacked courage and patriotism in upholding American rights; in other words, that he was controlled by British interests. When the President sent a retaliatory mes-

man of high culture as minister to Germany "would be received as a compliment by the German-American population here." In a speech delivered at the World's Fair at Chicago on "German day," June 15, 1893, Schurz praised the loyalty of the German-Americans to their adopted country, stating that they are proud of their citizenship, proud of our government, and proud of our mighty and noble nation. The German-American, said he, has never tried to mingle European politics with those of America, but has always wished that the friendship which has existed between the United States and Germany may never be troubled by a cloud of discord or even of misunderstanding. He referred to the fact that the Germans in the Fatherland never lost confidence in the ultimate victory of the North and that they lent millions of dollars to our government. Whoever does not honor our old Fatherland, said he, is not worthy of the new. He who does not revere his old mother will not truly love his bride. The hearts of German-Americans were stirred when Germany was unified. Then they could say, "At last Germans again have a Fatherland!" When we look at the great exhibits of the Fatherland at this fair, he concluded, we can say, "Look, this is Germany, the land that gave us birth!"

A few days after President Cleveland had startled and electrified the country by sending to Congress his bold message on the Venezuela boundary dispute, when there was grave danger of war between the two great English-speaking nations, Schurz, in a speech before the New York Chamber of Commerce, urged all good citizens to stand by the government in time of need, at the same time hoping that peace would be maintained. Alluding to the statements that some American citizens of Irish origin wanted war with England because they believed that war would relieve Ireland of

British connection, he praised the willingness of the Irish to fight for the United States. But as American citizens, having sworn allegiance to the United States, they should never forget that the republic has the right to expect of all adopted citizens, especially in questions of peace and war, the loyal and complete subordination of the interests of their native countries to the interests of the United States. All seriously minded Americans, he said, earnestly hope for the continuance of the long existing friendly relations between the United States and Great Britain.[1]

The time has not yet arrived for a trustworthy and impartial account of the rôle played by racial stocks in the political history of the United States. A few instances have been cited to show that there have been times when politicians have appealed to certain nationalities, with what success it is difficult to determine from the material available. It is not easy to fix the responsibility for racial cleavage, whether it rests largely with the "foreigners" or with the "natives." It is, however, safe to assert that neither class is free from censure.

Moreover, in dealing with the rôle played by race and religion in political contests it must be considered that issues relating to them are seldom brought openly into the forum of discussion. In contrast with the years following, issues vital to the immigrants prior to 1914 were far less important. In other words, "racial blocs" in a large way were not so much in evidence. By reason of their strategic political position the Germans have bulked rather large in political contests. On the whole, the Irish have been loyal to the Democratic party; the German vote, on the other hand, has been more independent and therefore more important and decisive.

[1] The speech was delivered on January 2, 1896.

CHAPTER XVI

THE YEARS OF NEUTRALITY, 1914–1917

When Woodrow Wilson was inaugurated president of the United States on March 4, 1913, there was every reason to believe that we were about to enter a period of constructive legislation designed to correct some of the errors into which the government had fallen during a half-century of unexampled development, when law had lagged far behind conditions. The President's inaugural address was devoted altogether to domestic problems. Four years later his inaugural was devoted to the appalling prospect of entering a great war which for three and one-half years had converted Europe into a shambles. It is the irony of fate that two great men to whom war was utterly abhorrent, Abraham Lincoln and Woodrow Wilson, should have been called upon to lead the nation into war.

It is doubtful if the immigrants, individually and collectively, ever had a more sympathetic friend in the White House than Woodrow Wilson, yet within a few months after his inauguration he was bitterly assailed as their betrayer.

It was unfortunate that a few months before the outbreak of the World War President Wilson was compelled to take a stand that branded him pro-British in the eyes of many. After the passage of the Panama Canal Act (August 24, 1912) the British government had formally protested against the provision exempting American vessels engaged in coastwise trade from paying tolls, on the ground that it was contrary to the Hay-Pauncefote Treaty as interpreted in the light of the Clayton-Bulwer Treaty of 1850. The matter was widely discussed in the press and in Congress and furnished a welcome opportunity to those who have always charged Great Britain with thwarting American ambition and rights. On March 5, 1914, Mr. Wilson appeared before Congress and in an address which is a model of brevity and straightforwardness urged the repeal of the exemption provision. "Whatever may be our own differences of opinion concerning this much-debated measure, its meaning is not debated outside the United States," he said. . . . "The large thing to do is the only thing that we can afford to do, a voluntary withdrawal from a position everywhere questioned and misunderstood." He closed the address with these pregnant words: "I ask this of you in support of the foreign policy of the administration. I shall not know how to deal with other matters of even greater delicacy and nearer consequence if you do not grant it to me in ungrudging measure." Congress was deluged with telegrams and petitions, many of them coming from Irish and German societies, declaring for an "American as against a British interpretation of the treaty." After weeks of acrimonious debate Congress granted the President's request, nòt, however, "in ungrudging measure." From this time on, nothing that Wilson could ever do or say would convince certain individuals that he was anything but an Englishman in American clothing.

When the war clouds unloosed their fury in the closing days of July, 1914, very few expected that the war would last more than a few months at most. When Lord Kitchener declared that the war would last at least three years, it is doubtful if his prediction was taken seriously. About three weeks after the beginning of war President Wilson issued an address to the American people counseling them to be impartial in thought as well as in action. "The people of the United States are drawn from many nations, and chiefly from the nations now at war," said the President. "It is natural and inevitable that there should be the utmost variety of sympathy and desire among them with regard to the issues and circumstances of the conflict. . . . It will be easy to excite passion and difficult to allay it. Those responsible for exciting it will assume a heavy responsibility, responsibility for no less a thing than that the people of the United States, whose love of their country and whose loyalty to its Government should unite them as Americans all, bound in honor and affection to think first of her and her interests, may be divided in camps of hostile opinion, hot against each other, involved in the war itself in impulse and opinion if not in action." Mr. Wilson's statement was bitterly assailed, but under the circumstances then existing it was the height of wisdom. However that may be, his words fell on deaf ears. Both sets of belligerents immediately began a campaign to win American sympathy. Probably it will never be known how many million dollars were spent for propaganda.

At first the newspapers trod the path of neutrality, but after a few months they swung sharply toward the Allies. The great mass of the American people took one side or the other, but up to the hour of the declaration of war by their government the majority was probably opposed to American participation. In the case of the foreign-born and their immediate descendants nationality largely determined their sympathies. The Slavs, because of the oppression and alleged oppression of their countrymen in Germany and Austria-Hungary, were pro-Ally. Those of English birth and descent were naturally in sympathy with the mother country.

The Italians, the Greeks, and the peoples of the Balkan states (except Bulgaria) were likewise opposed to the Central Powers. With their brethren fighting under every flag in Europe, the American Jews were no doubt divided in their sympathies; but remembering their experiences in Russia, Germany, and Austria, the countries from which the bulk of them came, many probably wished for the success of the nations fighting alongside the British, although hostility to Russia must have weighed heavily with a large number. The Scandinavians were divided. Speaking in general terms, as in the case of the other nationalities, the Swedes were pro-German. It was difficult, if not impossible, to convince a Swedish-American familiar with the history of his native land that Russia was fighting in the interest of democracy and for the rights of smaller nations. The Swedish-American clergy, whose influence counted heavily, were strongly pro-German. The Norwegians were more evenly divided, but the majority were pro-Ally. The Danes, with the background of the Schleswig-Holstein war, could not think kindly of Germany. The Irish and the Germans heartily wished for the victory of German arms.

Some day the part played by the different racial stocks during the years of American neutrality will be written; but for the present the historian must deal with the most obvious activities of the Germans and Irish and to some extent the Scandinavians. By reason of their numerical importance and from the fact that they were represented by various organizations, the most influential rôles were played by the Germans and the Irish.

Regarding the Germans the most contradictory things have been said: that they Americanize quickly; that they retain their language, customs, ideals, and attachment to the

Fatherland entirely too long. The Germans themselves lament that it is impossible to continue things German into the second generation. As we have seen, German immigration began in real earnest after 1848. The newcomers were known as the "greens" in distinction from the "grays," the older immigrants, who were denounced by the former because they had forgotten German. It is true that some German immigrants of the thirties and forties came expecting to form a German state, but just how seriously this was taken by any considerable number of individuals it is impossible to say. The important thing is that the Germans settled in communities and concentrated in certain states, although they are more generally distributed over the states of the Union than are any other group of immigrants. During all these years the Germans were welcomed and praised for their industry, thrift, intelligence, and patriotism. It is said that the Scandinavians are the most easily assimilated, but to compare them with the Irish and the Germans is unfair. The Scandinavians are comparatively few in number and have not had the means of continuing their language and of influencing politics. But even among them are found political organizations, such as the Swedish-American Republican Club of Illinois, societies to preserve the culture of their native lands, and churches conducting services in the mother tongue. Of course their membership and their influence are inconsequential compared with the Ancient Order of Hibernians and the National German-American Alliance. The most ardent nativist of today would hardly question the Americanism of Carl Schurz, but he himself was proud of the fact that in his home German was spoken.[1] There has always been opposi-

[1] Carl Schurz, *Speeches, Correspondence and Political Papers*, Vol. V, pp. 334-338.

tion to organizations like the Educational Alliance for the Preservation of German Culture in Foreign Lands, the Pan-German Alliance, the Knights of Columbus, the Polish National Alliance, and parochial schools; but in times of public excitement it is easy to read into them many things which exist only in the imagination. It is true that there is a certain degree of clannishness about these organizations, but the same can be said of secret fraternal organizations, of the Daughters of the American Revolution, and of hundreds of other organizations which abound in "good works."

During the hectic days of war the National German-American Alliance was singled out for special condemnation, and after the entrance of America into the war its charter was revoked by Congress. It was made up of local and state federations organized in 1901 and incorporated by act of Congress in 1907. The objects of the Alliance were to strengthen the sense of unity among people of German origin, to counteract nativistic encroachments, to maintain friendly relations between America and Germany, to encourage the use of the German language and to have it taught in public schools, to oppose restrictions upon immigration, and to prevent invasions upon personal liberty.[1]

As an example of the sensitiveness of the immigrant stocks, the resolutions adopted by the Western branch of the German-American Alliance of Pennsylvania in March, 1903, apropos of the remarks attributed to Admiral Dewey on the German navy may be cited:

[1] For anti-German accounts of these activities see two brief books written by Gustavus Ohlinger during the war-time hysteria: *Their True Faith and Allegiance* and *The German Conspiracy in American Education*. Similar in tone is an article by Reinhold Niebuhr, "The Failure of German-Americanism," in the *Atlantic Monthly*, Vol. CXVIII, pp. 13–18. Albert B. Faust, *The German Element in the United States*, is sympathetic.

Coupled as his undiplomatic statement was, with a eulogy of Great Britain's friendship for America, it would seem that the admiral's discourtesy to Germany was prompted rather by social prejudices than by true patriotism. A composite people like our own is bound by congenial and cultural ties to Germany no less than to England. To needlessly offend a people to whom we are so closely related, and to whom we owe so much, must arouse the disapproval of every fair-minded American.

During the years of American neutrality, when Germany and Germanism were attacked so bitterly, the membership of the National German-American Alliance increased greatly, reaching a figure near three million. This figure would probably never have been attained had it not been for the fact that many Germans felt that the attacks on Germany were unjust and that the loyalty of German-American citizens was impugned.

The Alliance used its influence effectively in inducing school boards and legislatures in certain states to make the teaching of German obligatory in the public schools. In Nebraska, for instance, the law provided for the teaching of a foreign language in grades above the fourth when the parents of fifty children attending any school by petition in writing demanded it. Parochial schools of whatever nationality have taught foreign languages, sometimes to the detriment of English. The Roman Catholic Church, by reason of its remarkably efficient organization, has been far more successful in establishing and maintaining parochial schools than have Protestant churches. Among the Lutheran bodies the powerful German Missouri Synod has been the most persistent and successful. Except in a very few rural communities, where the population is solidly Scandinavian, the Swedish and Norwegian Lutheran churches have long since discontinued the year-round parochial schools. A number of Lutheran congregations conduct brief summer schools, but their mission is primarily to give instruction in the principles of the Christian religion. Their motto is: "The faith of the fathers in the language of the children." It should not be forgotten, however, that the churches have a real obligation to the recent immigrants. They would be remiss in performing these obligations if they did not furnish them the opportunity of attending services in the language which they understand. Undoubtedly it is true that there are all too many instances of pastors and priests failing properly to represent the sentiments of the people whom they serve. The fact that a number of them were born and educated abroad has made them too reluctant to introduce English services. This, however, has probably accelerated "Americanization" by repelling the younger generation and causing them to desert the church of their parents in favor of other churches or to sever all church connections.

The foreign-language press has also made for solidarity among the foreign-born and, next to the church, has probably been the strongest bond of union; and as a general thing its influence has been salutary. Possessing the faults of every newspaper, the foreign-language paper has bridged the gap between the old country and the new and has brought the immigrant in touch with the affairs of his adopted country. After a few years, it is safe to assert, the immigrant rarely rests content with only the foreign-language paper; he cannot escape the ubiquitous American newspaper.

Upon the opening of the World War meetings were held all over the United States protesting against the exportation of arms and munitions. These protests were not confined to the foreign-born and their immediate descendants,—many of the old American stock attended these meetings,—but our interest centers in the part played by the immigrant stocks. The Germans and the Irish because of their numbers and hostility to Great Britain were the most prominent in arranging these meetings. They organized societies like the American Truth Society, the American Independence Union, the Friends of Peace, and the Teutonic Sons of America. The National German-American Alliance launched a campaign for new members, addressing Americans of German origin and calling them to a consciousness of their unity. "Germanism is embattled against half the world," said the appeal, "and we German-Americans owe it to our race to stand our ground as manfully as our brothers across the sea. We must be the hammer or the anvil, we must up and strike or receive the blow and perish." "We have long suffered the preachment that 'you Germans must allow yourselves to be assimilated, you must merge in the American people,'" said the president of the Alliance, "but no one will ever find us prepared to descend to an inferior culture. No! We have made it our aim to elevate the others to our level. . . . We must not allow our two thousand-year culture to be trodden down in this land." The Alliance sent resolutions to the newspapers of the country demanding that they follow a policy of impartiality in dealing with the cause of Germany. *The Fatherland*, a weekly issued in the interest of "fair play for Germany and Austria-Hungary," was established during the first days of the war. It was indorsed by the Alliance and, as was later proved, subsidized by the German government. The German-language papers increased rapidly in circulation.

The Germans, Irish, and Swedes attacked the policy of the administration by branding it unneutral and un-American.

They called it a hypocritical neutrality. Deploring President Wilson's policy with reference to the German submarine warfare and the exportation of munitions of war as morally wrong and bound to draw us into war, they favored an embargo on munitions and a resolution warning American citizens off the ships of belligerents. To their way of thinking the British blockade and the German submarine warfare were interlocked, the illegality and barbarity of the two differing only in degree. In the words of a distinguished German scholar, Professor Kuno Francke of Harvard University, they believed that "one may be a good American and yet venture to think that the particular way in which the President has attacked this problem has been unfortunate. One may be a good American and yet believe that it would have been better if the President, instead of putting the whole blame for this ferocious warfare upon Germany, had held both England and Germany to account for it."[1] The editor of a Swedish paper published at New York, while believing that America ought to try to remain neutral, asserted that the policy of Great Britain and Germany should be protested with equal emphasis. It was no worse to use dumdum bullets, submarines, and Zeppelins than to starve whole nations, he wrote. These things have happened in war; they cannot be defended, but they can be explained.[2]

To the men who took this position it seemed that Germany had been grossly misrepresented; that Germany was fighting a defensive war; that in Germany's situation every nation would do what Germany was doing; that there was no essential difference between German militarism and British navalism.

[1] Kuno Francke, *A German-American's Confession of Faith*, pp. 37 ff.
[2] *Nordstjernan*, February 19, February 26, and March 5, 1915.

It would be unhistorical and unfair to present only one type of pro-German. There were many German sympathizers, like Professor Francke, who heartily wished for the success of German arms but who resolutely refused to have anything to do with any movement which might embroil America in war with Great Britain. They denounced the attempts of native and foreign-born politicians to turn President Wilson's speeches into attacks upon certain immigrant stocks.[1] They claimed that the utterances of the extremists did not represent the bulk of the German sympathizers. A goodly number were disposed to trust the President, recognizing the difficult task which confronted him and believing in his peaceful intentions.

In the exciting days after Germany had horrified the world by sending a torpedo crashing into the *Lusitania* on May 7, 1915, causing the death of nearly twelve hundred men, women, and children, of whom over one hundred were American citizens, with the exception of the German-language papers the press of the country generally applauded the President's note, although there was a tendency in some quarters to stigmatize our neutrality as technical and to emphasize the fact that practically American citizens were aiding the Allies by taking advantage of the legal right to profit by the war by selling arms and munitions. It was said that the language of the American notes to Germany was sharp and threatening, whereas to Great Britain it was unusually polite and friendly.

On May 10, 1915, Mr. Wilson addressed four thousand newly naturalized citizens at a meeting at Philadelphia. In the tense foreign situation the speech attracted wide attention. Although there was no direct reference to the *Lusi-*

[1] See *Congressional Record*, 64th Cong., 1st Sess., pp. 11,253, 11,258.

tania, there were certain statements indicative of the proposed action of the government or thrown out as "feelers" of public opinion. The President was burdened by the great responsibility of the moment and conscious of the fact that the eyes of millions of naturalized citizens were upon him. Above all his speech was an appeal for their confidence in the government:

> You have just taken an oath of allegiance to the United States. Of allegiance to whom? Of allegiance to no one, unless it be God —certainly not of allegiance to those who temporarily represent this great government. You have taken an oath of allegiance to a great ideal, to a great body of principles, to a great hope of the human race. . . . I certainly would not be one even to suggest that a man cease to love the home of his birth and the nation of his origin—these things are very sacred and ought not to be put out of our hearts—but it is one thing to love the place where you were born and it is another thing to dedicate yourself to the place to which you go. You cannot dedicate yourself to America unless you become in every respect and with every purpose of your will thorough Americans. You cannot become thorough Americans if you think of yourselves in groups. America does not consist of groups. A man who thinks of himself as belonging to a particular national group in America has not yet become an American, and the man who goes among you to trade upon your nationality is no worthy son to live under the Stars and Stripes.

Touching upon the thought that must have been uppermost in the minds of his hearers—the possibility of war with Germany—the President delivered himself of a statement which was as much attacked as it was misunderstood.

So a nation that is not constantly renewed out of new sources is apt to have the narrowness and prejudice of a family; whereas, America must have this consciousness, that on all sides it touches elbows and touches hearts with all the nations of mankind. The example of America must be a special example. The example of America must be the example not merely of peace because it will not fight, but of peace because peace is the healing and elevating influence of the world and strife is not. There is such a thing as a man being too proud to fight. There is such a thing as a nation being so right that it does not need to convince others by force that it is right.

In a sense this carefully phrased speech gives the keynote of the President's foreign policy. It was the product of a mind deeply read in history and cognizant of the emotions which play on the human heart. It explains the President's firm policy tempered with caution. It explains the "open diplomacy" of the period of our neutrality. It reveals that the notes were written to steady the composite mind of America as much as they were written to reach the inflamed minds of the belligerents. To what extent they prepared the American people for the supreme effort of war cannot be determined with any degree of accuracy at this early date, but it is not without significance that men who had been critical of the administration paid tributes to the President's sagacity after he had decided that the time had come to lead the nation into war.

Mr. Bryan's dramatic resignation of the state portfolio at the time of the *Lusitania* crisis because of the fear that the President's note would lead to war won him the warm applause of the German sympathizers and the opponents of war. The former secretary appealed to German-Americans to bend their efforts to maintain peace between the two countries.

Although Germany after a fashion yielded to the American demand that she cease her unrestricted submarine warfare, the relations with the Central Powers remained unsatisfactory, and the President's policy was the target for most acrimonious criticism. In September, 1915, our government demanded the recall of the Austrian ambassador because of his attempted interference with American industry and his violation of diplomatic usage by employing an American citizen traveling under an American passport to carry messages to his government. About the same time the German government defended the sinking of the *Arabic* on the ground that the vessel attempted to attack the submarine.

The President's message, December 7, 1915, subordinated everything to national defense and security. The concluding paragraphs were a stinging rebuke to the "hyphenated" Americans, who put the interests of their native country above loyalty to their adopted land.

There are citizens of the United States, I blush to admit, born under other flags but welcomed under our generous naturalization laws to the full freedom and opportunity of America, who have poured the poison of disloyalty into the very arteries of our national life; who have sought to bring the authority and good name of our government into contempt, to destroy our industries wherever they thought it effective for their vindictive purposes to strike at them, and to debase our politics to the uses of foreign intrigue. Their number is not great as compared with the whole number of those sturdy hosts by which our nation has been enriched in recent generations out of virile foreign stocks. . . . America never witnessed anything like this before. . . . A little while ago such a thing would have seemed incredible. . . . Such creatures of passion, disloyalty and anarchy must be crushed out. They are not many, but they are infinitely malignant, and the hand of our power should close over them at once.

The President also censured native-born Americans, at home and abroad, who "have so forgotten themselves and their honor as citizens as to put their passionate sympathy with one or the other side in the great European conflict over

their regard for the peace and dignity of the United States."
The message was the subject of many favorable comments,
but the German-language papers continued to condemn
"Wilson & Co."

In the early weeks of 1916 Mr. Wilson made a series of
"preparedness" speeches in New York, Pittsburgh, Cleveland, Milwaukee, Chicago, Des Moines, Topeka, Kansas
City, and St. Louis. His Milwaukee address, delivered in a
strongly German city in a strongly German state, was obviously pointed at that particular audience. Brushing aside a
dogmatic interpretation of Americanism, and generously
recognizing the lingering memories of their Fatherland, he
appealed to his hearers to lay aside those prejudices which
weaken the fabric of American nationality. He expressed
confidence in the great body of American citizenship.

And so the trouble makers have shot their bolt, and it has been
ineffectual. Some of them have been vociferous; all of them have
been exceedingly irresponsible. Talk was cheap, and that was all
it cost them. . . . But you will know without my telling you that
the man whom for the time being you have charged with the duties
of President of the United States must talk with a deep sense of
responsibility, and he must remember, above all things else, the
fine traditions of his office which some men seem to have forgotten.

Without unduly minimizing the possibility of America's being
drawn into the war, he assured his auditors that he knew that
they were depending upon him to keep the nation out of war.

So far I have done so, and I pledge you my word that, God help-
ing me, I will if it is possible. . . . There may at any moment
come a time when I cannot preserve both the honor and the peace
of the United States. . . . If danger comes, I want to turn to you
and the rest of my fellow-countrymen and say, "Men, are you
ready?" and I know what the response will be.

The strategy of the speech-making campaign was to win the confidence of the country in his peaceful intentions and at the same time to prepare it for a hearty and spontaneous and effective response if it became necessary to resort to warlike measures.

Throughout the period of American neutrality the President had shown his hand: that he was for peace without the abridgment of the rights of American citizens in any respect; that he would bear and forbear until forbearance ceased to be either virtuous or patriotic. With the approach of the political contest of 1916 Congress became increasingly uneasy. Fearful of their political lives because of threats from Germans and Irish in their districts and states, a number of representatives and senators in February, 1916, favored the passage of a resolution warning American citizens against taking passage on the armed merchantmen flying the flags of the belligerents. Mr. Wilson met the situation by a *coup d'état*, which was as unexpected as it was bold and manly. He demanded that Congress speedily vote on the proposed resolutions, thus thwarting the wishes of the politicians to keep the question open and to provide a political football. While the resolutions were pending Washington was deluged with telegrams, and many papers, including the Hearst dailies, shrieked their approval of the resolution. By a vote of 68 to 14 the Senate voted to table the Gore resolution, but in doing so it clouded the issue by including in the motion to table resolutions of directly opposite meaning. In the House the issue was more clear-cut; by a vote of 276 to 142 it voted to table the McLemore resolution, although a reading of the speeches indicates that some of the representatives were angling for the votes of people of all shades of opinion. These votes were taken during the first week of March.

During March, April, and May—the period of the primaries—events moved rapidly. On March 7, at a great meeting in New York, the "Irish Sons of Freedom" denounced England and hoped for a German victory. Champ Clark of Missouri, the Speaker of the House and Wilson's rival for the Democratic nomination in 1912, was boomed as a presidential candidate. On March 26 a German submarine sank the French channel steamer *Sussex*. On April 18 the President dispatched the *Sussex* ultimatum, notifying the Imperial German government that unless it immediately abandoned its unrestricted submarine warfare, diplomatic relations would be severed. The editor of *The Fatherland* charged that there was a compact between Wilson and England, and thousands of telegrams from German-Americans and Irish-Americans poured in, demanding that America keep out of war. On April 26 the papers brought the information that a German ship attempting to land arms for the Irish rebels had been captured and that Sir Roger Casement had been taken prisoner. Sir Roger became the hero of the Germans and Irish, who compared him with George Washington. Mr. Wilson was accused of having "tipped off" the Irish rebellion to the British government. On May 4 the German government conditionally complied with the American demand that it abandon unrestricted submarine warfare and indulged in gratuitous sneers about the humanitarian pretensions of the American government. These sneers were not exactly distasteful to the pro-German foreign-language press. Thus matters stood when the opening guns of the presidential campaign were fired.

In renominating Woodrow Wilson the Democratic party had both the advantage and disadvantage of presenting a candidate whose foreign policy was clean-cut and public property. Among the men prominently mentioned for the Republican nomination Theodore Roosevelt was the most straightforward and outspoken. He had been unmerciful in condemning Germany and most bitter in denouncing the "flabby" foreign policy of Mr. Wilson. In a speech at St. Louis, shortly before the Republican convention, he had unsparingly flayed the "hyphenated" citizens. Of all the possible candidates he was the most obnoxious to the Irish and the Germans. The National German-American Alliance notified the Republican managers that it was unqualifiedly opposed to Mr. Roosevelt. In nominating Charles E. Hughes the Republicans chose the most "available" candidate. His position on the Federal Supreme Bench had sheltered him from the political blasts, and he had never made public what policy with reference to the belligerents he would pursue. His speech of acceptance was cautious, playing up Wilson's failure to bring Great Britain to terms, and his campaign addresses were equivocal. He was often heckled and asked what he would have done when the *Lusitania* was sunk. He evaded a definite reply until at Louisville, on October 12, he stated that he would have severed diplomatic relations. Replying to a heckler at Evansville, Indiana, on October 31, Mr. Hughes said that he was opposed to an embargo on arms and munitions and that he was not in favor of warning American citizens off armed merchantmen.

Mr. Hughes's speeches were very disappointing to those who believed the times called for plain speaking. His failure to outline a clean-cut foreign policy, contrasted with Mr. Roosevelt's sledge-hammer blows directed at Germany and at President Wilson's foreign policy, repelled many sincere lovers of peace and gave the impression that he was playing both ends against the middle.

Mr. Wilson's speech of acceptance was dignified, calm, and convincing. It summed up the record of his administration and dwelt on the reactionary nature of the Republican party. In defending his policy with reference to the belligerents he stated that property rights can be vindicated by claims for damages, but the fundamental rights of humanity cannot be. "The loss of life is irreparable. Neither can direct violations of a nation's sovereignty await vindication in suits for damages." Referring to "that small alien element amongst us which puts loyalty to any foreign power before loyalty to the United States," he asserted that he neither sought their favor nor feared their displeasure. Perhaps one of the most effective and unexpected strokes of the campaign was Wilson's telegram to Jeremiah O'Leary, president of the American Truth Society, a pro-German organization. Mr. O'Leary had addressed a rather insulting communication to the President of the United States. "I would feel deeply mortified to have you or anybody like you vote for me," said the President. "Since you have access to many disloyal Americans, and I have not, I will ask you to convey this message to them." Undoubtedly this message repelled many Irish and Germans, as it convinced many of the doubtful of Wilson's firmness and courage. Some days later the telegram became even more convincing when it came to public notice that at a meeting of some two hundred German Lutheran clergymen at Chicago the assurance was given that Mr. Hughes would bring Great Britain to terms. This was followed by the Democratic charge that Mr. Hughes had had a meeting with Jeremiah O'Leary, which the Republican candidate admitted, claiming, however, that at the time he did not know what Mr. O'Leary represented—a damaging confession in the judgment of a great many people. Contrasted with Mr. Wilson's methods, the efforts of a number of Democratic campaigners to smear the issue are not at all impressive.

Standing out boldly during the campaign was Mr. Wilson's great generalship. He refused to stay on the defensive. He played up other measures and policies of his administration: the child-labor law, the Adamson Bill, the Underwood tariff, the Federal Reserve law, etc. Taking advantage of the "pussyfooting" of the Republican candidate, he made a bid for the support of those elements who were opposed to war but also opposed to a "disgraceful" peace. He carried the former Roosevelt strongholds in the West, where peace was a passion, but where the volunteering for service was brisk after war was declared. He repelled the extreme pro-Germans. The Democratic vote fell off decidedly in Chicago and New York, where many Democratic voters of German and Irish origin deserted the party. The literature of the German organizations indicates that Mr. Hughes was their candidate. In the rock-ribbed Republican state of Minnesota, apostate only once before in a presidential election, when the Progressive candidate won it away in 1912, the Scandinavian voters deserted in shoals, the state going Republican by only a few hundred votes. The fact that Mr. Bryan, a man celebrated for the courage of his convictions and known the world over as an apostle of peace, supported the President for reëlection bore a significance not to be passed over lightly by the Scandinavians.

Perhaps never before in a presidential campaign were racial prejudices exploited to the extent they were in the exciting contest of 1916. The perspective of history will probably determine the measure of success which attended the efforts of campaigners to appeal to racial groups; for the present we must rest content to record their efforts.

CHAPTER XVII

THE WAR AND AFTER

With the vast bulk of the American people, native and foreign-born, the declaration of war by Congress in the early days of April, 1917, was the signal for submission to the sovereign will of the government and for sinking former differences in the common cause. That this was done reluctantly and grudgingly in many cases does not detract one iota from the splendid exhibition of loyalty to law and order which the magic of America instills into its composite citizenship. The majesty of American citizenship was demonstrated as probably never before when on June 5, only two months after the declaration of war, some ten million men between the ages of twenty-one and thirty, both inclusive, registered under the terms of the conscription act, with a minimum of disorder. Remembering that in the Civil War the government did not resort to conscription until after the war had been in progress for two years, the fact that Congress during the World War passed a draft law within six weeks after the declaration of war bears eloquent testimony to the confidence of the government in the people. It is true that Congress enacted the most drastic espionage law in our history, but precaution rather than necessity was its father. Considering the violent differences of opinion developed during the years of neutrality, the number of convictions were few. The vigilance of government agents and the effective educational work of the Committee on Public Information and the Four-Minute Men should not be lightly stressed, but the seed was sown on fertile soil and the harvest was abundant.

The violence of the controversies over the wisdom and justice of the President's policy and the responsibility for the precipitation of the war, sharpened still more by the animosities of the presidential campaign, had brought forth extreme statements on both sides; in consequence the entrance of the United States into the war placed some individuals in very embarrassing positions from which it was difficult to retreat gracefully and honestly.[1] This was especially true of the German-language publications, although some editors retreated both gracefully and honestly. The same may be said of other foreign-language publications and English-language papers supported by the foreign-born.

The declaration of war enabled the government, Federal and state, to take strong measures, some of them unnecessary and objectionable, defeating the purpose for which they were intended. A loyalty campaign is as successful as its leaders are judicious and tactful. In time of war, when patriotism and nationality are watchwords, anything remotely "foreign" is under suspicion. The mere fact that an individual's name was of German, Irish, or Scandinavian origin made him suspect. The foreign-born, on the other hand, insist that their citizenship entitles them to a free expression of their opinions. They resented the demands that they pledge their loyalty just because they conducted religious worship in a language unintelligible to the majority of citizens. They resented especially the campaign directed against the foreign-language press and the efforts to suppress religious worship in a foreign tongue. In the state of Iowa, to cite a specific

[1] Carl Wittke, "Ohio's German Language Press and the War," in *Ohio Archæological and Historical Quarterly*, Vol. XXVIII, pp. 82–95.

instance, the patriotic zeal of the governor, who on his own responsibility issued a proclamation forbidding public worship in a foreign tongue, defeated its purpose by arousing a spirit of opposition to the government. Its effect was purely negative: it united the various racial groups, regardless of previous sympathies, in a determination to withstand the assault on what they believed to be their rights. Parenthetically it may be added that aside from the matter of loyalty the effect of the governor's proclamation was salutary in that many congregations which were ready to adopt the English language, but were prevented from doing so by the conservatives, have continued the use of English, at least in a number of services.

The attempt to stamp out the use of foreign languages took four forms: the prohibition of religious services in foreign languages, legislation forbidding the teaching of foreign languages in primary and secondary schools, the suppression of parochial schools, and the prohibition of foreign-language publications.

In the matter of religious services the pressure came from public opinion rather than from legislation. In the state of Iowa the governor's proclamation was undoubtedly contrary to the letter and the spirit of the Constitution; it was plainly in violation of the principle of religious freedom, because many citizens unable to understand English were deprived of public religious services. Missouri passed a law eliminating German from religious services. This was bitterly resented by the various immigrant stocks in all states. It was the conviction of the *Lutheran Witness*, the organ of the German Missouri Synod, that "the devil has a hand in legislation which robs American Christians of the right to worship God in any language whatsoever, be it German, or Polish, or

Dutch, or Italian." "The legislators guilty of such oppressive measures may not have been conscious of the injury they were doing Christianity," it continued, "but this will not prevent us from saying that the devil certainly must rejoice when he sees the backwash of the world war destroying in large territories the effectiveness of the ministrations of the Gospel. Russia crushing out the language of worship in Finland, Poland in Lithuania, 'have nothing on' these American examples of interference with a God-given right."

Justice and expediency aside, the effect of the war and postwar agitation against foreign-language religious services was to hasten the transition to English. The change was inevitable in any event. The organ of the Swedish-Lutheran Church, in which 85 per cent of the preaching in 1921 was in Swedish, admitted that English must be learned, but deplored the efforts to force the use of English. The church was under heavy obligations to preach the gospel to the recent immigrants in the language of their native lands. During the war this body resolved officially that the immigrants and their children ought to learn English, the language of the country, but that Swedish ought to be preserved as a rich cultural inheritance as long as possible.[1] This probably represents the attitude of the leading churchmen among the old immigrants, although many exceptions could be found. The situation among the new immigrants is difficult to gauge, but with most of them the language problem has not become so serious. In the next generation their problem will be almost identical with that of the older stocks.

During the war and the year following the armistice over twenty states made English the only medium of instruction in both public and private schools. These laws were aimed

[1] *Augustana* (Rock Island, Illinois), July 4, 1918, and June 2, 1921.

mainly at the German language and were provoked to some extent by German propaganda. In the words of an American newspaper,

Those were the days when some of the symphony orchestras of the land did not dare play the works of such masters as Beethoven, Wagner, and Brahms, and when it would have been virtually taking their lives in their hands for certain German artists to appear in public in halls where, previous to 1914, they had been hailed with loud acclaim.

About the same number of states prohibited the teaching of foreign languages in any and all schools under the eighth grade. These laws were brought into the United States Supreme Court, which rendered a decision in 1923 (when the reaction against the war-time excitement had set in) that they were unconstitutional.

The agitation against all things German and, to a lesser degree, against all things "foreign" threatened the existence of the foreign-language press. Editors were arrested; their offices were attacked by mobs; editions of papers were confiscated or torn to shreds by excited citizens; and firms advertising in these papers were boycotted. By act of Congress, October 6, 1917, no foreign-language publication could print matter pertaining to the war without filing a translation with the postmaster unless the government was satisfied that the loyalty of the paper was unquestionable, when a permit allowing publication was issued. The most extreme law of this nature was enacted by the Oregon legislature in January, 1920, over a year after the armistice. This measure made it unlawful for any person, firm or corporation, or association of persons to print, publish, circulate, exhibit, sell, or offer for sale any paper, treatise, pamphlet, or circular in any other language than English unless those prints included translations. The effect of the law was to make it practically impossible to receive a foreign-language paper through the mails. Certain pastors were unable to read their own church papers. A Swedish paper commented as follows:

We have to go back to the Spanish Inquisition to find the like of such a law. No such measure was enacted in Russia in the flourishing period of the Czar and his despotism. What will Europe think of us and our civilization? When we were in Paris we read English papers published in that city. . . . The humiliating thing for us Swedish-Americans is that a member of the legislature born in Sweden introduced the law and two other Swedish-Americans voted in favor of it.

Notwithstanding the fact that the loyalty of certain foreign-language papers was questionable, the press as a whole rendered truly great services to the government by appealing to its readers to give unstinted loyalty to the government, by explaining the issues involved in the conflict, and by giving publicity to the Liberty Loan campaigns, the work of the Red Cross, and the necessity of conserving food. Thousands of people could be reached through no other medium. In all fairness another angle to the question should be stated. The very politicians who professed a horror for foreign languages had, prior to the war, favored compulsory teaching of those languages and had voted for laws designating foreign-language publications as official papers and authorizing public officials to publish legal notices in their columns. The sudden shift from coddling "foreignism" to chastising it was the occasion for sneers and contempt from citizens of all creeds and races.

The war furnished a welcome opportunity for the opposition to parochial schools to assert itself effectively. The only churches seriously affected were the Catholic and the German

Lutheran. As we have observed, parochial schools which compete with the public schools have all but died out among the Scandinavians. Except in a few concentrated Scandinavian rural communities it has proved impossible to maintain anything that remotely resembles parochial schools outside of a brief summer session in which the teaching of the Scandinavian languages has practically yielded to instruction along purely religious lines. The Scandinavians maintain colleges and academies, but out of the total number of eligibles only a very small proportion of young people are attracted to them. Among the Lutherans of German birth and origin the large Missouri Synod alone has succeeded in competing with the state system of education. Holding themselves studiously aloof from other Lutheran synods on doctrinal grounds, they have been remarkably successful in holding their members in the language and faith which they and their fathers cherished in the Fatherland. There are German settlements today where German is by far more familiar than English. Next to the Missourians, the Iowa Synod is the most conservative on the language question.

Of the leading religious organizations the Roman Catholic Church shows less change than any other American church. While possessing adaptability, its organization—the marvel of the centuries—retains all the essentials; and unlike other American bodies it retains its connections with Europe. While the Lutheran Church counts its greatest numbers in the country, the Catholic strength is in the cities. The activity of the church is also affected by the circumstance that every diocese and almost every parish harbors a considerable Protestant population, which is not always the situation in other lands. A surprising number of priests are Irish, showing that the organization is such that it can surmount racial prejudice. The Lutheran Church, on the other hand, is hampered because it is split up into numerous synods, the boundaries of which closely follow nationalistic lines or were laid early in the history of American Lutheranism. Back in the forties and fifties Archbishop Hughes of New York, one of the eminent American Catholic prelates, was extremely vigilant to suppress the first tendencies among the various nationalities in the church to divide according to respective nationalities. He was also opposed to those who tried to "Americanize" the church; that is, to trim doctrine and discipline to suit national prejudices.[1]

The rapid growth of the Roman Catholic Church has been due largely to immigration, and the steady stream of Catholic immigrants from 1840 to the present time has made the problem of caring for their spiritual welfare a constant one. The church considers the parochial school one of its strongest agencies in ministering to those under her care. The organization of the church, the sacrificing devotion of her members, and the concentration of the Catholic population has made the parochial-school system possible.

About 1840 the school question was vital in New York. Governor William H. Seward saw that the public schools did not reach the children of the immigrants and that at least thirty thousand of them were growing up without proper educational advantages. The governor was in close consultation with Archbishop Hughes, who believed that parochial schools should receive a share of the public money devoted to educational purposes. In his message of 1840 Mr. Seward made this recommendation and advocated the substitution of new school boards in New York City in place of the Commit-

---

[1] H. A. Brann, *The Most Reverend John Hughes*, pp. 128 ff.; *Brownson's Quarterly Review*, last series, Vol. II, pp. 81 ff.

tee of Public Instruction, a close corporation exclusively Protestant. The question got into politics. Seward's message antagonized the rank and file of his own party, the Whigs, largely because the foreign-born were chiefly Irish Democrats. Meetings were held denouncing the Catholics, and Archbishop Hughes assumed the leadership of the movement in favor of the governor's recommendation. The Catholics in 1841 named a ticket made up from candidates already nominated by the Whigs and Democrats. The upshot of the controversy was a compromise which was unacceptable to the archbishop, who set about to build up a school system independent of state support. Since that time the parochial-school question and the personnel of state school boards has been a bone of contention between Catholics and Protestants wherever the Catholics have been numerically strong. Stated briefly, the principal objection to the parochial school on the part of non-Catholics is the contention that the public school is the very best Americanizing agency. This belief sometimes takes the form of the slogan "One flag—one school—one language."[1]

During the war the Catholic Church was extremely active in giving support to the war and in ministering to the spiritual and material comfort of the men in the trenches and in the camps, as were the other churches. There was no difficulty in securing Catholic chaplains. In September, 1919, at the call of Cardinal Gibbons the Catholic hierarchy met for the purpose of organizing on a national scale every field of Catholic activity. This was the largest meeting of the hierarchy ever held in America. It was voted to establish the National Catholic Welfare Council, which is the Catholic hierarchy of

[1] H. A. Brann, *The Most Reverend John Hughes*, p. 70; Frederic Bancroft, *Life of William H. Seward*, Vol. I, pp. 96–101.

the United States acting as a composite unit. It has been very active in promoting a comprehensive program.

Partly to counteract this extraordinary Catholic activity the Ku Klux Klan came into being. As has been pointed out, the significance of the Klan lies in the fact that it is a symptom of hostility to "foreign" influence. One of the most striking manifestations of hostility to parochial schools is found in the so-called compulsory-education act adopted by the people of Oregon on November 11, 1922, by a vote of approximately 115,000 to 101,000.[1] The law, which was to become effective in 1926, compelled children between the years of eight and sixteen to attend the state schools. The responsibility for initiating the measure was publicly assumed by the Scottish-Rite Masons. The opposition to the measure presented a motley appearance, including individuals and organizations which had little in common except antagonism to this particular measure. The most effective opposition was presented by the Catholics and the Missouri Synod Lutherans, who were joined by the Seventh Day Adventists, private nonsectarian schools, certain Episcopalians, some Protestant ministers, and certain individuals of all creeds and racial origin who could not agree to the principle of the act.[2] It is said that some Catholics voted for the bill because they objected to the expense of contributing to the support of two educational systems.

Another aftermath of the war is the proposal to require aliens to register with county clerks or police officials once a year or more frequently if they move from one place to

---

[1] The law was declared unconstitutional by the Federal district court of Oregon in 1924. This decision was sustained by the Federal Supreme Court on June 1, 1925.

[2] Edwin V. O'Hara, "The School Question in Oregon," in *Catholic World*, Vol. XVI, pp. 482–490.

another. The American Legion has come out strongly in favor of this, and in the annual messages of 1922 and 1923 Presidents Harding and Coolidge urged the enactment of a law to this end. It is argued that it will facilitate Americanization by enabling organizations to come in touch with aliens, and that in time of war the government can place its finger upon enemy aliens. On the other hand, powerful objections have been urged. It is said that the proposal smacks of Prussianism; that it would entail a mass of red tape and require too many officials; that it would lower the standard of citizenship by unduly stimulating naturalization (aliens naturally wishing to avoid the expense of paying the registration fee and incurring the trouble of registration would speedily apply for citizenship); and that it would furnish a basis for action against political refugees. It is certainly true that one of the most appreciated advantages America offers to the immigrants is the feeling that they are not constantly under the surveillance of the government—a welcome relief from the regulations of the governments of Europe. Before the war the benevolence of America to the immigrant consisted in leaving him severely alone, allowing him to work out his own salvation. In a sense this was neglect rather than benevolence. The flaws and the merits of this policy are obvious; whether the former outweigh the latter is largely a matter of individual judgment.

Temporarily at least the war closed this chapter of immigration policy; the Americanization movement marks the beginning of a new one. We have seen that in the three decades preceding the Civil War the "Americanization worker" was the missionary sent out by churches and private organizations to convert the German, the Irishman, and the Scandinavian in the Mississippi Valley from Catholicism,

Lutheranism, and agnosticism to Puritanism. The modern
Americanization movement is quasi-governmental. "Before
the War we hardly realized that we had an immigrant population," writes one who is inclined to be skeptical of the
movement. "Most of us simply took it for granted when we
thought of it at all, and it was left for a few sociologists,
economists, and special workers in the field to deal with the
problem of assimilation from whatever angle their point of
view engendered. Opposed to these were powerful industrial
interests who thought of the immigrant wholly in terms of
'man power,' and to whose direct advantage it was to keep
him unassimilated, un-Americanized, and as isolated and
ignorant as possible so that he would be less likely to make
demands upon them." [1]

Although the term may probably be resented, present-day
Americanization is benevolent nativism. The spirit that ani-
mates it is not only the objection to "little Italys," "little
Germanys," "little Polands," and ghettos, but the feeling
that somehow or other the preservation of the heritage of the
fatherlands and the existence of bonds of language and common origin are incompatible with true Americanism and
retard the untrammeled development of a sound American
nationality. Assimilation, therefore, must be facilitated and
hastened by a hothouse system. Speaking in sweeping gen-
eralizations, the Americanization movement involves the
teaching of English, cultivating a friendly feeling between
natives and immigrants and between the various racial
groups, giving instruction in the fundamentals of citizenship,
preventing undesirable segregation in cities, and meeting the
demand for immigrants in desirable locations and occupations. In the promotion of this work the Federal, state, and

[1] Edward Hale Bierstadt, *Aspects of Americanization*, p. 19.

city governments coöperate with private organizations, churches, schools, employers of labor, the Knights of Columbus, the Young Men's Christian Association, the American Legion, the World War Veterans, fraternal organizations, and others. National, state, and city Americanization conferences have been held, and colleges and universities have added to their curricula courses designed especially for Americanization workers.[1] A number of bills have been introduced in Congress to promote Americanization by providing coöperation with the several states in the education of non-English-speaking persons and the assimilation of foreign-born residents, some of them carrying appropriations as high as $100,000,000.[2]

Conceived in a spirit of patriotism and charity, the Americanization movement fell victim in all too many instances to selfish interests and untoward incidents not even remotely connected with the movement as such. Inflamed by the war mania, some misguided exponents of Americanization, ignorant of the fundamentals of psychology and courtesy, approached the immigrants in a spirit calculated to repel. Not entirely without reason the immigrants associated the agitation against foreign languages and the raids on the "reds" with an undertaking which was designed to befriend them. A few—but entirely too many—not being able to wear the uniform of the country, took up Americanization as a fad. Without detracting from the solid achievements of the movement, it must be set down that it has a most serious handicap. The very approach of the Americanization worker is often

[1] Philip Davis, *Immigration and Americanization*, pp. 427–747.

[2] Interesting information and points of view are presented in the speech of William S. Kenyon of Iowa in the United States Senate, January 16 and 17, 1920, entitled "Americanization of Aliens." Consult the *Congressional Record* for these dates.

resented by the alien. Americanization is not a thing to be learned like the multiplication table; it is a growth. Like the kingdom of heaven, it cometh not with observation. It cannot be taken by violence. The mechanics of salvation are useful only if the whole lump is leavened.

Perhaps the point of view of the immigrant, new and old, has never been better stated than by an immigrant of the fifties, who wrote his reminiscences after a long and varied career of leadership:

The Americans consider themselves very tolerant, and are in a way, but in many respects they are very intolerant and prejudiced; but this is owing to the lack of knowledge of other nations. It is true that the immigrant is bidden welcome, and is generally well received, but he is expected to be content with shovelling dirt, chopping wood, carrying water, ploughing the fields, and doing other manual labor, no one disputing his right or fitness for these occupations. But when he begins to compete with the native American for honor and emolument in the higher walks of life, he is often met with coldness mingled with envy. It is exceptional that he is recognized as an equal socially. Children of immigrant parents, although born and brought up here, are often subjected to taunts and sneers by their more fortunate playfellows, even within the walls of the American public school.[1]

The troubled years of the World War and after revealed as never before to the American people the problems of a composite citizenship and brought forth efforts, intelligent as well as otherwise, to lighten the burdens of the immigrants and to facilitate assimilation. But from the advantages which have accrued from wisdom and philanthropy must be subtracted suspicion, hatred, and jealousy, generated by heated words and well-directed blows, the by-products of war and of political tumult and strife.

[1] Hans Mattson, *The Story of an Emigrant*, pp. 299, 300.

CHAPTER XVIII

NATURALIZATION

The nation that holds out inducements and enticements to the subjects of other nations, to leave their domicile of nativity, and become members of the community so tempting them, will be considered by other political communities as contravening a known and established law of nations; and if quarrels be the consequence, the nation so acting must fight it out. Our country has so acted. America *has* held out inducements and temptations to foreigners to come and reside here. Thousands have done so: thereby prodigiously adding to the stock of wealth, of knowledge, of enterprize, and in every possible way to the national prosperity. . . . We do not hold out to naturalized foreigners a limited, qualified protection, because we do not require from them a limited, qualified allegiance.

So wrote a man signing himself "An American" to the *American Weekly Messenger*, published at Philadelphia, October 2, 1813, at the time the United States was engaged in a war with Great Britain, partly to vindicate the right of a man to divest himself of allegiance to his native country in favor of citizenship in America. The theory underlying American citizenship, whether the individual be native or naturalized, is that it is a poor justice that is bounded by rivers and mountains; that although a man owes obedience to the government while he lives within its limits, the world is the theater of his enterprise.[1] On the other hand, the

---

[1] George H. Yeaman, *Allegiance and Citizenship. An Inquiry into the Claim of European Governments to exact Military Service of Naturalized Citizens of the United States* (Copenhagen, 1867).

Constitution of the United States is not a "pool of Siloam" in which all political disabilities are washed away.

Considering the development of international law since the beginning of the era of European colonization, it is little short of remarkable that the governments of the world have been so tardy in recognizing the right of expatriation. Not an inconsiderable portion of the diplomatic correspondence of the United States is devoted to the problems which have arisen over this question. Perhaps the increasing demand for military service during the nineteenth century, accompanied by intense national rivalries, has made the nations even more reluctant to admit the principle. For the United States, however, there was no alternative but to insist upon the right of expatriation. Americans have accepted it without question, and naturalized Americans have esteemed it without price.

We have seen that before the Civil War the United States engaged in a controversy with the Austrian government over the case of Martin Koszta, a former subject of Austria who had declared his intention of becoming an American citizen. Koszta was arrested outside of Austrian jurisdiction, to be transported to Austria for trial for participation in the Hungarian insurrection. The strong contention of the American government, that Koszta was subject to the protection of the government, was finally acquiesced in by Austria, but at the time European publicists regarded the American position invalid.

Another case involving the obligation of military service, although very different from the Koszta case, was that of Felix Le Clerc, a Frenchman by birth but an American citizen by naturalization. In reply to a communication from Le Clerc, Secretary of State Cass in a letter dated June 17, 1859, stated that the United States government would not undertake to protect him from arrest, fine, or imprisonment by France should he voluntarily return to his native land and be seized on account of delinquent military service. This letter was seized upon by Republican and foreign-language newspapers to discredit the Democratic administration in the eyes of naturalized voters. It was a very effective set-off to the two-year amendment adopted by the Republican state of Massachusetts, providing that no person of foreign birth should be entitled to vote or should be eligible to office unless he had resided within the jurisdiction of the United States for two years subsequent to his naturalization. The attitude of the American government and the rulings in American courts had been in harmony with the doctrine of the Le Clerc letter, but the political issue raised by the Republicans was very effective.[1]

President Andrew Johnson in an annual message stated that with the peace then prevailing in Europe, the time seemed to be favorable for an assertion by Congress of the principle so long maintained by the executive department, that naturalization by one state fully exempts one born a subject of any other state from the performance of military service under any foreign government, so long as he does not voluntarily renounce its rights and benefits.

Even before the Civil War the Prussian government made proposals regarding naturalization which were far in advance of anything that any government had previously conceded.[2] Until 1870 Great Britain steadfastly refused to recognize the right of expatriation, and even today the recognition by most European governments is tacit rather than formal. In specific

[1] Herriott, "The Germans of Iowa and the 'Two-year amendment,'" in *Deutsch-Amerikanische Geschichtsblätter*, Vol. XIII, p. 275.
[2] George H. Yeaman, *Allegiance and Citizenship*, p. 49.

cases the United States usually wins its point, although as late as 1910 our treaty with Russia was abrogated because Russia refused to recognize the validity of American passports issued to Jews of American citizenship. In the first year or two of the present century our government entered into diplomatic correspondence with Germany respecting the liability to military service of Americans of German birth who had returned to visit or reside in Germany.[1]

On the part of the United States the act of March 2, 1907, provided that "any American citizen shall be deemed to have expatriated himself when he has been naturalized in any foreign state in conformity with its laws, or when he has taken an oath of allegiance to any foreign state." This law also presumes that an American citizen becomes naturalized upon two years' residence in the country from which he came or upon five years' residence in any foreign state. During the World War a resident of the United States within the draft age who refused to surrender his allegiance to a foreign government waived all claims to American citizenship in the future. On the other hand, the government was extremely liberal in granting citizenship to aliens who entered the military and the naval service. By the act of May 9, 1918, the bars of citizenship were lowered in their favor and in favor of men honorably discharged from service, regardless of the residence requirement. A number of Japanese and Chinese were admitted to citizenship under the military naturalization law; but in November, 1922, the Federal Supreme Court decided that they were not eligible. During the Civil War foreign soldiers honorably discharged from service were given full rights of citizenship without going through the formality of taking out their first papers.

[1] *House Documents*, 57th Cong., 2d Sess., No. 1, pp. 448–462.

The liberality of our naturalization laws dates from the colonial period, when in effect the naturalized citizens had all the privilege of the native-born.[1] During the period of the confederation (1781–1789) naturalization was left to the individual states. The ratification of the Constitution gave Congress the power to establish a uniform rule of naturalization; and in 1790, shortly after the inauguration of Washington, was enacted the first naturalization act, which required a two years' residence and confined the benefits to free white persons. From 1790 to 1854 fifteen laws dealing with naturalization were adopted, the term "free white persons" being retained in all; and after 1802 five years' residence was required, this remaining substantially in force until 1906. The term "free white persons" excluded Indians and negroes, who were considered unsuitable material for the fabric of society. After the ratification of the Thirteenth, Fourteenth, and Fifteenth amendments the law of 1870 extended the right of naturalization to Africans and to persons of African descent.

During the nativistic agitation in the two decades preceding the Civil War the proposition to lengthen the period of residence to twenty-one years was agitated widely, but in spite of many bills embodying that provision, Congress looked upon it with scant favor. The demand was strongest in the East and South. The South desired it, because by depriving the immigrants of citizenship the voting strength of the free states would be curtailed; and in the East the fraudulent naturalization of thousands of aliens ignorant of American institutions was thought to lower the tone of politics. If such a law had been made permanent, the dangers from a large

[1] Cora Start, "Naturalization in the English Colonies in America," in Report of the American Historical Association for 1893, pp. 319–328.

disfranchised element would have been considerable, for with all its undeniable shortcomings universal suffrage is one of the best safeguards against violence.

While the Fifteenth Amendment was pending, the question of Chinese suffrage was of vital interest on the Pacific coast. The opponents of the radical Republican reconstruction policy of granting suffrage to the negro pointed out that the amendment wrested from the states control of suffrage within their borders, and that therefore Chinese suffrage would be taken out of the keeping of California. If the amendment does not mean Chinese suffrage, it was asked, why did the radicals in both Houses reject the resolution declaring it should not have that effect? The radical Republicans in California, hard pressed by their opponents, countered by saying that no pagan could become a citizen, because he was disqualified by "the good moral character" clause, and that no honest judge would naturalize him. Furthermore, no Chinese-born could satisfy the educational requirement.

When the amendment was before the Senate a resolution was offered as follows: "But Chinamen not born in the United States, and Indians not taxed, shall not be deemed nor made citizens." The opponents of this resolution were most positive in their statements. One Republican senator said that his party was committed to universal suffrage without any discrimination. Another wanted to invite to the United States negroes, Irishmen, Germans, Frenchmen, Scotchmen, Englishmen, and Chinese. And still another thought we ought not to exclude people from the most populous portion of the globe, a country which in many respects excels any country on the face of the globe in arts, sciences, and in her eminent scholars.[1]

[1] *Congressional Globe*, 40th Cong., 3d Sess., pp. 1029–1037.

In 1870 a bill to establish a uniform system of naturalization was introduced in Congress, and an effort was made to strike out the word "white" and to exclude the local courts from naturalization jurisdiction and transfer it to the Federal courts in cities where three terms of such courts were held during the year. Again the cry was raised that the purpose of the Republicans was to cpen suffrage to the people from India, Japan, China, and Africa.[1] The main purpose of the bill was to prevent the fraudulent naturalization that has been perpetrated in the larger cities. The representative in charge of the bill stated that in New York City two judges had naturalized 1147 persons daily for a period of twenty-three days preceding election. The immigrants were brought in in groups and platoons, and anybody who came along was sworn in.[2] At this time there was considerable ill-feeling toward the Irish because of the activities of the Fenians, some of whom had left the country to fight for the Irish republic and had been arrested and brought to trial in English courts. They appealed to the American government for protection. In some cases the Fenians had been fraudulently naturalized.[3]

In order to prevent wholesale naturalization the bill held up the completion of naturalization for six months after the second papers were taken out. The Democrats made political capital out of the bill, charging that it was designed to make naturalization difficult and to discourage immigration. "It comes here moved and inspired by their ancient hate and hostility to the Irish and German voter in particular and the Catholic population which we have received from foreign countries in general," said a representative from Wisconsin.

[1] *Congressional Globe*, 41st Cong., 2d Sess., pp. 752 ff.   [2] Ibid. p. 4269.
[3] For the diplomatic correspondence and accompanying documents on the Fenians see *House Executive Documents*, 40th Cong., 2d Sess., Nos. 157–180.

"Every line and letter of the bill breathes the infernal spirit of Know-Nothingism and the convent and church burning of Native Americanism." Republicans from New England took little risk in voting for the bill since the naturalized vote in their section was almost unanimously Democratic; but in the Western states they were embarrassed by the presence of a large Republican naturalized vote, besides knowing that those states were offering inducements to immigrants to settle within their borders. The bill was laid on the table by a vote of 102 to 62.[1]

The fact that the Chinese Exclusion Act of 1882 denied the Chinese the right of citizenship would indicate that a special act was required to accomplish this, but the Supreme Court has decided this question in no uncertain terms. In the case of a Japanese, Ozawa, in 1922, the court said in part:

Beginning with the decision of Circuit Judge Sawyer in *In re Ah Yup*, 5 Sawyer 155 (1878), the Federal and State courts in an almost unbroken line have held that the words "white persons" were meant to indicate only a person of what is popularly known as the Caucasian race.

The definition of the term was further clarified in 1923 in the case concerning a high-caste Hindu born in India who had been granted a certificate of citizenship in Oregon by the technicality of being a Caucasian. The Supreme Court stated "as a study of the literature dealing with racial questions will disclose, and while it [Caucasian] and the words 'white persons' are treated as synonymous for the purposes of the Ozawa case, they are not of identical meaning." The court held that the words are to be interpreted as synonymous with Caucasian only so far as that word is popularly understood, and therefore citizenship was denied to the Hindu. These

[1] *Congressional Globe*, 41st Cong., 2d Sess., p. 4284.

decisions, however, in no way affected the decision of the court in the case of Wong Kim Ark, a child born in California of Chinese parents (1897), when it established the right of citizenship by birth on American soil, regardless of race or descent. So that while Chinese and Japanese cannot be naturalized, they become citizens by virtue of birth. The Fourteenth Amendment, therefore, makes it impossible to deprive any person born in the United States of citizenship.[1]

In spite of a strong agitation in favor, no fundamental changes were made in the naturalization system until 1906, when the naturalization law revolutionized the whole process. While the act made no change in the period of residence preceding naturalization, it provided for elaborate machinery to eliminate fraud and to test with thoroughness the applicant's qualifications for citizenship.

Since the enactment of this law the tendency has been to guard more jealously the portals of citizenship, and at the same time more and more to judge the desirability of immigrant stocks by their eagerness to assume the responsibility of citizenship. That the assimilability of immigrants can be judged by naturalization statistics seems to be the popular opinion. This has resulted in a war of statistics, marshaled pro and con by partisans in the conflict. That this standard is faulty could probably be demonstrated by a searching study of the many factors that ought to be considered in determining the relative desirability; but the naturalization figures alone are inaccurate and misleading, as has been demonstrated by competent students.[2] Americans are not made

---

[1] For a digest of the cases cited in the text see J. W. Garner, "Recent Decisions of the United States Supreme Court affecting the Rights of Aliens," in *Journal of Comparative Legislation and International Law*, third series, Vol. VI, pp. 210-214 (November, 1924).

[2] See J. P. Gavit, *Americans by Choice*, pp. 197 ff.

by a hothouse system. The law naturalizes the old Adam; the heart may be naturalized before the immigrant leaves the land of his nativity. Any law that exerts pressure to stimulate naturalization is open to objection. A corrupt tree does not bring forth good fruit, and a good tree does not bring forth evil fruit. A Swedish immigrant of the forties was so impressed with the majesty of American citizenship that he refrained from active participation in politics. He was severely critical of the Germans and the Irish, who, he says, rushed into American affairs before they were familiar with conditions.[1]

I love the social order of a democracy, in which the people's majesty is truly a majesty in the presence of which one may have greater reverence than before a king's throne; and I believe that some day the American people, left to themselves, will reveal to the world this reverence, but when one sees European immigrants don the toga of democracy which on their shoulders is usually transformed into a fool's cloak; when one hears them speak of freedom and with a dictatorial mien pass judgment on public questions of great importance, of which the bulk of them know almost nothing, but are mere tools in the hands of politicians—then one can scarcely repress a smirk at the contemplation of what sort of republic the countries of Europe will find workable in the event that the modern apostles of freedom in those countries succeed in getting their principles adopted. Democracy in Europe will prove to be something different from American democracy.

With the exception of the races of Asia, and the negro down to 1870, immigrants have been admitted to American citizenship on most generous terms. To the layman it seems strange, not to say unjust, that high-caste Hindus and Orientals with college and university degrees should be barred.

[1] Gustaf Unonius, *Minnen från en sjuttonårig vistelse i Nordvestra Amerika* (Upsala, 1861, 1862), Vol. I, p. 335.

CHAPTER XIX

THE PROTECTION OF IMMIGRANTS

"If crosses and tomb stones could be erected on the water as on the western deserts, where they indicate the resting-places of white men killed by savages or by the elements, the routes of the emigrant vessels from Europe to America would long since have assumed the appearance of crowded cemeteries."[1]

The testimony of thousands of immigrants would have substantiated this gloomy statement, written in 1869 by a man who knew at first hand their experiences. The columns of the foreign-language papers, to say nothing of the English-language press, relate the experiences of individuals and groups who fell victims to the dishonesty and indifference of their fellowmen. The suffering, mental and physical, of some were so terrible that even a reminder of their voyage was a horror. Without sanitation, privacy, and moral safeguards until immigration had spanned many years, the number of victims of disease, insanity, and vice would be appalling if the facts were known. Sometimes the supply of food and water —all too frequently unfit for human consumption—was exhausted, leaving the immigrants for days on short rations or on no rations at all. In 1854 a select committee of the Senate prepared a circular containing fourteen questions relative to police and sanitary management of emigrant ships, copies of

[1] Friedrich Kapp, *European Emigration to the United States* (New York, 1869), pp. 20, 21.

which were sent to members of the medical profession, merchants, navigators, collectors of customs, presidents of benevolent societies, and others. The replies indicated that the diseases which particularly scourged the passengers were typhus, cholera, and smallpox. The causes of typhus were stated to be (1) the confinement of a number of people in apartments disproportioned to their requirements of wholesome respiration; (2) the retention in the same department of excretions from the bodies of individuals thus confined; (3) the exclusion of pure air.[1] The governor of New York in 1854 wrote in his message that the authorities were unable to account for the causes of the ravages of the mysterious disease cholera which had caused fearful loss of life on board a number of immigrant ships. Many of these ships, he said, bring over from Europe on each passage more than one thousand persons.

"Provide yourselves with food in case you are unable to eat the fare furnished on board ship," writes an immigrant in 1869 to her parents and relatives who are about to undertake the voyage to America. "When you land in America you will find many who will offer their services, but beware of them because there are so many rascals who make it a business to cheat the immigrants."[2] "It is a matter of almost daily observation by persons in the employ of the commission, that the frauds exposed in the report of the select committee, appointed last year 'to examine frauds upon emigrants,' continue to be practised with as much boldness and frequency as ever. A regular and systematic course of deception and fraud is continually in operation, whereby the

[1] *Senate Reports*, 33d Cong., 1st Sess., No. 386.
[2] *Yearbook of the Swedish Historical Society of America*, 1921–1922, pp. 94, 95.

emigrant is deprived of a large portion of the means intended to aid him in procuring a home in the country of his adoption," according to the report of the commissioners of emigration of the state of New York in 1847. The report of the following year states that many of the immigrant boarding-house keepers are as unscrupulous as the runners, in the advice they give to immigrants regarding routes to the interior and on matters connected with their sojourn in the city.[1]

The most dangerous of the sharks who infested Castle Garden and Ellis Island[2] were the countrymen of immigrants who by virtue of speaking their language were able more easily to insinuate themselves into their confidence. They cheated them in exchange, sent them to false destinations, lied to them about railway fares, and made impossible promises in order to deliver them into the hands of unscrupulous employers and land agents. The activities of the runners extended into the cities of the interior, to which immigrants flocked. At Chicago, for example, if the immigrants had railway tickets, they told them that these did not cover the transfer and transportation of baggage, and they warned them against the legitimate agents of railway companies.

The authorized agents of the railway companies were far from blameless in many cases. The railway companies ran immigrant trains on slow time or as extras, and they held themselves responsible for no particular time. The immigrants lived on hard, springless trucks for many days at their own expense, often without fire or water, owing to the neglect of employees who cared nothing for the "foreigners."

---

[1] *Annual Reports of the Commissioners of Emigration of the State of New York, from the Organization of the Commission May 5, 1847, to 1860, Inclusive*, etc. (New York, 1861).

[2] The immigrant station was transferred from Castle Garden to Ellis Island on January 1, 1892.

According to a report of a government inspector in 1871, the ticket agents received 15 per cent commission on tickets and 20 per cent on excess baggage charges, furnishing strong inducements to cheat, so that the charges for freight and baggage often exceeded the price of the tickets. "If Europe were to present us with 300,000 cattle per year, ample agencies would be employed to secure their proper protection and distribution," he wrote, "but thus far the general government has done but little to diminish the numerous hardships of an emigrant's position. . . . All legislation having for its purpose the good of the poor and lowly, will necessarily be opposed by those who make money off their ignorance and helplessness. . . . Since congress has assumed the power to protect the dumb cattle *in transitu* on railways, the power to protect passengers may be conceded. Yet all this extension of federal administrative influence is regarded with jealousy, and characterized as centralization."[1]

The protection of immigrants has been left pretty largely to states, cities, benevolent societies, racial organizations, churches, and foreign governments. Churches have maintained immigrant homes in cities like New York and Boston, where the immigrants not only receive the consolation of religion upon their arrival in a strange land but are assisted in various ways by pastors, sisters, and men and women especially trained for service. "I succeeded in getting a family to Chicago for eleven dollars, the regular fare being twenty-six, and today I persuaded a company to transport another by offering their effects for security," writes a missionary in 1865. "Some ask for bread, and I have been compelled to give what little I have until the supply is soon exhausted. I

[1] Report on Immigration etc., by J. Fred Meyers, in *Senate Executive Documents*, 42d Cong., 1st Sess., No. 73.

also write to their friends—for those who have them. . . .
I have received about $300 in exchange from different rela-
tives, the greater part of which has been disbursed to the
proper parties." Among the numerous organizations which
have ministered to immigrants may be mentioned the Sons of
the American Revolution, the Council of Jewish Women, the
International Committee of the Y.M.C.A., the Charitable
Irish Society, the German Society of New York, the Scandinavian Emigrant Aid Society, the National Catholic Welfare Council, and the American Legion.

In New York, where the vast majority of immigrants have
disembarked, the care and support of immigrants was left to
the general quarantine and poor laws or to local laws and
ordinances until 1847. With the rapidly increasing immigration in the forties these regulations proved inadequate, and
in 1847 a state board of commissioners of emigration was
created, consisting of nine members of whom six were appointed by the governor and three were members *ex officio*
by virtue of their positions as mayor of New York, president
of the Irish Immigrant Society, and president of the German
Immigrant Society. The states which established immigration commissions in order to stimulate immigration clothed
them with power, sometimes very inadequate, to give aid
and protection. The state legislature designated Castle Garden as the landing depot of all immigrants, a considerable
improvement over the open wharves, where the arrivals were
at the mercy of rapacious runners. The accommodations in
the Garden were meager enough, but at least a temporary
shelter was provided.

Prior to the Civil War the interest of the Federal government in the care and protection of immigrants was confined
to the enactment of laws designed to compel shipowners to

provide proper food and space and to correspondence with foreign governments to the same end. By the act of 1864 an immigrant office was established at New York in charge of a superintendent of immigration who should arrange for transportation for immigrants and protect them from fraud, but the appropriation was pitifully small. The law was repealed in 1868.

Petitions and memorials from state legislatures, immigrant societies, mass meetings, and the national immigration convention at Indianapolis in 1870 reminded the Federal authorities that there was a strong feeling among a considerable body of citizens that the time was ripe for Federal action.

In 1871 an official in the Treasury Department was instructed by his chief to visit the European countries which furnished the larger number of immigrants to ascertain and report on the conditions and character of immigrants.[1] The report recommended the establishment of an immigration bureau and an immigrant police court. No one thinks of dispensing with the Indian bureau, it said, though we have only three hundred thousand Indians in the United States, whereas nearly that number of immigrants arrives yearly on our shores. The machinery of the Federal courts was too slow, making it impossible for the immigrants to secure justice without unreasonably delaying the journey to their destination. These recommendations were followed by a special message from President Grant in 1872, asking for legislation along these lines. The immigrant does not know states or corporations, but confides in the protecting arms of the great free country of which he has heard so much, said the President.[2]

Federal immigration legislation has been primarily to protect the country from undesirable immigrants rather than to

[1] *Senate Executive Documents*, 42d Cong., 2d Sess., No. 72.   [2] Ibid. No. 73.

protect the immigrants. This is not to say that the immigrant has not profited greatly by legislation without special reference to him. His welfare has been promoted by the whole body of laws regulating interstate commerce and protecting the citizen.

It is to the states that the immigrants should feel grateful for laws establishing immigration bureaus, providing protection at ports of entry, regulating and creating employment bureaus, investigating housing conditions, regulating hours and conditions of labor, affording facilities for education, driving runners from the corridors of courtrooms, and the like.[1]

It must be remembered, however, that the protection of immigrants is a most difficult problem. The great majority come from small rural communities to the largest city in the world, ignorant of the English language and inexperienced in the ways of America. The reports of immigration commissions and welfare workers continue to relate the details of experiences which have blighted the hopes and aspirations of men and women who have come to share the blessings of the great republic.[2]

That conditions at Ellis Island might be improved is admitted by officials in the immigration service. Not only is the staff short-handed, but the facilities are not in every way adapted to conditions. This is a matter of concern to foreign governments as well. In 1922 in reply to questions in the House of Commons the undersecretary of foreign affairs stated that negotiations between Great Britain and the United States had been entered into with regard to the situation;

---

[1] See the chapter on "The Immigrant and the State," in Davis's *Immigration and Americanization*, pp. 440–496.

[2] See *Report of the Commission of Immigration of the State of New Jersey* (Trenton, 1914); Stanislaw Gutowski, "An Immigrant at the Crossroads," in *Scribner's Magazine*, Vol. LXXVII, pp. 185–192 (February, 1925).

and in the latter part of the year the British ambassador, at the invitation of the American Secretary of Labor, inspected the island. The ambassador's report lauded several features of the service and generously recognized the difficulties, but he saw considerable room for improvement. The buildings had been allowed to fall into a bad state; dirt had been allowed to accumulate; the sleeping-quarters did not provide proper moral safeguards; the quarters for medical inspection were badly accommodated; individuals were sometimes detained and kept in suspense for a considerable time. "After seeing Ellis Island and studying its problems," he concluded, "I believe that it is true to say that it is impossible to administer any immigration station under existing United States laws without hardship and tragedy. If a system could be devised which would prohibit persons desiring to come to the United States from sailing from Europe or elsewhere without the certainty of admission to the United States, the problem would be almost entirely solved. . . . It is quite certain that no other nation's immigration station has quite the same problem to solve, for the reason that the laws of the United States are not the same as those of any other nation."

It will be recalled that by limiting the number of immigration visas for each country the act of 1924 falls in with the ambassador's suggestion that a system be devised which prohibits persons from sailing from Europe without the certainty of admission to the United States. The first months' experience at Ellis Island under this law bears witness to the wisdom of this provision. "Ellis Island a gateway, not a hotel" is the aim of the officials.[1]

---

[1] Edith T. Bremer, "How the Immigration Law Works," in the *Survey*, January 15, 1925, pp. 441–445.

PART III. ORIENTAL IMMIGRATION

CHAPTER XX

THE CHINESE

If European emigration was a phenomenon of the nineteenth and twentieth centuries, Asiatic emigration may be a phenomenon of the future. Until the closing years of the last century China was "the sleeping giant" and "the hermit kingdom," but the present century knows of the "yellow peril" and the "menace of Asia." Even today it is doubtful if any considerable number of Americans have a clear understanding of the nature of the Oriental problem and know that we have a permanent and perhaps growing Asiatic population in our midst. A distinguished student of contemporary history has stated that the historian of the relations between the United States and China is confronted with a curious fact.

He has to recognize that the tale of the dealings of the American government with the Chinese Empire and with its inhabitants in their own homes is one story, and that of the treatment of Chinese immigrants to the land of liberty, by both government and people, is quite another. . . . In the first case the Americans can point with pride to their record; in the second they can feel no pride whatever; at best, they can fall back only on the plea of self-defence and of disagreeable necessity.[1]

[1] A. C. Coolidge, *The United States as a World Power*, p. 327.

The migration of the peaceful, industrious, sober, and adaptive Chinese to America began with the discovery of gold in California in 1848. These curious strangers were heartily welcomed because, at the time when everybody desired to find gold and people who were willing to perform the menial tasks of life were few, they satisfied a great need. With the beginning of the building of the Pacific railway during the Civil War Chinese coolies were imported to do the rough work of construction; and when in 1866 the Pacific Mail Steamship Company established direct communication between San Francisco and Hongkong, it was hailed as the beginning of a great development. Although the Chinese at first were welcomed because of their servile industry on railways, on fruit and vegetable farms, as laborers in certain kinds of industries, and as domestic servants, with the completion of the Pacific railway in 1869 laborers from the East began to arrive in large numbers on the Pacific coast, and hostility developed. In 1859 the California state superintendent of public instruction protested against the attempt to force "Africans, Chinese, and niggers" into white schools; and the following year a statute excluded them. Chinese were not allowed to testify in courts. In 1862 Congress prohibited the coolie trade. But thus far the hostility was largely localized on the Pacific coast, as the Burlingame Treaty of 1868 bears witness. By this treaty Chinese subjects visiting or residing in the United States should enjoy the same privileges, immunities, and exemptions in respect to travel or residence as might be enjoyed by citizens or subjects of the most favored nations, although the right of naturalization was denied them.

In California, however, the anti-Chinese agitation grew apace. In a riot at Los Angeles in 1871 fifteen Chinese were hanged; the same year the Federal Supreme Court decided that Chinese were not eligible to citizenship; and in 1876 both political parties adopted anti-Chinese planks in state platforms. The same year the California legislature appointed a committee of investigation, which rendered a violently anti-Chinese report of three hundred pages. The gentleman who presented the matter before a congressional committee said: "The Chinese are inferior to any race God ever made. These people have got the perfection of crimes of 4000 years. . . . I believe the Chinese have no souls to save, and if they have, they are not worth saving." About the same time a congressional committee report, based on insufficient and biased testimony, denounced the Chinese.

In 1877 the hatred of the Chinese took the form of the "sand lot" agitation, led by a demagogue named Denis Kearney. At this time California was in the grip of hard times, and labor felt the pinch of poverty. It needed only a spellbinder of the Kearney type, ably assisted by the newspapers, to lash the people into a fury against the Orientals, who were said to be depriving the American workingman of what little employment there was. On a large open space on the west side of San Francisco, called the sand lot, Kearney's "oratory" attracted the discontented part of the population, whose ranks were soon swelled by the more respectable element of citizens. "Like Cato with his *Delenda est Carthago*," says Lord Bryce, "Kearney ended every speech with the words, 'And whatever happens, the Chinese must go.'" Kearneyism was only one of many tributaries to a great stream of discontent which gave California a new constitution, submitted to the people in May, 1879, containing provisions forbidding all corporations to employ Chinese, debarring them from suffrage, forbidding their employment on public works, annulling all contracts for coolie labor, directing the legislature to provide punishment of any company importing Chinese, and imposing conditions on the residence of Chinese.[1]

The agitation against the Chinese was beginning to assume a more widespread significance; in the East, notably in Massachusetts and Pennsylvania, Oriental labor was being imported to break strikes. In 1875 a Federal law prohibited the importation of Chinese women for immoral purposes and of Chinese convicts; the importation of Chinese and Japanese without free and voluntary consent for the purpose of holding them to a term of service was made punishable by imprisonment or a heavy fine; and the importation of coolie labor was made a felony.

This measure was followed in 1879 by a bill abrogating the Burlingame Treaty of 1868. The bill was supported by Western and Southern senators and representatives, was opposed generally by Republicans, and was vetoed by President Hayes. "Up to this time [1868] our uncovenanted hospitality to immigration, our fearless liberality of citizenship, our equal and comprehensive justice to all inhabitants, whether they abjured their foreign nationality or not, our civil freedom, our religious toleration had made all comers welcome, and under these protections the Chinese in considerable numbers had made their lodgment upon our soil," said the President. The Burlingame Treaty was a great advance toward opening China to our civilization and religion and gave great promise for the future, he continued. The developments since 1868 may necessitate a revision of the treaty, but we should do nothing to wound the pride of "a polite and sensitive people." He regarded the grave dis-

[1] See the interesting chapter on "Kearneyism in California," in James Bryce's *American Commonwealth* (New York, 1914), Vol. II, pp. 426-448.

content of the people of the Pacific coast with the workings of Chinese immigration as deserving the most serious attention of the people of the whole country, but he denied the power of Congress to abrogate the treaty. Mr. Hayes feared the effect of the immediate withdrawal of the treaty upon the Chinese already in this country and upon American merchants and missionaries in China.

Under the Hayes administration, however, a new treaty with China was negotiated in 1880. The Chinese government agreed to allow the American government to regulate, limit, or suspend Chinese immigration whenever the American government deemed it necessary for the protection of its interests, but in no case absolutely to prohibit it. The treaty was specific on the point that the limitation or suspension should be reasonable and applicable to Chinese coming as laborers.

How far the Chinese question had entered politics at this time may be seen in the forged letter which represented Garfield, the Republican presidential candidate in 1880, as deprecating the agitation against Chinese labor. This document was circulated by the Democrats in order to discredit Garfield on the Pacific coast. Whatever may have been the effect of the Democratic tactics, only one Republican elector out of nine in California and Nevada was chosen.

Foiled by one executive veto, Congress was not to be denied the right to exclude the Chinese. Accordingly, in 1882, immigration was suspended for twenty years. This bill encountered the veto of another Republican president, Chester A. Arthur, who wrote in his message that a nation is justified in repudiating its treaty obligations only when they are in conflict with great paramount interests. He quoted from interviews between American and Chinese commissioners when the treaty of 1880 was drawn. The Chinese stated what they understood by "prohibit, limit, or suspend." The American commissioners explained that it might never be necessary to exercise this power, and that if the problem became acute in one section of the country Chinese immigration might be diverted to some other section. In the judgment of the President a twenty-year suspension was an unreasonable interpretation of the treaty. In regard to the provision of the bill which required passports and personal registration, since they were not required of other immigrants and were undemocratic, Mr. Arthur thought it ought to be omitted. He suggested a shorter period of suspension, and, taking him at his word, Congress passed a bill reducing the term to ten years. This law, as it proved, established the permanent exclusion of the Chinese.

The Chinese minister at Washington protested, and a Chinaman brought a test case in the courts in 1883. The judgment of the court was that although the act was in contravention of the treaties of 1868 and 1880 it was not on that account invalid, because a treaty can be repealed or modified at the pleasure of Congress. The court disclaimed the right of censuring the morals of the other departments of the government.

Subsequent legislation has tightened up the restrictions, requiring all Chinese in the United States to take out certificates, so that the authorities might know their whereabouts. Those found without certificates were liable to deportation. In 1894, at the request of China, a new treaty was negotiated. It provided for the exclusion of all Chinese laborers for ten years and allowed returning emigrants to reënter the country provided they had a wife, a child, or a parent, or property worth $1000 in the United States. The law of 1902 reënacted all existing laws and was to continue in force until a new treaty should be ratified. Upon the refusal of China to continue the treaty of 1894, Congress in 1904 continued all laws then in force and included the insular possessions within their scope.

In reviewing the legislation with reference to the Chinese certain facts stand out boldly. All but one of the measures were passed on the eve of an election, showing that the question was the football of party politics. Moreover, this is legislation in contravention of a treaty, and it has brought protests from the Chinese government and individuals and precipitated anti-American demonstrations, the most serious of the latter being the Chinese boycott of American goods in 1905, which "proved that, throughout China, there now exists a national resentment against the way in which the Chinese have been treated in the United States."[1] The Chinese minister stated to Secretary of State Bayard, "I was not prepared to learn that there was a way recognized in the law and practice in this country whereby your country could release itself from treaty obligations without the consultation or consent of the other party." With the development of means of communication in China, the knowledge of American discrimination and treatment will be disseminated and the problem of the American government may become grave. The economic boycott is loaded with great possibilities.

Many Americans have protested against the policy of their own government and people, and American judges have condemned the procedure in specific cases. For example, in the case of a Chinese sentenced to deportation in 1915 a judge declared that the essential safeguards of liberty were ignored: the prisoner was not allowed to see any of the witnesses

[1] A. C. Coolidge, *The United States as a World Power*, p. 338.

against him while they were testifying; all testimony against him was taken behind his back; and the prisoner was denied counsel. The fact that the Chinese are undesirable from many points of view does not justify brutality or injustice. Star Chamber proceedings in the case of one class of individuals may in the end affect other classes.

America stands in a peculiar relation to China. Our high-minded treatment of her after the Boxer uprising, the enlightened policy during the years when John Hay was Secretary of State (1898–1905), and the work of American missionaries have placed the American people and government so high in the esteem of China that we cannot afford to be dragged down. There is, however, no immediate prospect that the attitude of the Pacific coast will be abandoned. In the words of a California editor:

> The Pacific coast is the frontier of the white man's world, the culmination of the westward immigration which is the white man's whole history. It will remain the frontier so long as we guard it as such; no longer. Unless it is maintained there, there is no other line at which it can be maintained without more effort than the American government and American civilization are able to sustain.[1]

Oriental immigration has profoundly affected our whole immigration policy. In the debates on the drastic restriction provisions of the bills in 1924 the favorite method of disarming those who condemned the discrimination against the peoples of southern and eastern Europe was to inquire if the speaker was opposed to the exclusion of Orientals. The reply, invariably in the negative, was, of course, turned to the disadvantage of the speaker's argument.

[1] *The Outlook*, January 14, 1911.

In spite of legislation there has been considerable smuggling of Chinese across the Mexican and Canadian borders. Undoubtedly American officials have difficulty in detecting the transfer of certificates from one Chinaman to another, so that a Chinaman returning to his native land is succeeded by another whose entry is unlawful. In order to detect these individuals—and the Chinese are expert smugglers—American officials have employed methods bordering on brutality, and sometimes refined gentlemen, students, and distinguished visitors, have been grievously offended.

Regardless of provocation, the treatment of some Chinese residents, lawfully admitted before the exclusion policy went into effect, has been disgraceful. According to a former Chinese minister, "More Chinese subjects have been murdered by mobs in the United States during the last twenty-five years than all the Americans who have been murdered in China in similar riots."[1]

The policy of our government with reference to European immigration stands in sharp contrast with our Oriental-immigration legislation. An alien population localized on the Pacific coast and affecting directly but a small portion of the American people has vexed our diplomatists and legislators and has from time to time threatened to bring serious discomfiture to American missionaries and men of affairs.

[1] Quoted by A. C. Coolidge, *The United States as a World Power*, p. 336.

CHAPTER XXI

THE JAPANESE

"One of the saddest events in the history of the world is the estrangement of Japan and the United States."[1] These are the words of a discerning Japanese-American student of American-Japanese relations, and the judgment is substantially correct. The situation has come about from apparently irresistible forces. The estrangement has come since about 1900, when as the result of the Chino-Japanese War (1894–1895) and the Spanish-American War (1898), the two nations became rivals in the Pacific. In a certain sense the immigration problem is secondary, because it would not be so acute were it not for the larger considerations which have intensified the feeling between the two peoples.

Japanese immigration began about the time the Chinese Exclusion Law went into effect, in 1882. Before that time little was known about the Japanese in the United States. In 1860 a Japanese embassy visited the country and was accorded an enthusiastic reception from President Buchanan and in many cities throughout the country, including San Francisco. It is true that the tour was marred by some untoward incidents which greatly offended the visitors. Some uncouth Americans ridiculed and insulted them, and a California paper, commenting on the cost of their entertainment in Philadelphia and New York, said that the latter city "cannot afford to clean the streets, . . . but can spend $100,000

[1] K. K. Kawakami, *Japan in World Politics*, p. 1.

for the entertainment of a parcel of Japanese monkeys."[1] On the whole, however, when the Japanese immigrants began coming in the eighties their virtues were praised. With the cessation of Chinese immigration the need for cheap labor was felt; and it was said that the newcomers were cleaner and more attractive than the Chinese, that they came from a better class, and that they adopted American ways sooner.

But as their numbers increased, the Californians grew increasingly critical, and it became the fashion to compare the virtues and faults of the Japanese and Chinese, usually to the detriment of the former. The Japanese, unlike the Chinese, were not content to remain in inferior positions; they aspired to greater things and wanted to be treated as equals. They became business competitors. Unwilling to remain in segregated districts, they purchased or leased desirable business sites and moved their families into the better residential districts, causing the Americans to move away and take financial losses on their property. As farmers they proved not only efficient but aggressive, purchasing and leasing farms. It is contended on behalf of the Japanese that this menace is greatly exaggerated; that the total value and acreage of Japanese landholdings in proportion to the total value and acreage of the entire state is insignificant.[2] The people of California, however, maintain that while the acreage is relatively small, the effect is great, because the Japanese are segregated in the most fertile sections and remain "foreign" in all respects, creating friction and agitation.

The annexation of Hawaii and the Philippines was disappointing to Japan, and in the case of Hawaii a formal protest was made at Washington. For many years Japanese immi-

[1] *Semi-Weekly Southern News* (Los Angeles), July 25, 1860.
[2] K. K. Kawakami, *Japan in World Politics*, p. 75.

grants had been coming to Hawaii, and the annexation by the United States shattered the dream of a Japanese Hawaii.[1] Then came the Russo-Japanese War. At the beginning of this great conflict American sympathy was overwhelmingly with Japan, but there came a sudden reversal of feeling from rather natural causes. In Japan it was charged that the treaty of Portsmouth, which was not so favorable as the Japanese anticipated, was framed to a considerable extent under pressure from President Roosevelt. These developments coming at the time when the immigration question was becoming acute, raised a rough diplomatic sea.

Before 1900 labor unions and others in California had protested against Japanese immigration, and in 1898 W. M. Rice, an American commissioner of immigration, was sent to Japan to investigate the causes of emigration. In two letters to the commissioner-general of immigration he made what may be called a report, not at all complimentary to the Japanese. He says they are tricky, deceitful, immoral, and un-Christian and that American writers have greatly exaggerated their progress. They have a childlike attachment to the United States, but a very superficial understanding of the American people and their institutions. In his judgment the emigration societies in Japan and business men in America were largely responsible for emigration.[2]

On the heels of this came messages from the governor's office and resolutions from the legislature of California calling on Congress to extend the Exclusion Law to other Asiatics. Then came something like the sand-lot agitation of the seventies. In 1905 the *San Francisco Chronicle* published a series of convincing articles against the Japanese. In May of that

[1] A. C. Coolidge, *The United States as a World Power*, p. 346.
[2] *House Documents*, 56th Cong., 1st Sess., No. 686.

year the Asiatic Exclusion League was organized. The following year the country was excited by the widespread publicity given to the exclusion of the Japanese from white schools. The reason given for this action was that the presence of adult Japanese in the grades had a pernicious moral influence upon the children; but this, according to some, was a mere pretext; it was only another manifestation of the economic and racial antipathy. After the terrible San Francisco earthquake in the spring of 1906 the less responsible elements of society reaped a harvest for a time; and until law and order were restored the racial situation grew steadily worse.

The California Japanese protested against this treatment and appealed to the Japanese government, a circumstance which has given a most dangerous aspect to the whole problem. As we have seen, the American people insist that immigration is exclusively an affair of their own, to be settled without consulting any other government. Japan, while admitting the American claim, is very jealous of her national honor and insists that her government and citizens must be accorded the respect which other nations demand. Her attitude on the right of immigration is perhaps influenced unconsciously by the ethical conception that a people inhabiting a sparsely settled and rich territory ought not to exclude people who are living in a cramped and poverty-ridden portion of the globe. But the sore point with Japan is the matter of discrimination. She objects to having any government point its finger at her and declare, "Your people must not come because they are Japanese!"

At this time the Japanese, flushed with the victories of the war with Russia, were in no mood to be trifled with. The Federal government was embarrassed because of the dual nature of our government. Although foreign statesmen probably understand the division of power between state and Federal governments, foreign peoples generally do not. A controversy may assume such huge proportions that a foreign government with the best of intentions may not be able to weather the storm of public opinion. In 1891 the relations between the United States and Italy were strained to the breaking point over the lynching of Italian citizens in New Orleans. In reply to the protest of the Italian government Secretary of State Blaine stated that the Federal government was bound by treaty to protect Italian citizens only in so far as it could protect its own citizens, and that the courts were open to all citizens. The Italian government pressed the claim; and its ambassador hinted that unless immediate action was taken, he would withdraw. To this Mr. Blaine made the sharp retort: "I do not recognize the right of any government to tell the United States what it shall do. We have never received orders from any foreign power and shall not begin now. It is a matter of indifference what persons in Italy think of our institutions. I cannot change them, still less violate them." Although diplomatic relations were severed, the affair was settled peacefully. What the outcome would have been had the controversy concerned a government more powerful and aggressive and more favorably situated for hostile action than Italy, one can only conjecture.

In the case of Japan the problem has been further complicated by the introduction of bills and amendments to general immigration bills to exclude Japanese. The Japanese government has vigorously protested against these proposals, and the executive department of our government has with difficulty restrained the radicals in Congress.

At the time of the controversy in 1906 President Roosevelt had to steer a most difficult course. In a message to Congress and in public utterances he denounced the discrimination against the Japanese and sent a member of his cabinet to investigate the situation, but at the same time he made it plain that he was not to be intimidated by either party. To their credit it must be said that the American and Japanese statesmen kept their heads, realizing the difficulties which faced the respective governments. On their side the Japanese officials knew that the United States would not yield to a threat of force, and they recognized the good intentions of President Roosevelt. Furthermore, the Japanese government was not especially anxious to have its subjects go to foreign lands, preferring rather to divert them to Formosa, Korea, and Manchuria. The settlement which grew out of the strained relations is known as the Root-Takahira agreement, but is more commonly called the gentlemen's agreement of 1907.

The essential terms of the gentlemen's agreement were stated publicly in a letter of Ambassador Hanihara to Secretary of State Hughes in April, 1924, at the time when the House of Representatives had before it the immigration bill of 1924 proposing to abrogate the agreement and to exclude the Japanese by statute.

The gentlemen's agreement is an understanding with the United States government by which the Japanese government voluntarily undertook to adopt certain administrative measures designed to check the emigration to the United States of Japanese laborers. It is in no way intended as a restriction on the sovereign right of the United States to regulate its immigration. This is shown by the fact that the existing immigration act of 1917, for instance, applied to Japanese as to other aliens.

It was because of the fact that discriminatory immigration legislation on the part of the United States would, naturally, wound the national susceptibilities of the Japanese people that, after thorough but most friendly and frank discussions between the two governments, the gentlemen's agreement was made for the purpose of relieving the United States from the possible unfortunate necessity of offending the national pride of a friendly nation.

The Japanese government agreed not to issue passports good for continental United States to laborers, skilled or unskilled (except those previously domiciled in the United States), nor to their parents, their wives, or their children under twenty years of age. Although the Hawaiian Islands were not originally included, the Japanese government, according to the statement of its ambassador, enforced practically the same procedure in that case.

The Pacific coast insisted that the agreement was not kept in good faith by the Japanese, and figures were marshaled to show a considerable annual immigration. The "picture brides"—wives secured by Japanese residents in America by a "long-distance" marriage ceremony—were especially objectionable. The sentiment against this practice was so strong that after March 1, 1920, Japan issued no passports to immigrants of this type. Upon its own word Japan also exercised strict control over the emigration of laborers to countries contiguous to the United States in order to prevent smuggling across the borders.

It appears, therefore, that the Japanese government tried to conciliate the United States; but the difficulty lay in the fact that the enforcement of its terms depended entirely on the good faith of one nation, and, rightly or wrongly, the people on the coast questioned that good faith. Moreover, the race question persists because of the birth of Japanese children, although authorities and would-be authorities differ widely as to the rate of increase of the Japanese population in America.

isfy, if for no other reason than the temper of American public opinion. Undoubtedly the fear that immigration might come under the jurisdiction of the League of Nations played no inconsiderable part in discrediting it before the Senate and the people. In October, 1920, thirty-six Democratic senators voted for a reservation providing that the United States was not required to submit to the League any matter, including immigration, which it considered a domestic question. All the senators from the Pacific coast and Far-Western states voted for similar reservations. Senator Phelan of California said that if the other members of the League took the position that immigration or naturalization came under the jurisdiction of the League, neither the United States nor Great Britain would be able to protect itself.

In the latter part of 1920 the California legislature adopted an anti-alien land law designed to "put teeth" into the law of 1913. The act was submitted to the people for ratification and carried by a decisive vote. It forbids the ownership or leasing of land by aliens ineligible to citizenship and the purchase of land by American-born children of such aliens under their parents' guardianship. When such aliens already own land, the law removes parents as guardians of their own children. Aliens of this class are also forbidden to hold stock in American landholding corporations. Although the Japanese are not mentioned by name in this act, it was understood that it was directed at them. In May, 1922, the California supreme court declared the measure unconstitutional on three grounds: First, it violates the treaty between the United States and Japan. Secondly, it violates the Fourteenth Amendment of the Federal Constitution, which forbids a state to abridge the privileges or immunities of citizens of the United States. Thirdly, it violates an article of the constitution of California similar in purpose to the Fourteenth Amendment. Commenting on the decision of the court, the *San Francisco Chronicle* expressed itself as follows: "Obviously we would not set up our judgment in legal matters in opposition to the learned justices of the supreme court, but we are constrained to wonder how they reconcile this particular decision with the ancient legal maxim that no person shall be permitted to do indirectly that which he is by law prohibited from doing directly." In October, 1923, the Federal Supreme Court reversed the decision, holding that the legislation in question was neither in violation of the treaty with Japan nor contrary to the Federal Constitution.

Speaking generally, the gentlemen's agreement was accepted as a satisfactory solution of the Japanese-immigration problem throughout the country with the exception of the Pacific coast. In season and out the Westerners demanded the abrogation of the agreement and the exclusion of the immigrants by statute. The California Oriental Exclusion League, not content with demanding the cancellation of the gentlemen's agreement and the exclusion of picture brides, has urged that Asiatics shall be forever barred from American citizenship and that no children born of foreign parents shall be considered American citizens unless both parents are of a race eligible to citizenship.

When the general-immigration bill was introduced in Congress in 1923–1924, there was a strong sentiment in the House of Representatives in favor of excluding Japanese by statute, but very few expected that the measure would pass the Senate. This, however, was brought about by the ill-advised and indiscreet communication of the Japanese ambassador addressed to the American Secretary of State, in which it was stated very candidly that the enactment of the proposed measure would inevitably bring "grave consequences." Not only did the House adopt the measure, but with very little opposition the Senate, resenting the "menacing" attitude of the Japanese government, adopted it over the protest of the Secretary of State. It is difficult to understand why the Japanese ambassador departed from the proverbial courtesy for which his people and government are distinguished and addressed a communication calculated to wound the pride of the American people. On the other hand, it must be admitted that the policy of our legislators is difficult to fathom. By including the Japanese under the quota system, the number of Japanese admissible annually would have been only one hundred and forty-six, thus effectively excluding them and salving the feelings of the Japanese nation by allowing the gentlemen's agreement to stand. It is true that the quota basis in the act of 1924 is subject to change; and there might have been some ground for the fear expressed by congressmen that in the future the doors might have been opened wider to the Japanese, thus reopening the controversy. Speaking on the report of the conference committee on May 8, Senator Borah of Idaho stated:

So far as I am interested in this question I should not want it to turn upon the question that 67 Japanese, more or less, may come into the country between now and the 1st of March. That is not a serious proposition at all, to my mind; but there are two propositions involved in it which, it seems to me, are very serious. The first is the one . . . that we do by this procedure recognize the right of a foreign government to be heard when we propose to exclude certain people from our shores. Secondly, as I understand, now, for the first time, the conferees admit the quota principle with reference to Japan.

At the urgent request of President Coolidge and Secretary Hughes the conference committee agreed to postpone the effective date of the provision excluding the Japanese until

March 1, 1925, "before which time the President is requested
to negotiate with the Japanese Government in relation to the
abrogation of the present arrangement on this subject." This
action precipitated a most acrimonious debate in both Houses.
Mr. King of Utah, a Democrat, one of the Senate conferees,
stated on the floor of the Senate that he supported the provision "knowingly and was influenced very largely by my
knowledge of the wishes of the President of the United
States. . . . When a subject is presented by the Executive
department dealing with the relations between our government and other governments I shall, in so far as I can,
support the President, whether he be a Democrat or a
Republican."

The debate in both Houses revealed most strenuous objection to any recognition of the immigration question as a
proper subject for international negotiations. In the language of the leader of the Democratic minority in the Senate,
"If we recognize the right of Japan to stipulate the conditions
upon which Japanese can come into the United States we will
be confronted immediately with the demand from other nations which have equal rights to the same recognition."
Senator Johnson of California, a rival of President Coolidge
for the Republican nomination for president, called attention
to the fact that "between now and next March there will be
40,000 Japanese bachelors now resident in the state of California" who will return to Japan in quest of "kankodan"
brides, thereby eventually increasing the Japanese population of the country by 240,000.

In the House the chairman of the committee on immigration, Mr. Johnson of Washington, and others pleaded in vain
for compliance with the President's request. The possibility
of an executive veto; the desirability of extending courtesy

to a nation with which our relations in the past had been cordial and intimate; the danger of international complications; the small number of Japanese who could be admitted in the interval—all fell on the deaf ears of a majority, and the provision of the conference committee was recommitted by a vote of 191 to 171.[1]

In the effort to stave off any action that might cause international complications the President and the Secretary of State conferred further with the conferees, but they were informed that any proposal to extend the effective date of exclusion beyond July 1, 1924—the time fixed in the bill passed by Congress—would be overwhelmingly defeated. The upshot of it all was the adoption of the report of the conference committee in both Houses by majorities which indicated that the presidential veto would be overridden.[2]

It is fortunate that the Japanese problem in the United States is identical with that of the British Empire. Canada, Australia, and New Zealand are determined that their territory must remain "a white man's country." The people of these colonies bitterly resented the Anglo-Japanese alliance. In the words of a British weekly, *The Spectator*,

If the people of Australia and New Zealand were asked which side they were going to be on in a war between America and Japan they would not hesitate a second. They would not waste time in reading diplomatic papers or considering legal points. . . . There could be only one place for Canada in a finish fight between Japan and America—by the side of America, while South Africans would have the same answer. Nor would that be all. The moment they

---

[1] The debates and votes are found in the *Congressional Record* for May 8 and 9, 1924.

[2] May 15, 1924. The House vote was 308 to 58, or 64 in excess of the two-thirds majority to override the veto; in the Senate it was 69 to 9, or 17 more than two thirds.

realized what had happened, 99 per cent of the population would be stoning their own government for the criminal lunacy of backing Japan against their own flesh and blood.

The enthusiastic reception accorded the American battle fleet in Australian waters on its memorable cruise around the world in 1908–1909, just after the storm which preceded the gentlemen's agreement, and the tone of the press on that continent would indicate that the people claim the American fleet as their own in a conflict between the brown and white races.

In spite of the recent turn of events, which is indeed ominous, there are hopeful signs on the horizon. In 1915 the Federal Council of the Churches of Christ in America sent Dr. Shailer Mathews and Dr. Sidney L. Gulick to Japan to study the relations between Japan and America and to promote better relations. They found much hostility to America and learned that in some quarters a war was regarded as inevitable; but they also discerned signs of encouragement. According to these gentlemen it was the prevailing sentiment that Japan would welcome the expatriation of Japanese in America if the right of naturalization were extended to them.[1] The work of Christian missionaries in Japan also is promoting a better understanding. This optimism is not shared by the people of the Pacific coast, who claim that the Japanese maintain their own schools, where their language and loyalty to the emperor are taught; where the teachers are often Buddhist priests who, in order to resist Americanization, teach loyalty to Buddhism. Naturalization would be a mere formality, it is said, because the Japanese will forever remain alien in spirit. The fact that in the past the

[1] In 1924 the Japanese government formally recognized the right of expatriation.

Japanese have looked to their home government for protection undoubtedly prolongs their attachment to it. Resolutions from legislatures, chambers of commerce, American Legion posts, labor organizations, and various organizations on the Pacific coast hardly indicate a more friendly feeling toward Orientals.

It is true, however, that after the glow of indignation had paled, the American press felt that the senators had acted like schoolboys in response to the note of the Japanese ambassador. "When you can have your own way only by insulting another nation, there is perhaps a good deal to be said in favor of insulting it," said a Middle-Western editor. "But when you can have your own way exactly as well by not insulting it, there is then just nothing to be said in favor of insulting it." The explanatory note of the Japanese ambassador, which disclaimed any intention of a "veiled threat" may have convinced editors of Japan's sincere desire to maintain friendly relations. The fact that Secretary of State Hughes favored the continuance of the gentlemen's agreement and did not resent the Japanese note may have weighed even more heavily. Our presidents and secretaries of state have usually been far more conscious of the necessity and advisability of courtesy in dealing with foreign nations that have our congresses.

Judging by the tone of the Japanese press, the action of Congress was deeply resented. "Americans must know that we shall never cease quarreling with America so long as anti-Japanese clauses are not removed," was the sentiment of one editorial writer. At this writing it seems certain that the people of Japan will never willingly submit to the exclusion of Japanese immigrants by statute. That the American people will sustain the action of Congress, once taken, in an armed

conflict with Japan is equally certain. Whether the controversy will ever reach that stage is for the diplomatists to
answer. The time may come when public opinion in Japan
will become too insistent for any cabinet to ignore. The
words of the American Secretary of State in his letter to
the chairman of the house committee on immigration are
significant:

I regret to be compelled to say that I believe such legislative action would largely undo the work of the Washington Conference on
Limitation of Armament, which so greatly improved our relations
with Japan. The manifestation of American interest and generosity
in providing relief to the sufferers from the recent earthquake disaster in Japan would not avail to diminish the resentment which
would follow the enactment of such a measure, as this enactment
would be regarded as an insult not to be palliated by any act of
charity. It is useless to argue whether or not such a feeling would
be justified; it is quite sufficient to say that it would exist.[1]

The future will determine whether or not the American
and Japanese people are to pull farther away from each other.
At the present time it appears that church bodies are the most
potent voice of protest against the action of Congress. Ringing protests have already come from distinguished religious
leaders and from church organizations. The comfort in the
situation comes from the attitude of these organizations
and from level-headed individuals in both countries; the
uneasiness arises from the fact that in the past jingoes and
self-seekers have goaded nations into bloody combats over
disputes less irritating than the one which makes for discord
in the relations between America and Japan.

[1] Letter dated February 8, 1924.

PART IV. SELECT BIBLIOGRAPHY

BIBLIOGRAPHICAL AIDS

The material for a history of American immigration is so voluminous and scattered that a book of this character can list only a
few of the more important and easily accessible titles. The student
who aspires to an exhaustive study of the subject will begin by
consulting bibliographies and bibliographical aids, which may be
conveniently found in CHANNING, HART, and TURNER's *Guide to
the Study and Reading of American History* (1912), chap. iii.
A. P. C. GRIFFIN's *List of Books with References to Periodicals on
Immigration* (3d issue, 1907) is indispensable. PHILIP DAVIS's
Immigration and Americanization (1920) has a select list of
bibliographies, briefs, books, pamphlets, and magazine articles.
A. B. GREENE and F. A. GOULD's *Handbook-Bibliography on Foreign Language Groups in the United States and Canada* (1925)
gives a useful bibliography for each group and in addition data,
statistics, and brief sketches. In some of the books dealing with
individual immigrant stocks and special phases of immigration can
be found useful lists.

GENERAL: SOURCE MATERIAL AND MONOGRAPHS

The results of the most extensive and thorough survey of the
whole subject of immigration are embodied in the *Reports of the
Immigration Commission, appointed under the Act of Congress,
February 20, 1907* (42 vols., 1911). This is the so-called Dillingham Report, published in *Senate Documents*, 61st Congress. The
reports of the Secretary of State, of the Secretary of the Treasury,
of the Secretary of Commerce and Labor, of the Secretary of

Labor, and the Commissioner of L'bor, and the reports of commissions and committees, as well a, petitions and memorials,—all published in the *Congressional Documents*,—are indispensable. For statistics of population, naturalization, etc. see the census reports. Two monographs published by the Census Bureau are especially illuminating: *A Century of Population Growth from the First Census of the United States to the Twelfth, 1790–1900* (1909); W. S. Rossiter, *Increase of Population in the United States, 1910–1920* (Census Monographs I, 1922). In the *Report of the Commissioner-General of Immigration for the Year ending June 30, 1907* are published graphs showing immigration for eighty-eight years. A later compilation is *United States Bureau of Foreign and Domestic Commerce. One Hundred Years of American Immigration* (Daily Consular and Trade Reports, No. 254, 1919). A *Monograph on Immigration in the 19th Century* is printed in *House Executive Documents*, 49th Cong., 2d Sess., Vol. XXIV, No. 157. H. H. Laughlin's *Europe as an Emigrant-Exporting Continent and the United States as an Immigrant-Receiving Nation*, in *House Documents*, 68th Cong., 2d Sess., series 5A, is abundantly illustrated with charts.

General: Secondary Works

A number of books dealing with immigration generally have been written, but they approach the problem from the standpoint of the sociologist, the economist, and the special investigator. Among the most valuable of these are the following: R. Mayo Smith, *Emigration and Immigration* (1890); J. W. Jenks and W. J. Lauck, *The Immigration Problem* (1917); H. P. Fairchild, *Immigration* (1917); S. P. Orth, *Our Foreigners* (1920); J. R. Commons, *Races and Immigrants in America* (1907); E. A. Ross, *The Old World in the New* (1914); P. Roberts, *The New Immigration* (1912); E. A. Steiner, *On the Trail of the Immigrant* (1906); P. F. Hall, *Immigration and its Effects upon the United States* (1906); F. J. Warne, *The Immigrant Invasion* (1913).

GENERAL: ARTICLES IN PERIODICALS

Excellent charts and graphs are printed in the *Round Table*, Vol. II, pp. 241–273; in the *National Geographic Magazine*, Vol. XXVI, pp. 265–274; and in the *Journal of the Royal Statistical Society*, Vol. XLVII, pp. 496–516. JAMES BRYCE's "Migrations of Races of Men Historically Considered," in the *Contemporary Review*, Vol. LXII, pp. 128–149, is stimulating.

GENERAL: CAUSES AND EUROPEAN BACKGROUND

For an account of conditions in the various countries the following are the most satisfactory: *Reports of the Immigration Commission*, 42 vols. (*Senate Documents*, 61st Cong.); *Consular Reports*, 1886, 1887 (*House Executive Documents*, 49th Cong., 2d Sess., No. 157). The following books have general accounts: R. MAYO SMITH, *Emigration and Immigration*, pp. 12–52; F. J. WARNE, *The Immigrant Invasion*, pp. 1–52, 200–254; P. F. HALL, *Immigration and its Effects upon the United States*, pp. 14–35; F. A. OGG, *Social Progress in Contemporary Europe* (1912). Three illuminating studies are T. C. BLEGEN's "The Competition of the Northwestern States for Immigrants," in the *Wisconsin Magazine of History*, Vol. III, pp. 3–29; L. APPEL and T. C. BLEGEN's "Official Encouragement of Immigration to Minnesota during the Territorial Period," in the *Minnesota History Bulletin*, Vol. V, pp. 167–203; M. L. HANSON's "Official Encouragement of Immigration to Iowa," in the *Iowa Journal of History and Politics*, Vol. XIX, pp. 159–195. Among the articles in periodicals the following are recommended: W. B. BAILEY, "The Bird of Passage," in the *American Journal of Sociology*, Vol. XVIII, pp. 391 ff.; H. P. FAIRCHILD, "Immigration and Crises," in the *American Economic Review*, Vol. I, pp. 735–765; F. A. OGG, "Stimulated Emigration," in the *World Today*, Vol. X, pp. 418–424.

SPECIAL GROUPS: EUROPEAN BACKGROUND, CAUSES, AND
CHARACTERISTICS

The United Kingdom

S. C. JOHNSON's *History of Emigration from the United King-dom to North America, 1763–1912* (1913) is the best account of the whole subject and contains an exhaustive bibliography. J. VAN DER ZEE's *The British in Iowa* (1922), Part I, deals with the background. Important source material is found in *Hansard's Parliamentary Debates*, in *Reports of the Poor Law Commissioners*, and in *Reports of the House of Commons Committees on Immigration and Colonization*. Important articles are printed in the *Nineteenth Century*, the *Contemporary Review*, the *Edinburgh Review*, the *Quarterly Review*, and the *Fortnightly Review*. E. G. WAKE-FIELD's *England and America. A Comparison of the Social and Political State of both Nations* (2 vols., 1833) is a graphic picture of the distress of the people. The letters of an English immigrant of the forties, a representative of the hard-working middle class, are edited by M. M. QUAIFE, *An English Settler in Pioneer Wisconsin. The Letters of Edwin Bottomley, 1842–1850.* (Collections of the State Historical Society of Wisconsin, Vol. XXV, 1918). There is no satisfactory account of Irish immigration. The following references are suggested: T. A. EMMET, *Ireland under English Rule* etc. (2 vols., 1903); G. O'BRIEN, *The Economic History of Ireland from the Union to the Famine* (1921); S. BYRNE, *Irish Emigration to the United States* (1873); G. SMITH, "Why send more Irish to America," in the *Nineteenth Century*, Vol. XIII, pp. 913 ff.; *Edinburgh Review*, Vol. XLIV, pp. 49–74; Vol. LXXXIX, pp. 221–268; Vol. XCI, pp. 1–62; Vol. XCIII, pp. 475–498.

The Scandinavians

From the historical standpoint Swedish and Norwegian immigration has been exploited more thoroughly than the migration of any group with the exception of the Germans. K. C. BABCOCK's *The Scandinavian Element in the United States* (University of

Illinois Studies in the Social Sciences, Vol. III) contains the most satisfactory bibliography. O. N. NELSON's *History of the Scandinavians and Successful Scandinavians in the United States* (2 vols., 1900), G. T. FLOM's *A History of Norwegian Immigration to the United States from the Earliest Beginnings down to the Year 1848* (1909), and R. B. ANDERSON's *The First Chapter of Norwegian Immigration (1821-1840): its Causes and Results* (1904) are general accounts. Valuable references are given in T. C. BLEGEN's scholarly contributions: "Cleng Peerson and Norwegian Immigration," in the *Mississippi Valley Historical Review*, Vol. VII, pp. 303-331; "Ole Rynning's True Account of America," in the *Minnesota History Bulletin*, Vol. II, pp. 221-269. G. M. STEPHENSON's contributions contain references to and extracts from source material: "Some Footnotes to the History of Swedish Immigration, 1855-1865," in the *Yearbook of the Swedish Historical Society of America*, 1921-1922, pp. 33-52; "Typical 'America Letters,'" ibid. pp. 52-93; "Hemlandet Letters," ibid. 1922-1923, pp. 56-152. M. A. MIKKELSEN's "The Bishop Hill Colony," in *Johns Hopkins University Studies*, Vol. X, is good for the religious background. HANS MATTSON's *Reminiscences: the Story of an Emigrant* (1891) is written by a Swedish immigrant of the fifties.

The Germans

. A. B. FAUST's *The German Element in the United States, with Special Reference to its Political, Moral, Social, and Educational Influence* (2 vols., 1909) is the most comprehensive study and has a good bibliography. P. COLLIER's *Germany and the Germans from an American Point of View* (1913) is a sympathetic account of the German people and their institutions at the beginning of the present century. CARL SCHURZ's *Reminiscences* (3 vols., 1907) is a graphic story of one of the most distinguished German immigrants. GUSTAVE KOERNER's *Memoirs* (2 vols., 1909) is another interesting narrative. L. F. BITTINGER's *The Germans in Colonial Times* (1901) is brief and readable. The articles by J. SCHAFER, "The Yankee and Teuton in Wisconsin," beginning in the December, 1922, number of the *Wisconsin Magazine of History*, set a high standard. Interesting and reliable are the studies by MRS. K. E. LEVI, "Geographical Origin of German Immigration to Wisconsin," in *Collections of the State Historical Society of Wisconsin*, Vol. VIII, pp. 411–439, and by K. A. EVEREST, "How Wisconsin came by its Large German Element," ibid. Vol. XII, pp. 299–334. W. H. DAWSON's *The Evolution of Modern Germany* (1914) contains facts and statistics bearing on immigration.

The Dutch

J. VAN DER ZEE's *The Hollanders of Iowa* (1912) gives a good background. The same author has translated indispensable source material in "The Diary of a Journey from the Netherlands to Pella, Iowa," in the *Iowa Journal of History and Politics*, Vol. X, pp. 363–383. H. S. LUCAS has made the following important contributions: "The Beginnings of Dutch Immigration to Western Michigan, 1846," in the *Michigan History Magazine*, Vol. IV, pp. 642–672, and "A Document Relating to Dutch Immigration to Iowa in 1846," in the *Iowa Journal of History and Politics*, Vol. XXI, pp. 457–465.

The Italians

The excellent monograph by R. F. FOERSTER, *The Italian Emigration of our Times* (1919), is by far the best thing on the subject and is an example of what a book of that nature ought to be. B. M. TIPPLE's article, "The Emigration Crisis in Italy," in the *Methodist Review*, fifth series, Vol. XXXIX, pp. 442–453, is informing. C. M. PANUNZIO's *The Soul of an Immigrant* (1921) relates an interesting story of an immigrant, but is not typical of the average Italian. A. STELLA's *Some Aspects of Italian Immigration to the United States* (1924) presents the Italian point of view, but is not always sound. The following articles may be read with profit: J. C. VISMARA, "The Coming of the Italians to Detroit," in the *Michigan History Magazine*, Vol. II, pp. 110–124; E. SCHUYLER, "The Italian Immigrant," in the *Political Science Quarterly*,

Vol. IV, pp. 480–495; J. H. SENNER, "Immigration from Italy," in the *North American Review*, Vol. CLXII, pp. 649–657; A. H. WARNER, "A Country where going to America is an Industry," in the *National Geographic Magazine*, Vol. XX, pp. 1063–1102; L. LASKER, "Italy a 'Mother Country,'" in the *Survey* for February 26, 1921; J. F. CARR, "The Coming of the Italian," in the *Outlook*, Vol. LXII, pp. 419–431.

The Jews

The secondary material on the background is more satisfactory than for any other group. A concise, scientific study is S. JOSEPH's *Jewish Immigration to the United States from 1881 to 1910*, in *Columbia University Studies*, Vol. LIX. S. M. DUBNOV's *History of the Jews in Russia and Poland*, etc. (3 vols., 1916–1920) is a detailed historical account of conditions and events which produced the migration. I. FRIEDLAENDER's *The Jews of Russia and Poland* (1915) is a satisfactory short study. MARY ANTIN's *The Promised Land* (1912) is a personal narrative by a gifted immigrant. Of considerable value is I. M. RUBINOW's *Economic Condition of the Jews in Russia*, in *United States Bureau of Labor Bulletin No. 72*, Vol. XV, pp. 487–583. B. LAZARE's *Anti-Semitism, its History and Causes* (1903) is a translation from the French. Inquiries along the same line as the latter are B. DRACHMAN, "Anti-Jewish Prejudice in America," in the *Forum*, Vol. LII, pp. 31–40; E. J. KUH, "The Social Disability of the Jew," in the *Atlantic Monthly*, Vol. CI, pp. 433–439. L. LEWISOHN's *Up Stream. An American Chronicle* (1922) is a caustic narrative of the career of an American Jew. Interesting observations are presented in B. HENDRICK's *The Jews in America* (1923). C. ADLER, in the *Voice of America on Kishineff* (1904), has compiled newspaper comments and other expressions of public opinion. One of the recent manifestations of anti-Semitism is related in E. HEIFETZ's *The Slaughter of the Jews in the Ukraine in 1919* (1920). A mass of information is printed in the *Jewish Quarterly Review*, in the *American Jewish Yearbook*, and in the publications of the American Jewish Society. The Jewish situation during the World War and after is explained in *The Jews in the Eastern War Zone* (American Jewish Committee, 1916) and in *The Jews in Poland* (Official Reports of the American and British Investigating Missions, 1920).

The Slavs

E. G. BALCH's *Our Slavic Fellow Citizens* (1910) is the most comprehensive and satisfactory study. T. ČAPEK's *The Čechs (Bohemians) in America* (1920) is written in popular style. P. Fox's *The Poles in America* (1922) and J. DAVIS's *The Russian Immigrant* (1922) and *The Russians and Ruthenians in America* (1922) are superficial and add little to our knowledge of the European background. A study of the Dillingham Report would yield far more. P. R. RADOSAVLJEVICH's *Who are the Slavs?* (2 vols., 1919) is wordy and poorly arranged. M. O. WILLIAMS's "Czechoslovakia, Key-land of Central Europe," in the *National Geographic Magazine*, Vol. XXIX, pp. 111–156, is well illustrated and gives an interesting account of the customs. BARON LOUIS DE SEVAY's "The Hungarian Emigration Law," in the *North American Review*, Vol. CLXXXII, pp. 115–122, deals with the attitude of the government toward emigration. W. I. THOMAS and F. ZNANIECKI's *The Polish Peasant in Europe and America* (5 vols., 1918) contains a mass of information. A. H. SANFORD's "Polish People of Portage County," in *Proceedings of the State Historical Society of Wisconsin*, 1907, pp. 259–288, discusses the causes of the migration briefly.

NATIVISM

Know-Nothingism

There is no satisfactory history of the Know-Nothing party. H. J. DESMOND's *The Know-Nothing Party* (1905) is brief and superficial. In the absence of a study of the national party the two following monographs on the activity of the party in states may be used with profit: L. D. SCISCO's *Political Nativism in New York State*, in *Columbia University Studies*, Vol. XIII, and L. F. SCHMECKEBIER's *History of the Know-Nothing Party in*

Maryland, in *Johns Hopkins University Studies*, Vol. XVII. The contemporaneous literature is voluminous. For some references to this see G. M. STEPHENSON's "Nativism in the Forties and Fifties, with Special Reference to the Mississippi Valley," in the *Mississippi Valley Historical Review*, Vol. IX, pp. 185–202. The most valuable of these are *The Sons of the Sires; a History of the Rise, Progress, and Destiny of the American Party*, etc. (1855); J. P. SANDERSON's *Republican Landmarks* (1856); *Startling Facts for Native Americans called "Know-Nothings,"* etc. (1855). S. C. BUSEY's *Immigration: its Evils and Consequences* (1856) is an example of books dealing with immigration in this period. Among the historical works covering this period of American history the following contain useful chapters: J. F. RHODES, *History of the United States from the Compromise of 1850* (1893–1906), Vol. II, pp. 50–72 ; J. B. MCMASTER, *History of the United States from the Revolution to the Civil War* (8 vols., 1883–1912), Vol. VII, pp. 369–370; T. C. SMITH, *Parties and Slavery* (American Nation Series, 1904–1908, Vol. XVIII), pp. 136–148. Valuable special studies are A. C. COLE's "Nativism in the Lower Mississippi Valley," in *Proceedings of the Mississippi Valley Historical Association*, Vol. VI, pp. 258–275; G. H. HAYNES's "Causes of Know-Nothing Success in Massachusetts," in the *American Historical Review*, Vol. III, pp. 67–82 ; C. F. BRAND's articles on the "History of the Know-Nothing Party in Indiana," appearing in the *Indiana Magazine of History* during 1922. G. M. STEPHENSON's *Political History of the Public Lands, 1840–1862* (1917), pp. 149–177, 221–239, shows the influence of the public lands on the situation. F. I. HERRIOTT's articles in *Deutsch-Amerikanische Geschichtsblätter*, Vol. XIII, pp. 202–303 ; Vol. XV, pp. 181–254, give copious extracts from editorials in the German-American papers, showing the aftermath of Know-Nothingism.

American Protective Association

The material is voluminous and is found principally in the periodicals of the time. The following articles give a fairly good idea of the controversy. Three articles by W. J. H. TRAYNOR:

"The Aims and Methods of the 'A.P.A.,'" in the *North American Review*, Vol. CLIX, pp. 67–76; "The Menace of Romanism," ibid. Vol. CLXI, pp. 129–140; "The Policy and Power of the 'A.P.A.,'" ibid. Vol. CLXII, pp. 658–666. A. C. Coxe, "Government by Aliens," in the *Forum*, Vol. VII, pp. 597–608. W. DeWitt Hyde and E. Atkinson, "The Transformation of New England," ibid. Vol. XV, pp. 107–126. E. McGlynn, "The New Know-Nothingism and the Old," in the *North American Review*, Vol. CXLV, pp. 192–202. E. D. McCreary, "The Roman Catholic Church as a Factor in Politics," in the *American Journal of Politics*, Vol. IV, pp. 119–131. W. W. Quatermass, "A Defense of the 'Godless Schools' of the State," ibid. Vol. IV, pp. 574–586. C. Robinson, "The Threatened Revival of Know-Nothingism," ibid. Vol. V, pp. 504–525. G. P. Lathrop, "Catholic Loyalty: A Reply to the President of the A.P.A. and to Bishop Doane," in the *North American Review*, Vol. CLIX, pp. 218–224. A. Young, "The Coming Contest—With a Retrospect," in the *Catholic World*, Vol. LVIII, pp. 457–472. A. Young, "The Coming Contest—Have Catholics a Protestant Enemy?" ibid. Vol. LVIII, pp. 694–708.

The Ku Klux Klan

J. M. Mecklin's *The Ku Klux Klan: A Study of the American Mind* (1924) is the most satisfactory book. A series of articles "exposing" the Klan appeared in the *Cosmopolitan*, beginning in 1922. In 1921 a committee of the House of Representatives investigated the Klan, the hearings of which were printed (184 pages) but not distributed to libraries. The *Nation*, the *New Republic*, the *Outlook*, the *World's Work*, the *Forum*, the *North American Review*, the *Literary Digest*, the *Commonweal*, and other periodicals contain editorials and articles. In an article entitled "Know-Nothing and Ku Klux Klan," in the *North American Review*, January, 1924, pp. 1–7, W. S. Myers discusses the conditions which produced both movements. While hostile to both organizations, the article does not slur over the sins of the immigrants. "Nordic superiority," which partly explains the rise of the Klan, is reflected in the congressional hearings and debates on the immigration bills of 1924. That spirit is also present in books like C. S. BURR's *America's Race Heritage* (1922), L. STODDARD's *The Revolt against Civilization* (1922) and *The Rising Tide of Color against White World-Supremacy* (1920), and MADISON GRANT's *The Passing of the Great Race* (1921). J. J. SMERTENKO's "The Claim of 'Nordic' Race Superiority," in *Current History*, Vol. XX, pp. 15–23, takes sharp issue with these authors.

IMMIGRATION RESTRICTION

The important immigration acts are found in the *United States Statutes at Large*, but more conveniently perhaps in publications like the *World Almanac* and the *Chicago Daily News Almanac and Yearbook*. JENKS and LAUCK, in *The Immigration Problem* (1917), give the important provisions. The arguments pro and con are found as conveniently as anywhere in the debates on the bills in Congress in the *Congressional Record*, bearing in mind the endless repetition. The following documents are important: *House Reports*, 51st Cong., 2d Sess., No. 3472; ibid. 52d Cong., 2d Sess., No. 1333; *Senate Documents*, 57th Cong., 2d Sess., No. 62; ibid. 61st Cong., 3d Sess., Vol. XXI. M. K. REELY's *Selected Articles on Immigration* (1917) gives convenient summaries of important articles in periodicals. The *Hearings before the Committee on Immigration and Naturalization*, House of Representatives, 68th Cong., 1st Sess., serial 1-A and serial 2-A (1924), gives testimony and documents presenting many points of view. A list of magazine articles would be endless. For the liberal attitude during the World War and after, the *Nation*, the *New Republic*, and the *Survey* are the best. A series of articles by GINO SPERANZA, in the *World's Work*, beginning in 1923, "The Immigration Peril," presents the other side. The *North American Review*, the *Forum*, and the *Literary Digest* are rich in material. E. M. PHELPS's *Selected Articles on Immigration* (370 pages, 1921) is a valuable bibliography. Among the most important articles are the following: W. F. WILLCOX's "The Distribution of Immigrants in the United States," in the *Quarterly Journal of Economics*, Vol. XX, pp. 523–

546. H. P. FAIRCHILD replies to MR. WILLCOX in "The Distribution of Immigrants," in the *Yale Review*, Vol. XVI, pp. 296–310. F. A. FETTER, "Population or Prosperity," in the *American Economic Review*, Vol. III, Supplement, pp. 5–19. H. S. JENNINGS, in the *Survey* for December 15, 1923, pp. 309–312, gives a digest of the hearings before the House committee on immigration and naturalization, 1923 (*House Documents*, 67th Cong., 3d Sess., serial 7-C). He is favorable to the new immigrants. H. P. FAIRCHILD, in "Some Immigration Differences" (*Yale Review*, Vol. XIX, pp. 79–97), contrasts the old immigrants and the new, to the detriment of the latter. He points out how conditions have changed. M. J. KOHLER, "Some Aspects of the Immigration Problem," in the *American Economic Review*, Vol. IV, pp. 93–108. For the state of the post-war public mind see J. E. MILHOLLAND, "The Immigration Hysteria in Congress," in the *Forum*, Vol. LXV, pp. 68–76, and W. R. THAYER, "Throwing away our Birthright," in the *North American Review*, Vol. CCXV, pp. 145–154. C. C. BRIGHAM, in *A Study of American Intelligence* (1923), deals mainly with the army intelligence tests for immigrants and concludes that the immigrants are growing lower in intelligence. For material on the percentage plan see *Hearings before the House Committee on Immigration and Naturalization*, 66th Cong., 1st Sess. (June 12–14, 18–20, and September 25, 1919). For a digest of immigration legislation and detailed information about the administrative machinery a convenient volume is D. H. SMITH and H. G. HERRING's *The Bureau of Immigration: Its History, Activities, and Organization* (Service Monographs of the United States Government, No. 30. 1924).

PROTECTION OF IMMIGRANTS

Consult the reports of state immigration commissions, especially those of New York, New Jersey, and Massachusetts. References to important documents are given in the present work, Chapter XIX. Publications of church bodies, philanthropic organizations, etc. are important. C. G. O'BRIEN's "The Emigrant in New

York," in the *Nineteenth Century*, Vol. XVI, pp. 530–549, is interesting. *The Report of the Joint Legislative Committee of New York* (Legislative Document No. 76. Albany, 1924) is devoted to "The Exploitation of Immigrants."

NATURALIZATION

J. P. GAVIT's *Americans by Choice* (1922) is, all things considered, the most valuable single study, but has no bibliography. The footnote references, however, are of service. F. G. FRANKLIN's *The Legislative History of Naturalization in the United States* (1906) has a short bibliography, but is not an important contribution. The reports of the commissioner-general of immigration and the census reports furnish statistics.

IMMIGRATION AND LABOR

The History of Labour in the United States (2 vols., 1918), by J. R. COMMONS, is the most satisfactory account. *Documentary History of American Industrial Society* (10 vols., 1909–1911), by J. R. COMMONS *et al.*, contains source material. I. A. HOURWICH's *Immigration and Labor; the Economic Aspects of European Immigration to the United States* (second edition, revised, 1922) has a wealth of material. The reports of the annual conventions of the American Federation of Labor give definite information. *Some Reasons for Chinese Exclusion; Meat vs. Rice. American Manhood against Asiatic Coolieism. Which shall Survive?* (published by the American Federation of Labor, 1901) states the essence of the objection to Oriental immigration. The Dillingham Report (*Senate Documents*, 63d Cong.) has thirteen volumes devoted to industry and labor, a summary of which is printed in two volumes.

AMERICANIZATION

The volumes in Americanization Studies, edited by ALLEN T. BURNS (1920–1924), are special studies of immigration problems. P. DAVIS's *Immigration and Americanization* (1920) contains "select readings" on Americanization and a digest of the program of addresses made before the conference of Americanization specialists and workers held at Washington in May, 1919. E. H. BIERSTADT'S *Aspects of Americanization* (1922) is skeptical of the movement. C. ARONOVICI'S *Americanization* (1919) and "Americanization: its Meaning and Function," in the *American Journal of Sociology*, Vol. XXV, pp. 695–730, are hostile to the "hothouse" system. R. S. BOURNE'S "Trans-National America," in the *Atlantic Monthly*, Vol. CXVIII, pp. 86–97, is stimulating. C. S. STEWART'S "Prussianizing Wisconsin," ibid. Vol. CXXIII, pp. 99–105, partly explains certain manifestations of "radicalism" during the war and after. "Intellectual America," by "A European," ibid. Vol. CXXIV, pp. 188–199, is written by a Polish-American who is offended by the "self-satisfied" attitude of Americans. A. A. COSTA'S "Americanization and Reaction," in the *Living Age* for April 10, 1920, pp. 67–71, analyzes the attitude of the foreign-born toward the United States as the result of the war and the events following. S. B. HRBKOVA, "'Bunk' in Americanization. A Laudable Propaganda infected by Ignorance," in the *Forum*, Vol. LXIII, pp. 428–439. GINO SPERANZA, "Does Americanization Americanize?" in the *Atlantic Monthly*, Vol. CXXIV, pp. 263–269. "Beneficent America," by "One in the Government Service," in the *Catholic World*, Vol. XC, pp. 591–600, praises the loyalty of the foreign-born. *New York Legislature. Joint Committee Investigating Seditious Activities. Revolutionary Radicalism* (4 vols., 1920). This is the so-called Lusk Committee Report, extracts of which were widely published in the press. *The Interpreter* (published by the Foreign-Language Information Service) and *Immigrants in America Review* are illuminating.

POLITICAL ACTIVITY, RACIAL CONTRIBUTIONS, ETC.

General

The best source is the foreign-language press. R. E. PARK'S *The Immigrant Press and its Control* (1922) contains bibliographical footnotes. *Immigrants in America Review* reflects many-sided activities. *Foreign-Born. A Bulletin of International Service* is especially valuable, giving articles, immigration figures, legislation affecting the foreign-born, book reviews, etc. R. E. PARK's *Old World Traits Transplanted* (1920) and J. DRACHSLER's *Democracy and Assimilation* (1920) are volumes in Americanization Studies. *The Old World in the New* (1914), by E. A. Ross, is a series of essays on different stocks. *Our Foreigners* (1920), by S. P. ORTH, is brief and readable. The article, "Racial Minorities," by G. T. ROBINSON, in H. E. STEARNS's (Ed.) *Civilization in the United States* (1922), departs from the conventional point of view. A. E. S. BEARD's *Our Foreign-Born Citizens. What they have done for America* (1922) consists of a series of biographies. *Complete Report of the Chairman of the Committee on Public Information* (1920) is a satisfactory and sympathetic account of the part of the immigrants in the World War.

The Germans

A. B. FAUST's *The German Element in the United States* (2 vols., 1909) is the best general treatment. K. FRANCKE's *German Ideals of Today* (1907), *The German Spirit* (1916), and *A German-American's Confession of Faith* (1915) are written by a distinguished German-American scholar. H. MÜNSTERBERG's *American Traits; From the Point of View of a German* (1901) is the work of a famous psychologist. CARL SCHURZ's *Reminiscences* (3 vols., 1907–1908) and *Speeches, Correspondence, and Political Papers* (6 vols., 1913) record the career of a distinguished statesman. The article "Distinguished Germans in American Affairs," by O. BRAUN, in the *Magazine of American History*, Vol. XXV, pp. 469–488, is popular. E. BRUNCKEN, "Germans in America," in *American Historical Association Report*, 1898, pp. 347–353. J. GOEBEL's "The Place of the German Element in American History," in *American Historical Association Report*, 1909, pp. 183–189, makes a plea for the study of the background and culture of the Germans. J. FLYNT's "The German and the German-American," in the *Atlantic Monthly*, Vol. LXXVIII, pp. 655–664, is objective. F. W. HOLLS's "The German Vote and the Republican Party," in the *Forum*, Vol. XX, pp. 588–604, is decidedly "pro-German." R. NIEBUHR's "The Failure of German-Americanism," in the *Atlantic Monthly*, Vol. CXVIII, pp. 13–18, is hostile. *Deutsch-Amerikanische Geschichtsblätter* contains material on the history of the German element. *The Fatherland* (1914–1917), succeeded by *Viereck's American Weekly* and the *American Monthly*, was established in the interest of "fair play" for Germany and Austria and presents the extreme German side.

The Irish

J. P. BOCOCK, "The Irish Conquest of our Cities," in the *Forum*, Vol. XVII, pp. 186–195. "The Irish in America," in the *North American Review*, Vol. LII, pp. 191–234, is many-sided. "A New Ireland: A Reply to Lord Salisbury," by T. B. GRANT, in the *American Journal of Politics*, Vol. V, pp. 30–55, is an article compiled by authority of the Irish National Federation of America. A. G. GARDNER's "Anglo-American Issues," in the *Contemporary Review*, Vol. CXVIII, pp. 609–619, discusses the influence of the Irish in American politics and life. E. T. DEVINE's "Ourselves and the Irish," in the *Survey* for May 7, 1921, pp. 167–168, gives a sympathetic estimate of Irish character. O. WISTER's *A Straight Deal, or the Ancient Grudge* (1920) is violently anti-Irish. *The Irish World* (New York) presents the Irish cause. Biographies of distinguished men, like Archbishop Hughes, Cardinal Gibbons, Archbishop Ireland, are valuable.

The Scandinavians

K. C. BABCOCK, *The Scandinavian Element in the United States*, in *University of Illinois Studies in the Social Sciences*, Vol. III. This is a brief treatment. H. H. BOYESON's "The Scandinavians in the United States," in the *North American Review*, Vol. CLV, pp. 526–535, is eulogistic. H. WISBY, "The Scandinavian-American: his Status," ibid. Vol. CLXXXIII, pp. 213–223. A. O. FONKALSRUD's *Scandinavians as a Social Force in America* (1914) is brief and deals lightly with politics. G. M. STEPHENson, "The Attitude of the Swedish-Americans toward the World War," in *Proceedings of the Mississippi Valley Historical Association*, 1918–1919, pp. 79–94.

Other nationalities

The material is fragmentary. The books listed above may be consulted, but, with some exceptions, are rather unsatisfactory.

ORIENTAL IMMIGRATION

Bibliographies

R. E. COWAN and B. DUNLAP, *Bibliography of the Chinese Question in the United States* (1909); I. T. FIRKINS, "Japanese in the United States," in *Bulletin of Bibliography*, Vol. VIII, pp. 94–98; M. K. REELY, *Selected Articles on Immigration* (second edition, 1917). A. P. C. GRIFFIN, *Select List of References on Chinese Immigration* (1904).

The Chinese

H. H. BANCROFT, *Essays and Miscellany* (1890), pp. 235–279, 309–418. A most interesting description of conditions in the Chinese section of San Francisco. J. BRYCE, *The American Commonwealth* (2 vols., 1914), Vol. II, pp. 426–448, "Kearneyism in California." A. C. COOLIDGE, *The United States as a World Power* (1910), pp. 313–340; suggestive chapters. M. R. COOLIDGE, *Chinese Immigration* (1909), a standard book. TIEN-LU LI, *Congressional Policy of Chinese Immigration, or Legislation Relating to Chinese Immigration to the United States* (1916), a compact study. R. M. SMITH, *Emigration and Immigration* (1890), pp. 231–260, a sober account. E. E. SPARKS, *National Development* (1907), pp. 229–250, a clear, brief account. *House Reports*, 51st Cong., 2d Sess., No. 4048, the printed testimony taken before a congressional committee hostile to the Chinese. *Treaty, Laws, and Rules Governing Chinese Immigration. United States Department of Labor Bureau of Immigration* (third edition, 1920). *Annals of the American Academy of Political and Social Science,*

September, 1909, and January, 1921, special numbers devoted to the Chinese and Japanese; of especial importance. W. B. FAR-WELL's "Why the Chinese must be Excluded," in the *Forum*, Vol. VI, pp. 196–203, attempts to be impartial. H. L. DAWES's "The Chinese Exclusion Bill," ibid. Vol. VI, pp. 526–539, shows the change of public sentiment since 1868. T. MAGEE, "China's Menace to the World," ibid. Vol. X, pp. 197–206. W. A. P. MAR-TIN, "Does China Menace the World?" ibid. Vol. X, pp. 433–441. G. REID, "China's View of Chinese Exclusion," ibid. Vol. XV, pp. 407–415. S. PANG, "The Chinese in America," ibid. Vol. XXXII, pp. 598–607. M. J. DEE's "Chinese Immigration," in the *North American Review*, Vol. CXXVI, pp. 506–527, de-plores the lack of right investigation of Chinese immigration. G. F. SEWARD's "Mongolian Immigration," ibid. Vol. CXXXIV, pp. 562–578, by a former envoy to China, attempts to refute argu-ments in favor of exclusion. J. H. DURST's "The Exclusion of the Chinese," ibid. Vol. CXXXIX, pp. 256–274, favors exclusion. T. J. GEARY's "Should Chinese be Excluded?" ibid. Vol. CLVII, pp. 58–68, gives an affirmative answer. J. T. SCHARF's "The Farce of Chinese Exclusion Laws," ibid. Vol. CLXVI, pp. 85–98, offers evidence of violation of exclusion laws. Ho Yow's "Chinese Ex-clusion. A Benefit or a Harm?" ibid. Vol. LXXIII, pp. 314–330, is a plea for the Chinese. H. H. BANCROFT, "The Folly of Chinese Exclusion," ibid. Vol. CLXXIX, pp. 263–268. JOAQUIN MILLER, "The Ruinous Cost of Chinese Exclusion," ibid. Vol. CLXXXVI, 422–426. J. W. FOSTER's "The Chinese Boycott," in the *Atlantic Monthly*, Vol. XCVII, pp. 119–127, by a prominent American diplomatist, condemns America's policy.

The Japanese

A. C. COOLIDGE's *The United States as a World Power* (1910), pp. 341–374, is an excellent review of the diplomatic relations be-tween the United States and Japan. C. CROW, *Japan and America. A Contrast* (1916). S. L. GULICK's *The American Japanese Prob-lem* (1914) is a plea for a more sympathetic attitude. H. M. HYNDMAN's *The Awakening of Asia* (1919) is an objective study by an Englishman. T. IYENAGA and K. SATO's *Japan and the California Problem* (1921) is a discussion by Japanese observers who have resided in California. Contains a bibliography, the text of alien land laws, and a chapter on the background of emigration. K. K. KAWAKAMI's *American-Japanese Relations* (1912), *Japan in World Politics* (1917), and *What Japan Thinks* (1921) are by a Japanese-American who deplores the trend of events and hopes to bring about a better understanding. H. A. MILLIS's *The Japanese Problem in the United States* (1915) is a thorough study. A. M. POOLEY, *Japan's Foreign Policies* (1920), pp. 106–137, "Japan, America, and Mexico." J. F. STEINER's *The Japanese Invasion* (1917) is a brief, readable account surveying the entire field. I. TOKUTOMI, *Japanese-American Relations* (1922). Translated from the Japanese; a frank indictment of American "imperial ambitions." *California State Board of Control, California and the Oriental: Japanese, Chinese, and Hindus.* Report of the State Board of Control to Governor William D. Stephens, June 19, 1920 (231 pages, 1920). Contents: letter of Governor Stephens to Secretary of State Colby; population; birth rate; land; labor; picture brides; gentlemen's agreement; etc. Final Report of Secretary V. H. METCALF, "Japanese in the City of San Francisco," November 26, 1906, with accompanying documents, in *Senate Miscellaneous Documents*, 59th Cong., 2d Sess., No. 147. *Reports of the Asiatic Exclusion League* (organized in 1905). *Statistics Relative to Japanese Immigration and the Japanese in California* (Japanese Association of America, 1920). *Japanese Immigration and the Japanese in California* (Farmers' Co-operative Association, 1920). *House Documents*, 56th Cong., 1st Sess., No. 686, the report of W. M. RICE concerning his investigation in Japan. R. L. BUELL, "The Development of the Anti-Japanese Agitation in the United States," in the *Political Science Quarterly*, Vol. XXXVII, pp. 605–638; Vol. XXXVIII, pp. 57–81. R. L. BUELL's "Some Legal Aspects of the Japanese Question," in the *American Journal of International Law*, Vol. XVII, pp. 29–49, is a scholarly discussion of treaties, naturalization, and anti-alien legislation. H. M. DILLA, "Constitutional Background of the Recent Anti-Alien Land Bill Controversy," in the *Michigan Law Review*, Vol. XII, pp. 573–584. F. G. PEABODY's "Nagging the Japanese," in the *North American Review*, CXCVIII, pp. 332–340, is a protest against the American attitude. W. E. GRIFFIS, "Our Honor and Shame with Japan," ibid. CC, pp. 566–575. R. W. RYDER's "The Japanese and the Pacific Coast," ibid. Vol. CCXIII, pp. 1–15, by a California lawyer, thinks conditions are exaggerated. J. C. McKIM's "Japan and America," ibid. Vol. CCXIII, pp. 438–447, by a missionary in Japan, points out the danger of the anti-American propaganda in Japan. Critical of the Japanese press and fearful of war. A. M. KNAPP's, "Japanese Commercial Honor," in the *Atlantic Monthly*, Vol. CVIII, pp. 778–784, is a defense of the Japanese. P. J. TREAT's "California and the Japanese," ibid. Vol. CXXVII, pp. 537–546, is by a student of Japanese history and a resident of California. J. M. INMAN, "Japanese Aggression," in the *Forum*, Vol. LXV, pp. 1–8. By the author of the anti-alien land bills in the California legislature in 1919.

INDEX

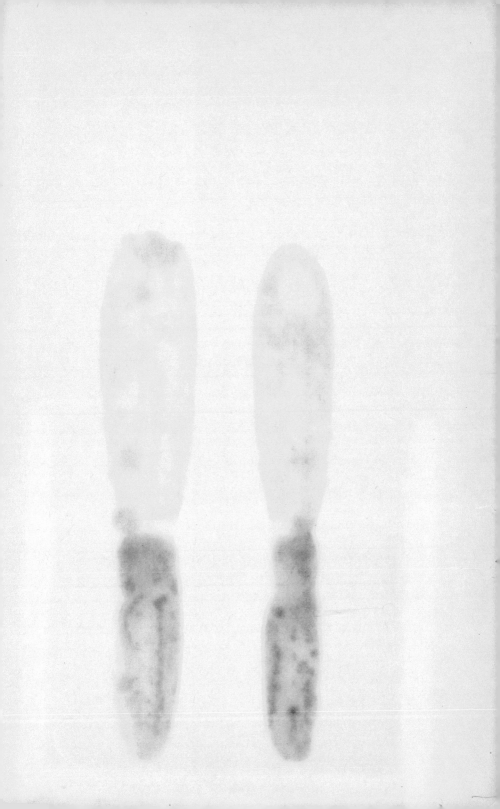

DATE DUE	
NOV 0 6 1996	
FEB 23 1999	
MAR 08 2000	